THE
Elemental
COLLECTION

- WRITE OUT YOUR DROPS
- SET FREE YOUR FLOW
- EARTH UP YOUR ROOTS
- FIRE UP YOUR FLIGHT

Selin Senol Akin

THE ELEMENTAL COLLECTION

COPYRIGHT © 2023 SELIN SENOL-AKIN

All Rights Reserved

The characters and events portrayed in this book (other than the memoir) are fictitious. Any similarity to real persons, living or dead, is coincidental and not intended by the author.

No part of this book may be reproduced, or stored in a retrieval system, or transmitted in any form or by any means, electronic, mechanical, photocopying, recording, or otherwise, without express written permission of the publisher, except in the case of brief quotations embodied in critical reviews and certain other noncommercial uses permitted by copyright law.

ISBN: 978-1-7346563-7-4

PRINTED IN THE UNITED STATES OF AMERICA

THE ELEMENTAL COLLECTION

Dedicated to anyone who's ever questioned the status quo (noting it of mere human formulation) and wanted to make their life experiences inspire beyond themselves and their immediate circles…

THE ELEMENTAL COLLECTION

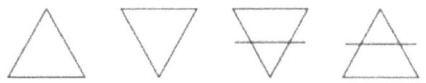

"You are the universe in ecstatic motion…"

–RUMI

"Everything was simple, physical, painful, exalting. The world consisted of the four elements: land and water, firepower, and distancing air…"

-SUSAN SONTAG

THE ELEMENTAL COLLECTION

Dear reader,

If you are reading this compilation, I thank you from the bottom of my ever-wide-open heart. I had never thought I'd even have a book published, let alone a suspense series and four books with a variety of stories told through prose and poetry, ranging from the deeply personal to the abstract and symbolic of the society we live in.

With each passing year, I tend to reflect on my life thus far through a retrospective glance at not only the events that have unfolded around me, but also on the choices I have made (and on whether or not I presently would have made the same ones). In doing so, I've come to recognize that I've often acted with a fusion of the four elements of Western culture: water, air, earth and fire. I've poured endlessly, flowing along with the direction of the wind in the moment. I've drawn nutrients from my roots wherever I went, setting fires while being lit myself.

We may not always foresee where our chosen journeys (chosen out of 'pre-determined' options available to each of us that some call 'kismet', or 'destiny') will lead, yet we can control the start at any moment, and focus then on enjoying the ride until that mysterious destination.

Some can start their journeys ('tis never a race, as no one is rushing to reach death) at various disadvantages based on their familial situations and/or physical inadequacies. Yet those can also be the ones who dream and strive harder- being able to reach a wider range of people to inspire through their recognition (case in point: look at the humble beginnings and various early setbacks of many- if not all- of your favorite notables).

THE ELEMENTAL COLLECTION

Regardless of where you have started *your journey*, you must first *recognize* yours: your unique path. Heed the signs. Heed to your call. Heed to the elements inside of you. For we are all a little bit of the grand universe, and hence- not so 'little' at all.

> the silver spoon (though now rusty)
> with which you were fed love
> my dear
> has never applied to me
>
> I learned to fight for it
> with my bare hands and soul
> like the feral hunter foraging for
> the last leftover in the savannah
>
> I was thought to be full
> and hence unworthy
> yet I was never given the lot of it I needed,
> though given pretty much everything else
> that I never really did,
> you see
>
> I learned to face any glimmer or ray of its hope
> fully and wholeheartedly
> like nyctinastic flowers tilting toward the sun
> only to wilt back with shielding petals
> upon seeing the dark approach,
> silently, daily
> coming undone
>
> I cannot treat lightly, my dear
> what I've secretly built my entire existence around:
>
> I **seek** *the sun*, and for those who need-
> I also **become**

THE ELEMENTAL COLLECTION

TABLE OF CONTENTS

WRITE OUT YOUR DROPS
POETRY   9-98

SET FREE YOUR FLOW
POETRY & MEMOIR   99-244

EARTH UP YOUR ROOTS
POETRY, STORIES & A PLAY   245-361

FIRE UP YOUR FLIGHT
POETRY   362-466

THE ELEMENTAL COLLECTION

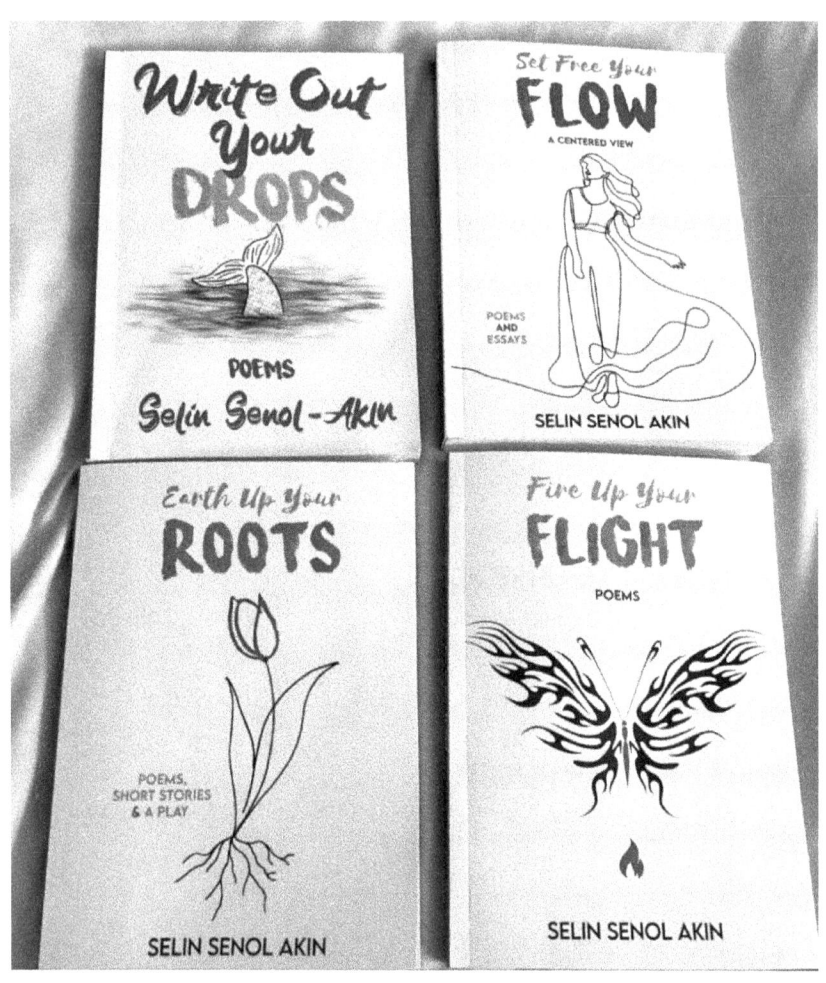

WRITE OUT YOUR DROPS

T HE OCEAN ASKS for your drops of rain.
The lover says, 'cry me a river'-
whether of joy or of pain.

The future asks for your blood drops-
for you to contribute your genetically inherited art:
bleed out your art…
bleed it out, through your heart.

Symphonies ask for your melodic drops.
Success asks for your hard work-
your perspiration drops...
the struggle never stops.

Go ahead- ride out the storm.
You can keep warm,
as long as you ***write out your drops.***

Photography: Ksenia Kolesova

WRITE OUT YOUR DROPS

Dear beloved reader,

Yes: you. If this collection has found its way to you, then I believe you to be an empathetic soul with many drops to pour into the globally-connective oceans as the collective human race. This- dear reader- makes you more beloved, and more valuable than you know.

I had written many of these poems before the onset of the tragic pandemic. In retrospect, I find that some of them about the new year and nature have eerily been foreboding. I sincerely hope these words find you and your loved ones in good health, and my heartfelt condolences to those of you whose loved ones were more negatively impacted.

The verses on these pages range from the very personal to the very objective, and as an observer of abstract art like in *The Ballerina's Catalysis* and *Tropical Loss*. My own name, Selin, translates to *your flood* in Turkish. As a believer in the universe somehow symbolically always trying to tell us something, I hope you can smile along with me in my love of play-on-words throughout the pages.

May your flood of teardrops, sweat drops, melodic art and the blood flowing through your veins all unite and rain onto the connecting oceans as your fluid imprints. I encourage you to express your own universal vision and bleed out your art and stories.

Write Out Your Drops. Write Out Your World.

as a young child
I knew in one sudden moment my destiny-
to share my stories in any way I could and
through any opportunity, not due to egotistical vanity
but because of my experiences' variety
and their Affinity
with Humanity

for my daughter, family, dear friends and all fellow empaths- especially ones attempting to break free of either societal chains and categorizations, or narcissistic abuse of one kind or another.

-Sel (*"your flood"* in Turkish. Author's nickname)

WRITE OUT YOUR DROPS

DROPS
OF
PRECIPITATION

nature

WRITE OUT YOUR DROPS

the dandelion

the winds of change
have begun to blow
even mightier than the unusual
rainy summer winds
of this already most unusual, viral year

the winds of change have shattered
any proximity in clinging to routines
and familiar daily visions and habits

they have caused an additional conundrum
at a time when long-hauled weights
had been begging to be finally released
from aching shoulders

it is said we take ourselves wherever we go
country to city, city to country
alone to partnered, partnered to alone
burdened to relieved, relieved to burdened

the cycle never truly ceases
as long as we're alive
the change itself may indeed be
the only fuel needed
to carry and drive on by

fate only exists to a certain point
after which you must decide
your own form of high

are you rooted to grow your flowers,
risking rotting?
or
a dandelion,
enjoying being blown along with the wind?

WRITE OUT YOUR DROPS

the value of the flower

                        valuable

                   never realized
              what has truly been
                     invaluable
     until the virus made all of us
                     vulnerable

          a glance from a mask
           a touch on the hand
     a question you're able to ask
      only over forced broadband

hoping someday to understand
            the purpose of it all

     the suffering you suppress
      you progress, then regress

     praying for some salvation
     before the last curtain call
     before we take that big fall

          all the world's a stage
     had said the theatrical sage

      on these emptier streets
full now of discarded gloves and masks
     whether or not tomorrows
       can still be promised-
  a blooming flower never asks

WRITE OUT YOUR DROPS

penitent souls

the ways of the past
could not possibly last
we knew the inevitable truths
we still ignored
thinking this generation
would be exempt from
the globe's defiant blast

Mother Nature was always
the force to be reckoned with,
even more powerful than love
in regards to both beauty and pain
she coughed a contagious poison-
global warming, and our sins, weren't myth

we try now to repent
living more simply and whole
holding down our families & forts
when we cannot even hold or shake
the hands of outsiders
lest we risk losing it all

let's apologize to nature
encompassing the trees and sky we see
as well as to the Being and Creator
that we don't

let's apologize also to our spirit
for seeking temporary outside validation
when we knew all along our duties to maintain its purity

bodies may die
but souls won't

WRITE OUT YOUR DROPS

pessimistic optimism

seasons come and go
the phrase has become
as cliché
as a winter with snow

this city that
doesn't sleep
hasn't seasonably witnessed
much of it lately, though

the new year
has indeed commenced
after everyone clinked
their glasses
and danced for hope-
with a January
catalyzing global trauma
instead

we've still got much to concern
ourselves with,
I'm afraid
up ahead

resilience

surveying the damage
after Isaias
the weather eerily wet and warm
catalyzes her to survey the damage of the past year as well:
trying to salvage any good she can
from the remnants of the storm

teardrops, year after year,
increasingly cease
from free-falling
and rather lump up in the throat,
after betrayal and strife
with hidden shameful mourning

they call it *experience* and *maturity*
she hides that it's necessary adaptability

majestic trees,
now merely unrooted debris
lie sideways as a neighbor takes a selfie

she, too, is at time defeated
by Mother Nature

yet resilience
is also *her* best feature

daisies

winter can take you
by surprise
with a sudden and inconvenient
slap of frost
when you'd been expecting a longer *fall*
with lingering moments of warmth
still not lost

allow *summer* to reign
inside your heart
disregarding the cold pain of memories
spring will surely return once again
blossoming hopes
alongside the daisies

esteem

it's a mother's nature
to care for and nurture
until fatigue sets in
and patience runs thin
in which case we turn into
a most angry creature

Mother Nature gave us bliss
the loveliest Scents and sights
but we did not value its glory
so, it released its viral fury:
now what we can no longer do
we miss

so, please, tell me this:
when can we ask for forgiveness?
when can we again have her mercy?
before all mothers, let us show courtesy

WRITE OUT YOUR DROPS

one-sided

with the sun comes expectations:
warmth for our skin
healing from within
our heart beats faster with palpitations
hormones kick in
let the summer begin

no one considers the sun's sensations,
the one-sided duty it's performing
aiding you with warmth
no matter who you've been

redeem

why is it
that the beautiful sun
peeks out
from the clouds
just as the day
is ending?

why is it
that the hurtful lover
with the shout
only succumbs
to softness
just as the relationship
is past mending?

why is this
human nature?
can we redeem ourselves
to enjoy what we can
while we are able?
let's ponder
and enjoy the sun, not thunder

WRITE OUT YOUR DROPS

lunar

it's not that the moon
doesn't hurt or care
but she knows how to share
the message that, to truly shine
it must also persevere through
solo moments of despair

the moon exists in the day
yet doesn't shine as brightly
as it does nightly
just remains rather gray
and instead-
allowing the way
for the sun to keep the cold away

the tree and the forest

oh, to be like a tree:
rooted deep
yet swaying from time to time
without falling over

surrounded by beings to whom you can relate
and trust
to coexist with you
without needing to glance
over your weary shoulder

unlike us
trees can trust:
no worries of rust

reawakening

when a flower is stomped on
it tilts
its will crushed
it wilts

with every disappointing, darkened shade
the once-beating Red
goes through a fade

the flowers decorate the yard
as the thoughts of you surround
my daily ponderings

I contemplate what you're doing right then
at a particular moment,
just as I wonder:
when exactly did the petals on that blush-pink peony fall off?
and
when did our occasionally watered rose wither?

how did those other roses,
in that other corner,
unexpectedly bloom?
I'd lost all hopes on those white ones
yet there they are: fluffily adorned in spring

no- I decide.

I shan't yet let go hope
of what our own
reawakening
may bring

WRITE OUT YOUR DROPS

shade

clouds are underrated:
without their cozy covering
the sky is an infinite yet eerie shade of *blue*
reaching the vast, unknown cosmos

yet clouds exist only to hydrate our lives
on the proud, *green* and *brown* earth

we are special to the clouds-
a fact overlooked by most

but which shade art thou?

are you a *red*, instead?
closer to *orange*- like a scorching flame?
in proximity to light *pink*- of sweetheart fame?
a darker fuchsia, befitting a classy dame?
or are you more Cardinal
like the Sin?
do you too err in judgement
after which nothing
can remain the same?

with each sunset, our cheeks blush
a different shade of rose
whether innocently or of shame

the clouds, however, never falter
hydration and shade: their only game

floral grace

petals too can fall from grace-
tossed over a bride after the ceremony,
settling on the concrete ground
after brushing her made-up face

having once been rooted to a stem,
which in turn clung proudly for life
deep inside the charcoal earth

they'd stood dainty yet strong under the sun

to think, they could now be hurled like trash-
a prism of splendid hues,
lustrous still despite being used

a confetti of true allure
cannot be handled by everyone.

WRITE OUT YOUR DROPS

the rain's joy

with the rain,
comes expectations
of cozy sweaters tickling the skin,
and other such sensations

not too hot, not too cold
catalyst October
is rather quite bold

after old leaves have been shed
new opportunities can be bred
unlike us,
joy from traversing crunchy leaves never grows old

with each chilly breeze
you get weak in the knees
like a warm cardigan
or a wondrous kiss
autumn holds bliss

pumpkin spice & everything nice
with routines and habits
there's no need to think twice

living ordinarily but standing out
through true happiness-
grandiosity can feel amiss-
simple joys sometimes just have to suffice

DROPS
OF
TEARS

emotions

WRITE OUT YOUR DROPS

the offspring

what happens to love
when the relationship that formed it
is in turmoil?

does it weep, too, along with the lover
like a helpless child
or burn like petrol oil?

can it be transmitted to the next lover
like a stepchild, pet, or plant
despite missing its original soil?

perhaps that love will always live on,
in infinity and beyond
in memory-a baby you can never spoil

shout

why glance above
for affirming signs
of what you already know from inside out?

why deny a love
which you can,
but do not want to live without?

why distance an embrace
when it leaves a smile on your face?

do you hide from the soul's request
and risk a permanent pout?
or mount yourself on a proverbial
mountaintop or rooftop
and simply let it out?

Shout!

WRITE OUT YOUR DROPS

the gazelle

what good is it
being the pursuit
when all it leaves you with
is less spirit than before?
life had already taken a toll on her heart
before the hunter aimed the arrow
straight to the core,
by the fragile bone marrow
exuding control
she held on to her art,
while distracted
by persuasive suggestions
to let go of it all

after its energy has been stolen
or compromised:
does the bear- left without life
feel flattered
that it has been the Hunter's prize?

she was convinced
to lower her shield for social gain
ultimately the thrills, though,
were never worth the pain

she should have seen
through the front,
from the always
dubious start

the trophy
was both the game and the prize
and once obtained
it'd be placed
high on a self
collecting dust
…never cared for
from then on
…merely smiled upon
as a memory
though it'd long been left to rust

the shield breaker

when he coyly smiled at her
a few seconds longer than the rest
her willpower to combat forbidden love
had at once been put to the test

when he boyishly wrote to her
a few verses more personal than others
her brain sensed a rush, and thought
this love frees, more than it smothers

when he nervously held her hand
with a few extra kisses, like a princess
her soul could never predict
that soon all would become a mess

when he purposely halted his chase,
cursing their speculated fate
her tears transformed from drops
into a sea of enamored hate

WRITE OUT YOUR DROPS

lay versus lie

lay all your cards on the table
you've been too good at
bluffing
too good at Poker

taking off your proud mask
shouldn't be such a difficult task
be my Batman
don't be Joker

let's lie down, watch the stars
don't think about taking it there for once
let's ponder something that can become an inside joke instead:
Like, 'what if we were living on Mars?'

I too desire the kisses on fire
and that firm grip, *oh my*
but this time lay your heart on the line
and promise
not to lie

WRITE OUT YOUR DROPS

diamond in the rough

to feel the sting of sin
upon our moral scale of the self

like unread yet most attractive, clean books
full of colors and verses
of the most-descriptive hooks
grabbed and devoured
abruptly from the
shelf

a demure sense of emotion
set off-balance by a desire set in motion
a pure sense of duty
set ablaze with heat sparked in the body

what good is love
if left to rot inside?
what good is a diamond
if it must always hide?

WRITE OUT YOUR DROPS

the unloving flatterer

what good does
constant flattery
inflict
when you see the roving eye
more than you care to admit
in order to avoid
conflict?

when the lover
simply loves beauty
it isn't the true you
they forever seek,
rather continuously
chasing images
in which to find
their 'perfect'

when you're made to feel
truly special
for all that you are
within and throughout,
that is the one your soul
won't question
and give its all for

if it's *you*
they don't want to live without
your heart to them
will remain
devout

WRITE OUT YOUR DROPS

love on a diet

it starts off as grand as the universe-
an explosion of fire in the heart and stars in the eyes,
tender sweetness spilling from the lips

it then loses weight-
like flowers drinking water less and less frequently
bulging love handles gradually withering away, revealing thinner hips

love of passion finally remains a skeleton of what once was-
sometimes glorious like an ancient mummy,
still holding onto some of its old teeth and hair
other times- completely rotted and bare
unaware
of the stare
from the soul that had once also been there

upon the discovery of a hole,
love drips and dips

the bee vs. the fly

the humble yet exquisite flower
can never deny its nectar
which, despite their large amount of fear,
pulls those verbose-when -enamored near

tell me, oh amorous being in the sky:
are you ultimately a pesky little fly
just interested in a temporary feed or high?

or a bee- buzzing royally nearby
with intent to receive benefit
but give it as well?

don't lie

WRITE OUT YOUR DROPS

dependence

patterns
are good to knit

patterns
are good to raise a kid

routines mean expecting
habits are humbling

when the world outside
is thundering,
settling is
soothing &
trusting

until it's not

until patterns abuse
until habits misuse
patterns can be hard
to break
but some must be broken
before they break
your self-respect
and boundary rules

be your own officer
and dignity defender:
your own muse

illicit

>you and the lover
>are on the same boat
>don't forget
>
>remember the law of karma
>before you take an action
>you'll eventually regret
>
>your feisty eyes
>burn the soul of the other
>a blooming surprise
>of emotions flood the ether
>
>catch them as they fall
>without a promise of safety,
>a dangerous love affair
>isn't worth it at all
>
>for even the strongest of flames
>get put off by the winds of time
>and tides of change
>when future possibilities
>are small

WRITE OUT YOUR DROPS

escape

after a certain point
you've learned
upon countless experience miles
you've earned

that being smart is different from
acting smart

a dubious, tell-tale start
disguised as art,
or kind words for convenient gain
don't equate to having a heart

that forgiveness and appreciation
aren't always reciprocated
sometimes you're stuck doing
what you once swore you hated

that imploring eyes
can best disguise
a wolf in sheep's clothing
full of narcissistic lies

no one is perfect
and neither are you
yet if you've done all you could
what's done was at least true

WRITE OUT YOUR DROPS

flying in chains

though contemplation takes hold
on a daily basis
as the hours pass on by,
there are some things
I still cannot fathom

people get hurled and chastised-
unappreciated when you've actually got 'em

and the blood in our veins
said to be thicker than water
can pump more painfully
when expectations are forced
rather than whatever comes naturally

another birthday has arrived
with much still lost
despite several gains

momentous occasions
to distract from the unpleasantly-packaged gift
of recognizing the cold truth of our chains

WRITE OUT YOUR DROPS

the exception

the sun has set

its view is surely gone
and we cannot get it back

though we are still lucky
and must consider ourselves so

for we've caught it

and we still see the traces
of purple tinges in the sky
as two French-speaking boys on bikes
speed on by

and we'll always have its trace
in memories
never underestimating, though
that we've actually caught *it*
as well:
the *it* many search for

the sunset by the lake
swinging with your hand in mine
glances intertwined

                                            perfection

WRITE OUT YOUR DROPS

the ballerina's catalysis

she rushes backstage after her abrupt exit
bursting into the tears long held back

there they are
she spots them on her changing-room counter
his final bouquet, she presumes

congratulations, the note indeed begins
yours always in heart, with immense pride, it stops

she chuckles with disgust:
 it appears the note too has an unexpected start
 and a short end.

she glances her reflection in the mirror

the image of his chiseled face in the audience will not leave her mind
his stare- intense and green as the leaves in the vase
his firm hands-
his left one in particular had been holding on to the small of her back just last week
as they'd been strolling amongst giggles in the park-
it was now being covered by another woman's right hand-
the sparkling on her right finger visible and blinding from the front row

so the woman had received the present she'd been waiting for after all
though not his heart
or,
perhaps she had received that as well
and it was only this ballerina who had been fooled

no longer
actions were the thing
words were futile, she'd forcibly learned

                                                                  "CRACK!"

WRITE OUT YOUR DROPS

braver

after it's over
you lean back on the pillows and turn your head toward the window
the curtains quiver in the soft wind,
in waves, as the pleasures in my body had just been

after it's over
you no longer light your cigarette-
you quit with my help, though I could not quit you

clichés were never your thing either
never a candlelit dinner getaway
or flowers for a lady in May

after it's over
you lose yourself in your soulless, skin-driven life
without any intention of making or keeping a wife

swearing you never want to be like the father you'd never known-
yet didn't he, too, cause many immeasurable strife?

after it's over
you're stuck in your darkness still,
swearing that it causes you glee
this quality of being forever unattached and free

after it's over, my wounds have still yet to close, it's true
but the one who loves wholeheartedly
is the real winner through and through

I'm braver than you

four seasons of a beautiful betrayal

in that moment
when the first dawn rays
hit my humble room
I often reflect back on our days of viscous *Summer* together
to appease my gloom

Spring in New York is the loveliest in the world, it is said-
surpassed only by the allure of its *Fall*

I loved you
despite all of your seasons and intricate flaws:
with your harsh brutal *Winter*
of sharp icicles on my back and all

tropical loss

the tropics with my beloved, I shall never forget
though to this day, I must admit, I live on with some regret

I wore my linen dress, long and flowing, as free as a canary in the wind
my hair had been pulled up high on the top of my head, to avoid that sweat to the skin

let's reproduce right here on this island, he'd said, ever the romantic
we've got all the time in the world, I'd responded, *don't be so dramatic*

the vessel took us that afternoon to the shimmering coastal shores
we'd signed up on a whim
….the sunset took my beloved away from me
a part of me, too, drowned there
right along with him

WRITE OUT YOUR DROPS

acquiescence

science tells us that heaviness sets to the ground, while lightness floats
yet it is your evil
that still haunts me and hovers around my ceiling the most

how many souls had your charcoal spirit already trapped,
when upon my heart's wall door you'd stumbled
and rather so loudly tapped ?

must this lingering haunting, be my punishment for believing?
must I awake still with nightmares,
despite still tearing up with yearning for you every other evening?

I shall long for your love no longer-
and only desire now to exorcise your memory's malice and venom
yet if your malevolent spooks leave, without my conciliation-
would they not take me, too, with 'em?

roller coaster

to the one who cried love
who'd seemed at first to have been sent from above
a savior from the routine
a daily switch to either lift my spirits
or sink them to the pit of my stomach-
never anything in between

my reason to start my day
to dress up my hours and face-
even when I'd been feeling quite gray

you return now to cry love once more
just as I'd finally boarded another ship-
away from your rocky shore

do I board your roller coaster?
self-control,
is something I still have yet to master

WRITE OUT YOUR DROPS

deny

amorously, eventually
I fall-
you deny making me
I react-
you deny provoking me

on your Hunter's lies
I choke-
you deny overfeeding me

with my last remaining
ounce of sanity and strength
I run away

and deny you

the clown fisherman

the foolish clown
at first impression
follows around the queen missing her crown
breathing life into her silent depression

my savior by fate
she now opines,
with surprising admiration
not realizing that the minute it's reeled in-
some fishermen can hurl the fish right back into the ocean

lost ones merely crave the attention
of an undeniably prestigious spirit
craving first for their dark soul to gain recognition
only to later back off of purity:
with a heart never truly in it

WRITE OUT YOUR DROPS

the unfrequented sin

you were a country I hadn't frequented before
I got lost without a map along the rocky shore
you approached wise beyond your years
I'd never seen a face so fierce
until my heartbreak fed your ego more

you're too good for me
was the line that'd reeled me in
made me feel safe along your translucent skin

I envy your thorough preparation, though
you knew the precise point at which to let me go
I just wish I'd known in advance, too, before the sin

a cut of you

cut it out
your 'humor' hurts and the words linger

cut it off
your long hair has witnessed much anger

cut it out
your heart's shape from a paper of color

cut in
any fake conversation you may see
between myself and another

and give me that part of you to keep
I'll swallow it into somewhere deep
your heart will remain in me forever

WRITE OUT YOUR DROPS

belittled

with every sunset,
her externally inflated expectations of love
disappear too, like the sun's rays-
little by little

expectations can only
genuinely
be raised internally

an organic feeling of faith in a union's future
that either exists, or doesn't really

she shall grow up, finally
the age of her spirit may still be little
but it must not
accept being belittled

the mermaid's selective memory

only the waves of good memories were allowed to wash over me
the cold truths were kept at bay-
waves of bad memories
didn't make it to the shore

but don't forget:
I'm a Mermaid
I can swim galore

when you need it again
the most,
I will
actively and purposely
not love thee anymore

WRITE OUT YOUR DROPS

proposals

make me an offer,
one that can't be refused

for promises have been broken
and good intentions, overused

with opportunities given
trampled
enthusiasm has finally been
dampened

yet I still want to believe:
it is the truth you wear on your sleeve

clueless disgrace

we borrow hearts
and lend our own
like library books
away on temporary loan

we unknowingly rent out
our arms to embrace
only to let go with the homeowner's return
attempting to then save face

whether we're acting in love-
something innocent, or taboo
our minds can tell us one thing
while the hearts don't have a clue

WRITE OUT YOUR DROPS

the phantom of the library

borrowed hearts, one is unable to own
like library books, away on temporary loan
I'd once written, romantically
they've since been tossed-
though once a possibility
to now mourn

my pleas- went to deaf ears
my tears- ignored by blind eyes
without healing the roots to grow:
by the flower, you were mesmerized

with each word
I walked on eggshells
my unvalued love became suppressed
along with my inability to speak
as I wept silently, to avoid yells

lasting love between opposites
is a myth
and gold can best be appreciated
only by a goldsmith

and my heart, sinking to the bottom
my jokes- you barely even got 'em
allow me to now sing my goodbye
and borrow from 'the Phantom':

and all the tears I might have shed
for your dark fate
have now grown cold, and turned into
tears of hate

DROPS
OF
PERSPIRATION

struggle

mata hari

World War Three exists
every season
between my heart, my body
and sense of reason

I attempt
foolishly
to mediate

yet I can never quite satiate
nor could I ever concentrate
when my tears for all three casualties
fall quite often

when I cannot choose
I am often imprisoned
for treason

psychology

there's apparently a void in me-
I discovered it in therapy-
which I fill with anyone and anything
to avoid facing that feeling of 'empty'

yet I'm not a gas tank
must get my alone-time back
no toxic cycles repeated, just for a good month or so
for too many times my heart has cracked and sank

maybe Freud said it best-
a girl abandoned by her father
can't fully feel whole

in peace may they both rest

WRITE OUT YOUR DROPS

mental curse

to fall into the abyss-
whether by
tripping, jumping, or,
being thrown-
but still survive
after being magnetically
pulled to the bottom core
into that land unknown

you sling right back up
like a shooting star
in reverse
try to maintain
your positivity
and sanity
through a forced smile
or a verse

many can't truly know
how mental suffering
can be a curse

yet like Disney princesses
with their own
some curses disguise
blessings
behind the scenes
shown

WRITE OUT YOUR DROPS

walking in the urbanite's shoes

city life
isn't always opportunities and lights
this morning on the train
it's disgusting smells, sounds, and sights

the proverbially greener pastures
on the 'other side':
they too rot without daily care

life can bore you
slower than a tortoise at times
only to later shake you to the core
and grab you by the hair

beauty isn't always as happy
and together as it appears
you'll never know when- inside-
strife has struck its youth
and added rapid years

a friendly greeting
becomes a façade
a way to hide
all the kryptonite
of the urbanite

WRITE OUT YOUR DROPS

settlements

to be settled
wise elders say
is cozier than excitement

a house that's familiar-
a home despite its flaws
an imperfectly familiar companion
a ring that made them yours

children to settle into bed
or a pet you're snuggling
truly are lovelier predicaments
as long as you're not settling

the undeceivable one

the cheater on quizzes
and later on lovers

becomes eventually
a most surprising addition
to the world of mothers

she sinks and rises
before being thrown overboard again
and later hovers

floating above the water,
in a realm of limbo-
more heated than heavenly
she must not cheat, her child, though
from precious, fleeting time with her company

the cheater must remember:
a child's memory, in retrospect,
is one that rarely falters

WRITE OUT YOUR DROPS

a mother's humility

the best gifts I've received
were painfully harsh
and brutally cold
life lessons

depression
comes to visit
from time to time now:
she strikes suddenly,
no longer in waves of longer
seasons

for the angel of purpose and pure light
shines before my eyes daily
so brightly

if it weren't for her, of golden-brown curls
I would be lost, when faced with what evil hurls

a poet's best friend

poetry weaves a web of protection
on the poet's emotions

allows us to feel both universal support
and acceptance of our fluid devotions

come what or who may
the verses will lay
in their realm-
for a read or write,
awaiting

they can never leave us, either
our mutual interdependence quivers
anticipating

WRITE OUT YOUR DROPS

innocence lost

blue
I'm blue
a young girl wrote, once upon an adolescent time
feeling stuck on these same old emotions, like glue
she'd continued-
she did always love to rhyme

I'm a bird, trapped in my cage
she'd also written
yearning to break free
like I could, long before harsh realities in this world, began to follow me

her heart was pure, her rage was raw
she'd witnessed things no child should ever say they saw
how was she to know, then, that a child would one day hold her hand
and that child would have a doll named *Blue*?

how was she to know, then,
that that child's father would indeed become that caged bird,
despite his innocence,
after the great injustice which had occurred?

I know that my wings will mend, and I CAN fly again
she'd begun the last verse
of her high-school-published ballad

though it will never be the same
she'd concluded:
a conclusion which to this day remains valid

for, following the storms, her rainbows have indeed appeared-
but they can never be luminous
just- rather pallid

WRITE OUT YOUR DROPS

the poet's fidelity

don't fall in love with a poet
you'll be disappointed before you know it

yes, you'll feel at first
immortal
as a subject in their verses'
portal

but we are more enamored with
love
than a human
beloved

the giver

it is excruciating
to be misunderstood
when understanding
is the goal of your livelihood

different from
culturally-set norms
since childhood
I've stood out, alone:
some praised this,
others never could

I blush-it is not shyness
I've just been raised
with manners and kindness

I love-it is not meekness
I smile when I can make another smile
this is my habit- not weakness

resolutions

can newness
fill in
the deficiencies,
left over
from the past?

can novelty
erase away
prior mistakes,
so their effects
don't last?

can the New Year
human-invented, not of nature
have the power of healing?

does it really matter,
though,
when it's all in our
states of mind?

so, never stop trying
and living
ignore, that we're born
simply for dying

WRITE OUT YOUR DROPS

the great forgiver

who determines what we deserve?
destiny?
where is the freedom to choose?

moral vs *immoral* reactions to pain
can we pretend to win when we lose?

no one can judge
if they have not been in the other's shoes
and faced the exact type of excruciating loneliness

only when I can't forgive, and judge *myself*
that's when God has judged as well-
though I believe in His eventual
forgiveness

years

15 candles
on her birthday cake
she didn't know the direction
her forced-to-bloom-early life would take

25 was 'the milestone',
they'd said
it didn't have to be your dream job
as long as you'd gotten paid

35 still holds promise
as it reluctantly nears
this time she's more realistic-
made wiser through her tears

WRITE OUT YOUR DROPS

day-to-day

avoid sustaining
a pout
whenever life throws a curveball
your way

whether apathetic
or devout
holding on to pain
will be your
downfall
however often
you pray

living with
regret
must not be
a safety net

own well-intentioned
choices
respect those
voices
in your head

any day could be the last
brave each sunset

WRITE OUT YOUR DROPS

true

tame your ego
not your
hopes
squander expectations
that wound you up in
ropes

style your soul
to your maximum
best
without rehearsals
of
feigned verses
to pass someone else's
test

like a fingerprint or snowflake
uniqueness
can sometimes be more than what they can take

whenever you feel reflective
there's always an alternate perspective
stay true to you- don't be fake

the fewer, the truer
commit to being You
And the True
will commit too.

WRITE OUT YOUR DROPS

the north star

feast your eyes upon
the loveliest star-subjective
out there on the horizon
never stop to think whether it'd always shined as bright
each and every previous season

when it's shining, you're smiling
when it's shooting, you're complaining

the star can't win

if it cannot be accepted as it is-

in all its majestic yet sometimes troublesome reality
tell me- what good is it being a most precious jewel in the galaxy?

if even amongst all the others
the star stays afloat
in the dark

desolate and lonely?

duality

she is a peculiar one
they say
her eyes burn dark
but skin caresses soft
like a flower in May

she wears her accumulated adornments loudly
each one reflecting petal off-springs of the rainbow

yet her wide-brimmed ebony hat and clothes remain fixed, proudly
if not for the darkness, the master thinks, *how would all my prisms show?*

WRITE OUT YOUR DROPS

cappuccino

the foamy sip
of cappuccino
enters my mouth
gradually
forewarning
either a warm
or
scorching
hot sip

reminding me of foamy waves
approaching the shore

they could wash over me
or swallow me whole
yet alive

I
must
take
a
dip

its cappuccino- foams rising higher and higher
the waves approach me as I rest on the shore
with my body on the wet sand
seashells scratch my hand

the water could indeed swallow me whole
I remind myself once more

or it could subside as it nears

I'll just have to take my chances
life's full of surprising circumstances

regardless of our tears and fears

WRITE OUT YOUR DROPS

sharp communication

mercury is in retrograde
it's your time of the month
you've been having a rough day
I've got a lot of other problems on my mind

it's amazing the excuses we can make
the variety of sources on which we can shift the blame
for our hurtful or ice-cold words

a single word-or lack thereof
can singlehandedly create the sharpest knife-
reaching down deep
and cutting out the very life and root
of any glimmer of hope, belief, or smile

the knife can carve out
the most excruciating and disfigured shape in our hearts,
adding unwanted emotions of anger and nervous regret
to the always welcomed and pure base of affinity
upon which we had initially built our behavioral coziness

we are the choices we make
do we really not see?
we are the creators of our own words, just as we are of our worlds

destiny can play a hand- sure- but astrology?
a bad day? physical sluggishness? financial or family issues?

would we use these sources to blame a murder?
when we don't choose our words carefully
with the most precious and intimate people in our lives
that is exactly what we commit:
we slowly become murderers
murderers of trust
murderers of love

WRITE OUT YOUR DROPS

social media mornings

mornings once started
with opening our eyes to peek outside of our windows
for a glimmer of sunshine behind the clouds
or sounds of raindrops tapping
or heavy gusts of wind-howling
or the gentle whisper of pristine snow falling

mornings once started
with the desire for some tea, juice or coffee
warm crispy bread toasted to perfection with butter

mornings once meant curiosity
about real current events
and intellectual stimulation to activate our minds,
flipping through the newspaper to sniff that wonderful print-smell
or turning on the television to listen to expert commentaries

mornings now?
still waking up with the desire
to observe, sense, and satiate curiosities
but technology has replaced the weather taking place outside our windows

social applications
have ingested that cup of coffee, or toast we could smell in our minds,
even before those had been prepared

they have even gobbled up our traditional paperbacks or hardcovers

in the mornings now, we shall be in mourning
For telecommunications are observing *us*
curious about *us*
devouring *us*

WRITE OUT YOUR DROPS

woman

                                                                                                   girl

wakes up, looks out the window
tall building's chauffeur starting up the Ferrari to drive her to school
maid cleaning up after her breakfast of scrambled eggs and French toast:
all the other girls envy her

                                                                                                   girl

lonely inside

                                                                                                   girl

wakes up, looks out the window
gets out the door of the car, mother sleeps in the driver's seat,
goes next to mom to wake her up-
to ask her where they will be looking for a home
and breakfast that particular foggy morning:

                                                                                                   girl

hope in her heart

                                                                                                   girl

wakes up, her friends- the ants and bugs crawling on the street-
tell her *good morning*
needs to find her younger brother,
they need to somehow escape
yet into another city in hopes of surviving that day's awaited bomb

                                                                                                   girl

tears in her eyes

                                                                                                   girl

wakes up, turns on the T.V.
watches the news, thinking about
how she could make a difference for the better
picks up her homework,
meets up with her friend as they walk to class that day

                                                                                                   girl

determination in her soul

                                                                                                   girl

give her a chance, listen to her, care for her

                                                                                                   girl

don't let anyone undermine your beauty and intelligence

                                                                                                   girl

take charge, make a difference, help those around you

                                                                                                   girl

WRITE OUT YOUR DROPS

use whatever you have,
whether it is your money, your willpower,
or your heart,
and do something good with it

girl

know that you deserve to be listened to,
appreciated and respected

girl

have faith, and know that no matter what you're going through,
you will learn from your experiences
and blossom into a magnificent
and strong being:
a loving, caring, intelligent, smiling through her tears, loved

woman

DROPS
OF
MUSIC

art & individuality

WRITE OUT YOUR DROPS

'rappin' for Queens'

♠ Aces of Spades: the ladies of Queens
♦ Brave Kings of Diamonds who'd go to extremes
the borough holds all flags
from Peruvian to Chinese hubs
the most diverse in the nation-
its people dance their soul in Clubs ♣
picket fences look at co-ops,
juxtaposed- industrial...commercial...residential
I became a true American here
to my hometown- I remain partial
the most loyal of Queens
you welcomed me in '92...thank you
you remain forever youthful in all your residents' Hearts ♥
no others can compare to you...for you do you

like versus love

this city is made up of bridges-
once you're on the path of one
there's no way out
must face the consequences
waiting on the other side
whether your apathetic
or devout

the city is full of dirty noise:
one of many things about it
beyond your control
you must force yourself
to enjoy the fast-pace
even when you're weary
and jaded after it all

you don't *like* New York
it can never make you feel whole
yet you *love* it...breathe it
the city where you root your soul

66

WRITE OUT YOUR DROPS

senses

listen
only to that voice inside
ignore unsympathetic whispers
trying to exert control
you know your melody
the best

they can't know
your spirit
as a whole

keep away
from those
always bellicose
save your own
soul

observe

the eyes
read poetry
the soul
hears a melody
the heart
registers the verses
the spirit
feels music's magical curses

WRITE OUT YOUR DROPS

the thrill of creativity

close your eyes
does it appear underneath your eyelids?
the last time you'd actually aspired to accomplish a feat?
and not merely go through the motions of duties- obsolete?
aspirations set upon yourself by your own conscience and will
can you visualize the last time you've actually felt that natural,
authentic thrill?
never let that teenager inside of you stop dreaming
for when that fire stops burning
we cease growing
and expanding

dancing mermaid

the melodic hymns
of her soul
sometimes take
utter control

like sirens,
singing with heavy breaths
luring captains
to their untimely deaths

the music of her heart
possesses her fragile
and tired mind

it won't let her start
another day with his memory left behind

WRITE OUT YOUR DROPS

wishful thinking

I don't know quite when
not sure quite how
vulnerably-catalyzed me
has been able to survive
without crumbling by now

the struggle of trying to always reach out,
prove my worth and instill
the same self-confidence in another
has often been taken advantage of
as they've drained my pure energy
to recharge their souls,
leaving me weaker in my ether
and often alone as I later suffer

how much longer can I keep up appearances
of strength and forgiveness, and onward fight?

how much longer can I swallow my tears?
how much longer can I hide my fright
and persevere with might?

may I no longer be forced to smile
 as I hide my scream

may I no longer troop on alone
may the nightmares transform into a dream

WRITE OUT YOUR DROPS

sober inebriation

summer birthdays
full of bittersweet daze
tears welling up
hidden by the sun's rays

growing younger as we get older
earning wisdom in exchange for
one disappointment
and another

stay strong, my brother
don't sell out, my sister

be drunk on life
while remaining sober

silenced victims

as he loosens
his buckles
with nervousness- not consent-
she chuckles

calculates ways out of her cage
to escape and open a clean page

he purposely ignores her age
as well as her secret rage

she hides her fear
only to have food & shelter near

it's not her choice
please allow her a voice

WRITE OUT YOUR DROPS

the fooled teen

glasses, frizz
unpainted fingernails on her hand-
a teenage girl
doesn't aim to, nor should she ever
attract a man

adored by those her age
even at her nerdiest
yet the words of the legal adult
had proved to be the cleverest

a predator is hard to notice
when he's given a girl her first real kiss

if there could've been a chance to do it all over again
she'd have gone to her family or the police station
right there and then

she had bottled up all her rage
to her surprise- today it still spills onto the page

the pain hasn't made her a helpless victim
nor some all-knowing sage

she simply continues to bleed her art
each day can become a new start

and the world truly is her stage

WRITE OUT YOUR DROPS

the mother

people always have a sense of wonder
when they see a woman standing alone
without another

is she a good one?
is she a sinner?
is she a free spirit?
or is she a protector?

labels haven't helped anyone
my friend
for in the end
life is simply how you react in the moment
and in particular shoes
when an event summons

we've all got
both our angels
as well as our demons

theatrics

if you deny
satiating your soul
for the sake of others

then who are you,
when you can't truly breathe
under masks and covers?

some wear visible masks
only in October
others wear invisible ones
the rest of the year-
their various truths hidden
behind a cover

umbrellas
yes- against the raindrops
can provide shelter

while self-defense shields
could certainly-
when faced with fate-
falter

WRITE OUT YOUR DROPS

yin and yang

the professional
professor
the nurturing
mother
the majestic
angel
the demonic
devil

she can be all she is called
yet she is ultimately none

always a battle persists
one which can never be won

a woman can try to achieve
everything possible under the sun

it remains, regardless of progress
a man's world
for boys are still allowed more fun

WRITE OUT YOUR DROPS

anticipation

I wait for my destiny
to rear its either ugly or stupendous head
out from the blanket of slowly-passing time
under which it's been hiding

I'm not choosy-
I wait like the passenger waits for the train
to catch the next appointment with a loved one,
a professional opportunity or disappointment,
even with death

I wait, you see
without any supposition

when you feel the call of destiny
everything else is merely a check-off list
until you can finally feel at peace-
at one with your own unique place in infinity

bare

I will allow the sun to shine
no shades
I will fight for what is mine
no shades

I will brave the feared
I will weather the storm
I will pray to be healed
I will defy the norm

I will be who I am
regardless of grays
I am both the dark and light
throughout all of my days

I will face those rays

the savior

it's indeed strange
how wisdom and
true self-acceptance
only come with age

I'm neither a model
nor an hourglass
I'm a guitar
with strings of brass

I'm neither a superstar
nor a CEO
but I feel fulfilled
being my own hero

the traveler

the sightseer
thought to be
always seeking
novelty
in reality
seeks conformity
in the innate ability
of people with new visions to see
to welcome with glee
her familiar eccentricity
however different
they all may be
from one another
in actuality

WRITE OUT YOUR DROPS

the protagonist

books
on shelves
describe Santas
more than the elves

the prominent
receive prominence
while the aides
are described
only through
their obedience

fair or not
we must play that part-
become the protagonist
of your own heart
of your own art

---

the blind archer

I am a blind archer
captivated by the target, despite a visionless sight
I am the prickliest rose in the orchard- useless for fruit production,
though dangerously lovely in the light

I am the messiest neat freak- OCD with symmetry,
though cleaning makes me shriek
I am the most exciting bore
the most thrilling wh... chore
I am the craziest sage- insane and wise to my very core

I am the owner of a biography to make you weep- reading through my roller
coaster chapters-
you'd finish me in one sweep
I am the simplest mystery
I am Duality, and Duality is me

WRITE OUT YOUR DROPS

the cat and the 'soul-met'

the images provoked in my mind-
invoked by a sunset or a sunrise-
bring memories of different people's eyes

I feel like a cat-
in that I've already lived through 8 of my lives
and that I'm on my final one,
still humorously looking for *the one*

but I now believe- we don't get one soulmate
but rather we get one 'soul-met'-
a soul our souls have crossed during one particular moment
for a reason

a soul we have simply 'met'
and said *hello* to

through a kiss, a hug, a look
a summer, a winter, or a catalyst heartbreak

I've learned not to take any experience for granted
but to not attach myself to anything either
for whatever life sends us…we can take

WRITE OUT YOUR DROPS

royal folklore

the ice queen
suffers forced isolation
despite playing like a child-
freezing everything during procrastination

the Arabian princess
suffers duties and responsibilities
before Aladdin-family and country
preceded other amorous possibilities

you are my queen, he claims
with eyes begging for more
she sighs, and cannot be flattered-
her pristine loyalty, to them soon feels like a bore

the happiness of royalty is folklore

hope

they won in the end
a haunting past and isolated present
for both him and I

he watches now only from afar
and I, like a fool, still have kept my door slightly ajar

hope should sometimes be a sin
for it can allow either devilish or foolish thoughts
to creep in

yet other times I get confused
and I feel it to my bones
for the accumulation over time of the smallest glitters of hope
can also erode even the hardest of stones

WRITE OUT YOUR DROPS

the peace

a piece of chocolate
melted in the mouth
as if the cocoa has the power
to manipulate brain cells
into believing all will be well

a piece of information
ingested with utmost curiosity and satisfaction-
if originating from a source of someone
who makes you feel swell

a peace of mind
is the rarest jewel to discover
and be able to spread throughout the mind,
for it is the only one the soul needs to survive.
the success or failure of which
only time can tell

the floater

life often provides timely signs-
ignored
yet recognized in retrospect
you actively live in the moment
not fully utilizing your head

harsh consequences, however,
can ultimately haunt the adult
floating like a teenager
void of responsibility

some haven't fully grasped this yet

if it makes us smile in a moment
all later pain-we tend to forget
under a pretense of *no regret*

WRITE OUT YOUR DROPS

dear new year

dear tomorrow

could you please help me overcome
all of my inner sorrow?

can each anxiety attack
alongside of OCD
I conceal
finally become appeased
through a sense of belonging
and settlement,
with just a dash of zeal?

can you help me
to help myself?
to do so
but still be myself?

sounds like a silly thing to ask

but self-acceptance
in implementation
is truly a difficult task

WRITE OUT YOUR DROPS

pink means go

when you have to be given the 'green light'
go 'pink'

go your own way
resist that traumatically-bonded
pull to stay

don't overthink

if they had been
true blue
a real one, through and through
you would have felt welcomed from the start
anyway
permission isn't needed
to be yourself
on any day

the strugglers

to *speak now*
or forever hold your peace
the cliché at weddings
is much deeper than it seems

to keep inside
a monster of truth
yearning to break free-
could never bring serenity

revel in the color of your gut
it's rarely seen to the outside world
but courage shan't be problematic
for without it
we merely exist and accept our lot

WRITE OUT YOUR DROPS

the variation of violence

knives on the street
punches and slaps indoors
we can hurt life rivals
as cruelly as the ones we claim to love the most
and we wonder why
the human race still can't prevent wars

the monsters within
often wait for the next opportunity
lurking beneath the skin-
desiring confrontation
in close proximity

we must choose our words
even more carefully
than our battles and swords

karma chases heart-crackers
as well as those folks
who remain cement-hard
and bellicose

WRITE OUT YOUR DROPS

the shield of humor

the
fake
snake
in the lake
made my body shake

tremors and panic attacks
caused by surprise tricks
hurt the most when one lacks
self-defense against stones and sticks

feigned
love
feels ordained
from above

until harsh reality pokes
and suddenly you'd prefer the jokes

WRITE OUT YOUR DROPS

the officer

faithfully
I execute my task

the dutiful officer
of fulfilling an expectation
of countless subjects,
without much protest or sensation

if I've reaped any benefits as well
they never ask

the goldsmith

dimming others' sunshine
won't brighten the ones you emit
it can even diminish your own rays entirely over time
only a Goldsmith can appreciate Gold
even if that gold is thrown into mud and smothered in slime
gold is gold
and its value doesn't depreciate
solely the thrower's value degrades:
drowning in the hate

WRITE OUT YOUR DROPS

DROPS
OF
BLOOD

family

WRITE OUT YOUR DROPS

'Sel'

August 8, 1984
a baby-unwanted by her father
came into this world

she's a gift
he'd told his wife that Wednesday
you wanted a baby so much
the 'gift' would grow up
without knowing a father's
protective touch

growing up amongst duality
of clashing cultures and her own personality
she was always searching,
the 8-8

soul-eaters fed off of her energy
you're a princess they all said
yet in regards to what she needed-
they could not care less
and did not appreciate
nor
genuinely reciprocate

November 25, 2015
her world changed
she'd no longer act like a teen
motherhood didn't develop
as planned and arranged
life became simpler yet serene

WRITE OUT YOUR DROPS

my rock

she is my rock
she keeps me grounded
both sweet and adventurous
she's quite well-rounded

she's my daughter after all
she's not always a picnic
but still is my closest ally
as Gud must have intended

she can make me smile through my tears
I can't always comprehend it
I've had so many more downs than ups,
but somehow still
I can be made to feel
that I've 'made it'

the foam's advice

where is my Captain?
the mermaid asked
he's been captured after the vessel's shipwreck
the foams answered

'what do I do now?'
she whimpered

*float on rough waters
by continuously flipping your own tail
and turn the tide in your own favor*
the foams encouraged
he may be gone, but you can be your own Savior

WRITE OUT YOUR DROPS

humility

colorful books
stacked before a
hand-print marked
window sill
exist now more for art
whereas reading
had once been
my daily pill

she used to nap
and I would smile
a book could distract me
for a while

now my toddler pouts
when I'm without her
in her young life
she's been through
much grief
and many goodbyes to incur

she's my entertainment now
and humbly I'm grateful
a child's a blessing
many wish for
so,
perhaps
that's more
beautiful

maternal guilt

on these cruel city streets-
I can be exhausted
to the max
yet I'll still carry her
if she needs me to
they say *let us help you, relax*
but it's me
whose eyes she implores
for it's me
whom she thinks sometimes ignores
not knowing my heart
explodes, and explores
ways to make up to her
all of my shortcomings
and the patience
my spirit lacks

the biggest fan

and in this life;
you may turn out to be
my only real fan
and my only real friend
yet in the end
I'll fight on alone
if I have to
with our without a plan
or a man
for it is you
I can never reprimand
for you always understand
as long as I live,
I will never let go of your hand

birthday woman-child part 1

this is 35
what you don't know is that in my family
no one has really lived past the age of 70
and so I would be considered midlife already
that is, if I'm even lucky
for trauma always pursues me relentlessly
my biological father himself died at 50
so what could possibly await me?
Only God knows the reality
but I'll keep dancing to my own tune,
and suffer fools gladly
as long as I can be there
for my baby

birthday woman-child part 2

this is 36
too many words
have hurt more than sticks
a dream admired
six figures desired
but my weary soul is getting tired
a prisoner of circumstance
stuck between conscience and chance

double standards
hypocrisy
no more highs
off of pointless jealousy
phantoms who lead to nowhere
just leave me be
I feel more loved on my own
than by words verbally expressed
but never shown

WRITE OUT YOUR DROPS

socio-political genocide

rotting away in boxes
is my only 'settled' life
one I'd barely gotten to know
with the role of a dutiful wife

I search for my baggy sweater
for without him, too, I feel bare
like the coziness of dear packed-away furniture
it also just isn't there

must be in one of the killed-memory holders of cardboard

forced evacuation
shunned by half a nation

will any of us reunite?

it too remains unclear

I'll maintain a sense of
settlement
as a vagabond
this new role I've found
praying for justice
year after year

WRITE OUT YOUR DROPS

medea

you are my sunshine
I sang to you, before you were even born
I had been amongst strict military crowds
feeling misplaced, and rather forlorn

you developed and came so peacefully,
wrapping your fingers around my pointer
I had unpreparedly become something much idolized-
I'd become a mother

with its good and bad,
life as we knew it changed in one night
despite innocence we were displaced
yet history will write the truth, and the schemers
will become the ones disgraced

just as we've gotten comfortable
with our new order
attempting peace through the chaos
of our new shelter

old demons re-emerge

and if they try to take away
our sunshine together?
hell indeed have no fury
like a scorned child-bearer

I'll let that thought linger

WRITE OUT YOUR DROPS

bloodline tears

red, red eyes
blood-red eyes
painfully-pink eyes
they cannot disguise

they cannot pretend
that they've poured for some hurtful friend
for in the end
it's the most painful downpour, you see
when your tears, have fallen due to family

some bridges are meant to be crossed
some are meant to be burned
some connect briefly
while others are earned

at the end of this one, which I'm on
I realize now, I can see
that it is only she
who alone with compassion and understanding
is waiting for me

she is neither my mother-
warm-looking with words of stone
nor my daughter-
my untimely yet beautiful source
of motivation to go on

she is my future reflection
She is Me
and she alone is no one

red, next-morning-puffy eyes
they attempt to disguise
a mentally-abusive lover:
a proud vessel
whom the world only sees the surface of on the water
unaware of the painful propeller
my tears have been my truest lifelong friend
to them I will now respectfully add *humility*,
as we continue to walk that bridge, until the very end

WRITE OUT YOUR DROPS

hero nostalgia

nostalgic songs
haunt me from the radio
I used to reminisce
smile
and then let it go

been getting harder and harder
however
to do that, you know
for too many sunsets have passed
and soon it will again be time for snow

my loneliness becoming increasingly highlighted
even in a crowd
longing to be more
than my own fellow, my own beau
I yearn both *for* and *to be* a hero
guess I need to be my own, though

WRITE OUT YOUR DROPS

unappeasable expectations

                the heaviness on her shoulders
                    could not be appeased
          by any soft massage done at the salon
         those shoulders can't heal with a squeeze
            regardless of how much she needs
                      another's to lean on

          she's taken on the sins of her father
                  who has been long gone
but whose betrayal still haunts her mother:
    her fiery eyes turn to *his* in her eyes
   each time the daughter confronts another

despite the new generation that has arrived
            the burden still will not let go
           a daughter who has miraculously
                            survived
  shouldn't suffer for the sins of her father
this- the grandparent now has simply got to know

WRITE OUT YOUR DROPS

when you can't write, dance it out

the best part of parenthood
so far
has been being given a second chance
a do-over
to re-witness every single endeavor of life
from the exquisite to the irksome
and view it from the outside in
like a moviegoer

children don't change
just age
lives rearrange
do we fit on the same page.?
separate the fool from the sage
sometimes we belong in a cage
I'm more than my rage

thoughts..thoughts..thoughts-

hush!

stillness

I throw my child a glance…
and I'm an angel before the fall again
and with purity I shall dance

AFTERWORD

when faced with the unknown
your inner voice and light
are sometimes
the only paths shown

before the advent of technology
a lighthouse- a star on earth- was shone
showing boats
in the ocean
'home'
despite standing alone

the 'ripple' effect
or
'butterfly' one
somehow,
it's all been coined
and done

yet clichés exist for a reason
they hold true through every season

we are all a mere drop in that ocean
you see
we shan't hold back any story
that will one day become history

for collectively,
we are the human community
we are family

SET FREE YOUR FLOW

L IKE THE TIDES OF THE MIGHTY OCEANS
receding before flooding the shores,
and rivers catapulting
into rapids & waterfalls

You too have a *flow*-
an inherent inclination
of which way to go.

Mother Nature must outpour
when it feels that call:
just as your own essence,
the one of your very soul.

Yet the society-pressured logical mind
can repress,
life choices the spirit wishes
to express.

Like wind currents harnessed into energy-
forces of your duality, in unison,
can create synergy.

Set free your glow. Set free your flow.

SET FREE YOUR FLOW

SET FREE YOUR FLOW

to be lost
in the **flow**
in that focused moment of
creativity

your artistry
and authenticity
safe and sound

no need to be found
no disillusioning distractions
that make your heart pound

to soar the world
in mind and spirit
with both feet
firmly on the ground

SET FREE YOUR FLOW

she made me do it
my divided soul
the one I cannot control

for when, using logic, I try to do so;
she shatters, like glass ensuing freefall
and I ultimately risk losing it all

so here I go,
I unleash her truth
as I best know
the urban and the floral
the liberal and the moral

I set free her flow
perhaps, thus, we can
finally heal and grow

SET FREE YOUR FLOW

"The happiest people spend much time in a state of *flow*- the state in which people are so involved in an activity that nothing else seems to matter; the experience itself is so enjoyable that people will do it even at great cost, for the sheer sake of doing it."

"To overcome the anxieties and depressions of contemporary life, individuals must become independent of the social environment to the degree that they no longer respond exclusively in terms of its rewards and punishments. To achieve such autonomy, a person has to learn to provide rewards to his/herself. He/she has to develop the ability to find enjoyment and purpose *regardless of external circumstances.*"

— **Mihaly Csikszentmihalyi**, *Flow: The Psychology of Optimal Experience*

SET FREE YOUR FLOW

Dear reader,

Yes, you. If this collection has found its way to you, then I believe you too to somehow have felt at one point to be in the eye of the storm called *identity*. Smack in the middle: *centered* between right and left. Geographically. Ideologically. At times attempting to mediate between the two forces. At others: to be 'centered' and 'aware' enough to actively enjoy being in the present, rather than constantly reflect on the past or future. Admittedly, I have only been able to do both through biographical self-analysis in retrospect, and sometimes still face the same struggles I will delve into here in this collection.

According to the late social psychologist Peter Weinreich:

"A person's identity is defined as the totality of one's self-construal, in which how one construes oneself in the present expresses the continuity between how one construes oneself as one was in the past and how one construes oneself as one aspires to be in the future…One's *ethnic identity* is defined as that part of the totality of one's self-construal made up of those dimensions that express the continuity between one's construal of past ancestry and one's future aspirations in relation to ethnicity…"
(*Theories of Race and Ethnic Relations*. Comparative Ethnic and Race Relations. Cambridge: Cambridge University Press. 1988)

What makes you *you*? And What makes me *me*?

Splendid literature has been written by bi-cultural authors (mostly vis-à-vis their biracialism in particular), discussing the difficulty of a *dichotomous* life a character experiences while growing up.

But these are *my* drops. My autobiographical 'contribution' into the bucket of human collective stories forming global oceans: akin to what psychologists have called a 'global consciousness'.

And who am I? No one special. No one with any mission other than being a storyteller. A voice for the less-frequently voiced, if even at all.

General details of my childhood are known by those who know me in real life. Some are also known by my likely-annoyed language students, for I've repeatedly shared with them biographical anecdotes in an effort to motivate them whenever I sensed the confidence in their language prowess begin to dim. Most frequently, I've relayed my 'Storytelling Contest' representation of the public school I attended in the 4th grade, just one year after immigrating to the United States with my mother.

In retrospect, I would consider this my first sense of 'accomplishment' in this country, as well as a 'catalyst' sign intended for eventually dedicating my life to becoming a storyteller. My subjective 'drop' of storytelling to pour into that 'global consciousness' of human interconnectedness (addressed mostly in my premier poetic collection, *Write Out Your Drops*) has been a little bit of many things. In Turkish, we have a coinage: *'ortaya karışık'*. It roughly translates to 'a little bit of everything mixed together in the middle' and is mostly used to order a variety of appetizers in restaurants (if you've never ordered eggplant appetizers at a Mediterranean restaurant, you don't know what you're missing).

'Ortaya karışık'. That's exactly how I felt growing up as an *Istanbulite* child in New York City: smack in the 'center' of various dichotomies. East and West. Villager and Urbanite. Traditional and Modern. Politically correct and political outcast. The family pleaser and the black sheep.

Through my musings, I attempt to not only provide you with *a view from the middle* (my first intended definition of 'a centered view'), but also increase my own sense of balance and self-awareness ('centeredness') through self-reflection. And, in doing so, hopefully allow you to be able to do the same for your own *self*.

Empathetic reader. You will be reading the following short essays and poetic verses from a woman-child who was raised as a bi-cultural person in the United States. (I was raised here, yes, yet even at the age of nearly 37 as I write this: I'm not sure whether or not I've yet grown up). An overly-sensitive woman, as well as an empath to other people's pain- who's been let down countlessly with the expectation that such sensitivity would be returned to me. I have been called 'childish' many times and by many people: with both good-natured intentions in using that word, and bad.

By blood I am Turkish, and by cultural upbringing: an American. I am equally Turkish and American. I am equally East and West. (Some pan-European Turks would argue that Turkish culture is not very representative of the East, but I'm a realist who begs to differ. I'm of the view that while geographically and ethnically Turkey is most certainly Eurasian, many of its cultural expectations and customs have more in common with the 'East'). And I strive every day simply for balance: grateful to be alive.

In theater, middle rows and 'center' seats are often favored: they're an easier-on-the-eyes 'view' of the performance. You can view the main event on stage from all sides, from different vantage points. I write now my own such view.

It was the great Shakespeare, wasn't it- who said that the world is a 'stage' and that we are all merely 'the players? What if we're more so the *audience*, observing natural events and how all living things go about fulfilling the various necessities for survival- albeit from different angles in accordance with our world views and social identifications?

I've come to follow various animals in my backyard lately; sparrows have built a nest in one corner of our roof, for example, while a showier male cardinal in his red glory chirps every morning alone. From my 'view from the middle' of both a liberal and traditional perspective, I imagine the birds in the nest as having built a traditional home as a family, while the cardinal chirps alone in a melancholy tone. The cardinal searches, I imagine, for a home or at least a partner of his own with whom to roam. 'The Settled' versus 'The Vagabond', I title them. Whenever I view them, I smirk.

SET FREE YOUR FLOW

I was raised smack in the middle of the storm where East and West would often clash, just like my dreams. I've now come, however, to not only accept my bicultural identity (which I'd spent my entire life running from, in order to 'fit in' better just in one category) but actually to be empowered by my duality. I feel this has allowed me to become more 'centered' and present in the here and now. Without being ashamed of my past, nor worried about the future.

I hope this personal overview of what has 'catalyzed' me into becoming the teacher and author that I am today makes you smile. Regardless of your background: if you can relate at all, and feel inspired even a teensy bit? Well then, my various 'drops' to ultimately form these 'collectively-oceanic' flowing waters will have been worth it. My nickname growing up, 'Sel,' after all, translates to a 'flood'.

With *Write Out Your Drops*, drops of sweat from my struggles and the drops of emotional tears I shed created a waterfall. With this collection, I aim to create an over*flow* of individuality *blowing* through people's souls- winds that are not filtered by cultural expectations and limitations. So that we may create hurricanes of a better kind than the destructive one of nature: hurricanes of art and authenticity so strong that dogma cannot diminish them.

I thank you in advance for allowing the ramblings of my consciousness and memories into your precious reading time and mental space. I hope my 'centered view' of self-knowledge and cultural observations allow you to *set free your own flow*.

XOXO

Selin Senol Akin

SECTION I:
Flowing Through the Veins

LINEAL LEGACY

A CENTERED VIEW

who can hold your hand,
when cannot you extend it?

why you have to be a storm, to thrive and keep warm
they'll never comprehend it

juggling two worlds
palms full
heart wary

you're dual, in one individual
and two can become heavy
for the soul to carry

delicate balance,
indecision and responsibility

your vulnerability
bare
let them judge
if they dare

tears flood your soul
whilst you feign not to care

ESTEEM

how enchanting
it would have been
to be transported to time gone by
merely through a wish,
or touching historic marble

then again- we can do so, can we not?

old neighborhoods
old loves
old joys and smells
old flaws

causing nostalgic retrograde

we're all living legends
to someone or other on this earth
realize your value and worth

before you are merely like that stone

immortalized
long after you can
recognize

SET FREE YOUR FLOW

Books Over Looks

When you tell a fellow Turk you're from the historically popular city 'Istanbul', they often follow up with, 'how about your homeland-*memleket?*' Istanbul, after all, is the Eastern twin of New York City- and I by no means believe it to have been random coincidence that I was meant to have been raised as an equal part of both places.

In my family's case, we could be considered relatively 'original' Istanbulites, I suppose. Istanbul is where my grandparents emigrated to from their native Bulgarian city of Plovdiv, following Communist repression of Muslims in the early 1950's.

It's funny. My 'duality' had begun before I ever moved to the United States with my mother at nearly age 8. Long before becoming a Turkish-American citizen, I had frequently felt torn between the often-discussed 'two different Turkeys' in my home country of Türkiye: the 'secularist' and the 'traditional'.

I'll never forget walking in a relatively 'conservative' part of Istanbul one day as a young child holding my mother's hand, and hearing a little boy around my age call to his headscarf covered mother: "Look mommy, wh*res are passing by…"

Now, I'm happy to say that Turkey has come a long way since the early 1990's in regards to the mutual acceptance of and friendship between Muslim women choosing to cover their hair and those who don't. But at the time- and, especially as a little girl who didn't even fully understand the degrading term in Turkish-

I was shocked. Not only by the boy's verbal outburst at my mother- who had just been dressed casually in jeans and a baggy t-shirt- but by the random action in itself.

What must have that little boy heard about 'uncovered' women at home in order to so casually have made such a remark, as if pointing out to his mother some zebras at a zoo? Furthermore, what must have become of that little boy, I wonder, as a man now around my age?

Has he been able to evolve from such flawed thinking stemming from his childhood, or, sadly- gone to mistreat and judgingly-label more women in his subsequent life?

This recognition of there being a socially-perceived 'dichotomy' between two types of women in Turkey began, therefore, when I was a young girl in Turkey- and only escalated over time.

Whenever I met a Turk here in the United States who didn't seem to understand why I wasn't as 'excited' about our traditional cooking, holidays, and customs as they were- they often talked to me with judgement. Their words and looks in response to my indifference would almost always make me feel as if they were looking down on me, their attitude coming across as thinking, *'so you think you're too cool and Americanized for our customs now'*? But what they didn't get was this: even back in Turkey, I hadn't been raised to prioritize such customs, either.

My late grandmother, Emine, with her trendy two-piece suits, light green eyes and chestnut curls looking 'Hollywood' in photographs, began to cover her hair in her later years with a bonnet and prayed five times a day in accordance with the Koran.

My paternal grandmother, Hafize- equally lovely and an immigrant from Bulgaria herself- remains similarly pious to this day, wearing a more traditional headscarf. Yet this is where their similarities would end. Emine was a 'city girl' reared toward becoming a professional woman and kept her spiritual life mostly to herself, while Hafize went on to reproduce five children and lived mostly in a domesticated lifestyle. Both my late grandfathers- whom I remember for their warmth (Hasan, descending from Georgia and Ismet, from Bulgaria)- were never really the 'strict' types either. They both smoked cigarettes heavily, enjoyed convivial spirits in the home, and rarely went 'macho' on their spouses or offspring.

Perhaps, dear reader, even by birth and genetics, therefore, I was never from very typically 'traditional' roots. Perhaps if my Zafer (more on him in the next section), had chosen to remain in my life and I had been raised with his family's influence rather than my mother's, I could have somewhat been more into Turkish holiday celebrations and various customs, as most of my cousins tend to be. But, alas, I was not. I was raised mostly by my mother and her small family. No big *Ramazan* celebrations. No encouraged hand-kissing of the elders. No baking something 'special' every week for 'big family dinners'. No observable 'Turkishness' aside from an inherent love of our cuisine, historical attractions and music, which remains to this day.

Perhaps this, perhaps that. Allow me, dear reader, to cut to the chase. Whatever 'Turkishness' I had learned as a young girl, I learned predominantly from my relatively more 'liberal,' working/then-single mother (I was never around my relatively more traditional set of grandparents geographically). But, of course, Turks I met growing up in New York couldn't have known that. They would view me as 'snobby' or somehow as 'forcibly westernizing' myself each time I expressed disinterest in Turkish customs. In reality: I simply wasn't familiar and had never felt an inherent (or environmentally-enforced) inclination towards such traditions. My 'centered view' is thus, quite literally, from the middle of not only Turkish and American cultures, but also a traditional and liberal worldview in general.

While I aim to express my unique view, I cannot ever state, in fairness, that I was distinctly 'torn' between my mother's 'eastern' ways and the relatively more 'western' ones of my Americanized upbringing (with my Turkish-American stepdad, and more on him a litter later as well). In hindsight, in fact, I can now hypothesize that the two parents who've influenced me were equally torn between the 'right' and 'left' themselves!

While one parent clearly was more center-right while the other was more center-left- relatively speaking- I was never directly pressured or reprimanded by my mother or stepdad for having chosen any one side over the other in my decision-making.

My bicultural duality and dichotomous struggles were caused more so by my own self-identity and image; by how I never felt able to 'fit in' among any of the social circles I'd frequent. I didn't want to disappoint anyone- and hence often ended up disappointing myself.

My mother, stepfather, as well as many friends growing up would themselves often experience feeling torn between a stern mindset and an open one. The definition of 'strength' whenever I'd hear her name- my mother, Aysu- for example, didn't lead a traditional lifestyle, yes, but her mindset certainly was as such. She'd grown up among a repressed yet curious generation in Turkey that had unknowingly planted the seeds of the dichotomy many of us as their children being born in the 1970's and 1980's would face. I'd even go so far as to liken Turkey's cultural dichotomy to the neighboring Persian one- with the only difference really being our secular laws contrasting with their theocratical ones. Like the character Nassrin of the renowned Azar Nafisi novel, *Reading Lolita in Tehran,* describes: knowing "…what it means to be caught between tradition and change (having always) been in the middle of it…"

Even in our native Istanbul- trendy clothes and discotheques would scream 'West', while ultimately becoming silenced with the daily calls to prayer from mosque minarets. My mother wanted to see me become a 'career woman', yes, but never make love to a man I wasn't married to. She and many other similar mothers of her generation would expect their children- especially daughters- to remain virgins even if marriage had to be delayed until well into one's 30's to be able to advance professionally.

My maternal grandmother continuously praised feminist-leaning ideals and never implied to me that a woman's main role was purely based on domesticity and marriage. 'My granddaughter is going to be a doctor,' she would fantasize in the letters she'd written to me after we moved to New York. (Sorry, *anneanneciğim*. I haven't become a doctor. But I am an academic. I hope that can still make your spirit smile somehow. In Turkish, both professions are, after all, addressed as *Hocam*).

My mother, her matriarchal heir, took such feminist ideals up a notch. My books always took precedence over my looks. In fact, whenever a family friend told my mother I was 'pretty'. she'd brush it off with that dreaded Turkish sarcasm *çirkin kızım benim* ('my ugly daughter'), in order to avoid that other cornerstone of Turkishness- *nazar* ('evil eye'). Whenever someone would suggest marriage, she'd tell them, half-jokingly, that I was still momentarily 'married to my books'.

My life status was preached to be elevated through self-advancement, not purely through marriage or customary feminine 'roles'. My late grandmother witnessed war. My mother witnessed her marriage crumble by infidelity and betrayal. They were both working women interested more in earned respect and social status than perfecting or promoting their traditional parsley and cheese pies- *börek*. (I'm not exaggerating. Most Turkish women- young or old- are somehow always pressured to preach something they cook or bake especially well. 'Oh, whoever marries our Ayşe will be lucky- her baklava is spectacular!') And there I was- reared to develop my 'Turkish-feminine' identity through traits somewhere between those of the two women; *always smack in the middle* of something or other. Just like the time I was sitting- literally- between my late grandmother and my mother on a Turkish Airlines flight from New York to Istanbul. My mom had been relishing in the pride of a daughter having shown her mother the 'new world' for the first time in a 'look ma I've made it' moment. And that flight happened to make it onto the Turkish newspaper the following day for falling in the air for about a good 10 seconds during severe turbulence.

There I was. Seated 'smack' in between them- my grandmother of the stern exterior and romantic, musical interior (she'd sing like a canary about heartbreak every time I saw her), and my heartbroken-about-men mother. And we were all praying and holding one another's hands as we were lifted up in our seats during the freefall (despite the seat belts), imagining our end and praying for some sort of familial reunion on 'the other side' after the pending doom.

The pilot luckily regained control and the plane didn't crush anything except my sense of bravery on any flight ever since (I still redden with panic attacks and repeat every Islamic prayer I ever memorized in my head at the slightest turbulence).

I liken myself sometimes to the main character in the popular children's tale *Goldilocks and the Three Little Bears*. You know, Goldilocks- the girl who prefers the porridge, bed, as well as the seat of the youngest bear for being 'not too hot/cold, not too big/small, not too hard/soft, but in the *middle* as being 'just right'.

The things I've lived through have felt 'not too traditional' but 'not too liberal', either. Though I grew up feeling in limbo over the difficulty of choosing or appeasing one 'side' or the other, I've now- at nearly 37- come to welcome the nostalgia of having experienced 'a little bit of both worlds'. This fuels my inner need to empower others through my particular vantage point's storytelling, in fact. I can empathize with people from traditional backgrounds, as well as liberal ones. I can empathize with a myriad of minority groups struggling to 'belong' in certain settings: black or white, hijabi or non-hijabi, gay or straight.

Life is beautiful, but full of so many challenges already:

economic, romantic, professional. So when 'social' categorization enters the mix- if you don't feel like you 'fit in' to live 'freely' as the flow of your soul dictates you to- you cry rivers while projecting rainbow smiles. The 'flow' inside me begs not to forcefully blow to 'sway' readers in any particular direction, but rather to be the 'wind' beneath their wings and behind their sails, aiding them along in their own journeys.

Before I end this portion of my prose, I cannot avoid one other elephant in the room- namely, the political one. But before I get to the international one that's trapped my daughter's innocent father behind bars later on in the book, I'd like to start with a snippet from my domestic experience with politics.

I was a former intern at both the Clinton Global Initiative and the United Nations. In fact, I was-what I'd deemed- a 'professional intern' for years after graduate school. Like many things in my life, my life was looking 'good on paper' to our Turkish-American social circle, though I wasn't getting much personal satisfaction, professional progress or financial benefit of any kind.

Most recently, right around the time when the pandemic first hit, I'd had the 'redirection' (I don't believe in empowering the word 'misfortune' by labeling it as such) of not only having my first novel 'The Catalyst' be published during such a timing, but, encouraged by local registered Democrats, running for local office in the primaries of my local Electoral District in Queens.

During the quarantine, with less opportunities for face-to-face interaction while attempting to obtain the required signatures from my neighbors to even be on the ballot for the basic/immediate-neighborhood-blocks-representing position, I was only able to end up receiving about one third of the vote. I lost to a neighbor I was curious to never see campaigning, until the mystery became solved when I later found out she'd had 'connections' and was a 'top-down' appointee who didn't exactly need to hustle like I did.

At the same time, I'm also someone who's voted for a Republican or two before, citing some policies- especially foreign- with which I agreed more. Why aren't I, then, registered as an Independent, you may ask? Metaphorically, yes, I suppose that would have been more befitting. As someone suffering from something I'll call *bicultural neurosis*- that mental struggle of tottering between 'am I fulfilling my full potential?' versus 'am I bringing honor to my family?'- I have often felt disturbed, in fact, by the American electoral system of having to choose between two polarized political parties, for any realistic poll victory. The reality that as an 'Independent,' a candidate I support, or, heck, even myself at the local level would have no real chance for any position with teeth, 'catalyzed' me, I suppose, in choosing one side once and for all.

I could never say, 'Screw Turkish customs, mom- I'm American, and 18, so I'll be moving out now and you can't interfere in my decisions' (No such Hallmark-movie moments for this one here). I also could not only never say 'Screw Westernization'—which, in this globalized day and age, would be hard for almost any young person in the world to do anyway- but also never 'screw American individualism and idealism'.

I wanted my individualistic dreams to come true, but also somehow be able to form a home where Turkish food and music was welcome. Whenever I would try to have both, circumstances would always somehow leave me to fend for myself alone- and I could never quite muster up the courage to lose the benefits of both. I have a poem in my premier poetic collection- *Write Out Your Drops*- entitled 'Mata Hari' about this. "World War 3 exists every season, between my heart, body, and sense of reason," it begins. "...When I cannot choose, I am often imprisoned for treason," it ends. Indeed, I observed that when we couldn't 'choose', it'd truly feel like we 'lose' in life.

So, I eventually learned to dim the fire I felt for both, projecting a lukewarm sense of comfort in the two cultures instead. In my opinion, because I couldn't choose just one side to fully 'live out' and 'set free' in my bicultural identity, I felt empowered in the forced decision to choose one political party to support and run under.

Political parties haven't been the only dilemma. The choice of a soccer team- a huge deal among Turks everywhere that has even been known to ruin friendships if you support 'the other side' in any crucial match- has also always felt troubling.

I was raised as a supporter of *Galatasaray*, for example, having been influenced by my dear late uncle Aydın, with whom I even attended a major game against our archrival '*Fenerbahçe*' in their home-base of Kadıköy, Istanbul. As someone from Kadıköy (who not only would stay there during summer vacations but also lived there to teach English on her own for a few years as an adult), I felt socially tormented by not supporting the team all my local friends had been supporting so adamantly, including a guy I was dating at the time. Luck would have it that later I'd end up marrying a fervent supporter of neither Galatasaray or Fenerbahçe, but of the 'third' major team- Beşiktaş! And, according to him: the question of which team our daughter was 'born supporting' was always a no-brainer. That's right- Dalya was one of those babies with 'I love Beşiktaş' onesies.

Political affiliations and sports teams being but minor components, socialization- last but not least- became my kryptonite. My traumatic weakness which at times also had the power to catalyze me toward 'better' pastures. It often felt like long-lasting friendship cliques I observed were subconsciously based on either their members' shared periodic experiences or cultural 'sameness' in one way or another.

Friends swearing closeness 'forever' often faded out with the end of common addresses or mutual benefits and experiences. You had a car, for example? People befriended you, but often didn't reach out when they didn't need to be driven around anymore for whatever reason. I didn't drive at the time, but I did have a social mother involved heavily in Turkish-American civil society- which often aided in annual Turkish parade placements or event entrances. I had one specific Turkish-American friend, for example, whose suddenly-frequent phone calls to hang out curiously faded just as 'suddenly' when my mother's second term as the head of a particular women's civil-society group ended.

Even recently in my life as a parent, I've noticed that many mothers engage one another in conversation when their kids take classes together, only to disengage when those classes end.

Why do I mourn this rather widespread social phenomenon, you may ask, in a poetic look at biculturalism? This is the reason, dear reader; although cultural similarities didn't really seem to make a difference as a basis for friendships when such women had shared experiences- when those commonalities ended, the same women seemingly always kept their friends of similar socio-cultural backgrounds in one form or another.

Where would this leave me? I was 'Turkish' but not 'Turkic' enough to feel zeal about observing cultural holidays perfectly or greetings house guests with the sanitary *kolonya* (in retrospect, not a bad idea in our pandemic times). I was 'American' but not 'red, white and blue' enough to care much for ball games, hot dogs (still associated by many to have *haram,* pork ingredients even if they're said to be made of beef) or watching reality shows while baking apple pies.

Many fellow Turkish-Americans I was hanging out with during the aforementioned 'periods of convenience and common experiences' were experiencing similar confusions. They loved dating, but often in secret. They loved clubbing until early morning hours, but had to frequently inform their parents of their whereabouts. They loved trendy clothes, but the girls had to watch out for miniskirts or décolletage that would be deemed 'unmarriageable' by their moms' circles- often eyeing them as potential spouses for their sons or nephews. It should be no wonder the periodic friends I had tended to be either such fellow Turkish-Americans, or immigrants from other cultures who were also able to commiserate with me.

Where did we fit in? Some would say that a 'melting pot' city like New York City was the perfect place. Yet whenever I agreed, and felt 'normal' riding a subway car full of a myriad of colors and nationalities, the 'traditional voice' in my head (interestingly often sounding like the one of my mother) didn't quite feel at ease trying to avoid the strong stench of Koran-banned bacon, for example, or watching teenagers making out heavily in public.

I heard someone say once that if a child grows up with an absentee parent, they never quite feel like they 'fit in' anywhere wholly, no matter what. These verses, dear reader, that 'flow' from my soul truly feel that it was my cultural upbringing's uniqueness which also defined the uniqueness of my frequent feelings of loneliness. But allow me to play the devil's advocate for a moment. Perhaps 'psychology' has had an influence too, as good old Sigmund Freud would have said. So, a little now about my absentee father.

Him

I only have three, very vague memories of my late father. Chronologically, the first is of an avid soccer fan shooing his 4-year-old daughter away from the television screen when she had been trying to get his attention during a soccer game. This image haunts me every time I find myself writing a caption for a post on social media, for example, and my little girl now tries to capture *my* attention.

I don't exactly shoo her - of course- but I tell her, 'Wait, Dalya, hold on,' and as soon as I do, my guilt-ridden conscience feels as if I've shunned her from my presence. As if I've locked her in her room, screaming 'leave me alone' or something else similarly extreme.

Perhaps I'm too hard on myself at times, or even too inattentive to my daughter's requests for continuously playing her made-up games with me (my attention span tends to dip after five minutes). But that memory- my first of *him*- creeps up, and I'm hit. I try my best to make it up to her. In a way he never did- and, having passed away without making amends, will never be able to do so as her grandfather by blood.

I try to make things right. In a way that my stubborn mother sometimes cannot. She loves in the best way she knows how, I suppose, and sometimes even shows affection- so rarely so that it's preciously beautiful and causes both of us bittersweet tears. But I know that 'tough love' was never a relating form I was comfortable with and have spent my entire life searching for an affectionate one.

I try to actually learn from the past and become better, rather than continue to linger there and curse it. In this way- I am not acting in a customary or a liberal fashion (where, I suppose, I wouldn't even really think of such conscience dilemmas). I'm observing from the middle: trying to evolve in a 'centered' way through incorporating the 'best' I can observe from two different perspectives in my life.

The second memory? After my parents divorced, my father had at first tried to 'see me' for a brief period of time when I was in kindergarten, to be fair. I remember my working mother dolling me up in fashionable clothes before leaving for work, and that my late grandmother, Emine, would take me to school.

One day sticks out in particular- because it's so often juxtaposed with another memory that I've combined them in my recollection here; the day I was so afraid to face my father when he came to visit me that the teachers had to beg me to see him at the school's lobby. He subsequently tried two more attempts to see me that I recall. One was when he bought me a bicycle and left it at the door to our house (once again I remember being afraid to greet him at the door even at least to say 'thanks'). The other was when he left a VHS tape of the then newly-released *The Little Mermaid* Disney movie at our neighbor's house- where I was on a playdate- and I just thanked him quietly at the door. No hug. No going off anywhere with him. I just froze- numbed, emotionless- and I suppose at that age, only after being nudged by my teacher and neighbor who was babysitting me, respectively, thanked him to be polite.

I cried with his memory as my daughter had a mermaid-themed 5th birthday party- more because her own father calls her his 'little mermaid' in his letters, and has always coincidentally called me his 'mermaid'. Being a Turkish navy man, Kemal has always likened himself to a ship's 'captain,' and hence the romanticization of the titles. I never told him about my father's memory in connection with a 'mermaid' until the prison letter I wrote to him to describe our daughter's birthday party. The prison thing is merely one of the many 'random,' 'movie-like' melodramatic aspects of my life; so much so that I've come to accept discussing it on a whim. Perhaps even as catharsis, in an attempt to normalize all the craziness I've experienced.

For a week or two prior to my father's gift gestures, I'd witnessed him walking violently toward my mother during their unamicable divorce process, breaking the door to our apartment before he'd done so. I'd hid behind a couch in the living room and shut my ears and eyes. My mother later told me he'd come for some off his stuff. He hadn't said goodbye, apologized or anything to acknowledge my presence and utter shock at the entire situation as his offspring before he left.

My father had, knowingly or not, left the bicycle as his 'parting gift' at the door. I was never able to ride a bicycle since. The artist who could create amazing charcoal drawings had given me his creative genes, though not his ability to say goodbye.

A therapist I've been talking to for 'post-traumatic stress disorder' (after my husband's imprisonment) has in fact shared with me how it truly does appear that my 'inability to say goodbye' to hurtful people and situations in my life stems partly from never having been able to obtain closure with the abrupt absence of my father.

But I digress. I come now, dear reader, to my third major memory of 'him'. Walking with *the other woman*. The woman fulfilling his ambitious side, as she'd promised him a life in England. They'd end up getting married and living in England, where my half-brother Cemre was born and raised; for many years until our father's death, I'd had a half-brother without my knowledge. In the direction opposite to their walking path, my mother and I had been in the backseat of the car my late uncle Aydın was driving. We were heading to the shopping center to exchange a Mother's Day gift (a green t-shirt I never forget) I'd bought my mother in the wrong size.

My mother saw that I saw. Because she hugged me and tried to get me to turn around. My uncle tried to distract me.

But I'd seen him, and he'd seen me. And he knew he'd been

seen. Right as the car had slowed down to a stop at the traffic lights, I turned around to look him in the eye from the back window. And he'd turned around- still holding her hand, despite having a sheepish look on his handsome face. We locked eyes. That was the last time I ever saw my birth father. I was five years old.

I tried contacting him as a teenager at the Turkish embassy of London, where I knew he was living with that woman. But he turned down my requests for communication. He died of cancerous stomach/intestinal complications at the age of 50, right as I'd been turning in my final graduate thesis paper. Accordance to letters he'd written to his brother (my paternal uncle Sefer gave them to me after his death), he was 'full of regrets' and never got to achieve his big 'Western' dreams. I never got to ask him 'why did you leave ME too?' and my mother never got to ask him 'how COULD you!?' She's been haunted with his betrayal for years and years- occasionally haunting *me* still, as his 'viceroy', through that brutal phrase I grew up hearing: "You're just like him".

Sometimes it was about how I looked like him or was artistic like him (the man could draw and apparently did interior design in England). But most of the time it was whenever I'd done something 'liberal' my mother did not approve of. "You're wild and ungrateful for your family, like he was."

I was him, yes, but I was my mother too.

I still am. Both of them. Both 'east' and 'west,' 'good' and 'bad' (whatever that means- I believe it's all about perspective), 'traditional' and 'liberal', 'conservative' and 'free-spirited', etc.

I grew up with dualities, dear reader. Therefore, I was torn not just between different cultures, but also between pretty much every other polarizing adjective one can think of: symbolically characterized to me since childhood through 'my mother' versus 'my father'. I write this 'drop' out. I am bleeding out this ink as art onto paper: this 'blood' drop, lineage portion of my centered view.

Father, I will never fully understand why you could not face contacting me- even in your dying days and even after you'd found me on social media as you told your brother. I could have gotten closure that may have helped me to be stronger in my mostly vulnerable relations with men during my entire life.

Mother, I will never fully understand why you could never see that I am literally half of him- yes, but also half of you- and, in unison, all together a THIRD and neutral, separate human being. Why did I have to grow up hearing about all his wrongs constantly- making me afraid of the similar characteristics in my own self? Why did I have to suffer, in a way, for *his* mistakes?

However,

Father, I forgive you.
Mother, I forgive you.
Out of respect, love, yes.
But, ultimately now in my thirties: because I forgive myself.
I forgive myself because in hindsight and reflection, I understand better why I did everything that I did. The parts of me that were at times judgmental and traditional, and at other times 'wild' and liberal;
I understand and forgive them all.
I accept my familial, lineal trauma.
And in that acceptance and forgiveness,
I heal.

Inheritance

I first read about the possibility of humans 'inheriting' lineal trauma in the James Redfield novel, *The Celestine Prophecy*- and it resonated with me immediately. I have often thought the same as many of the premises of the book: not only the part about familial-trauma inheritance, but also the concept of universal oneness. The novel- if you're unfamiliar- discusses the concept of superhuman capabilities for awareness and enlightenment, going through 'shifts in consciousness' and observing 'signs from the universe', such as people beginning to think and feel the same things and gradually recognizing their strengths. (Perhaps it was no 'coincidence' but rather a 'sign,' then, that I thought the same).

In *Write Out Your Drops*, I bring forth the idea that our individual 'drops' or stories into the collective 'whole' of the human race (or, 'ocean') can actually resonate more with some people than we can ever fathom. The individual can be more universal than we realize. We can 'inherit' not only familial genes and traumas, but also the issues of those in our social circles- including people with whom we share similar cultural experiences.

In that vein, allow me to now briefly go into 'individual' drops with details that could potentially resonate with a reader who- at first glance- perhaps wouldn't even think they have much in common with myself. I've already discussed my grandparents and mother and dedicated a subsection to my birth father. I would now like to do the same with my beloved late uncle (*dayı/m*) Aydın as well as my stepfather, 'daddy,' Mert (in the following sub-section): and my 'inheritance' from the both of them.

Let us take a literal, palpable approach to inheritance-namely, a financial one. My mother was in a painful legal battle over real estate with my cousin following the untimely death of my maternal uncle from Alzheimer's (quicker so, we opine, after poor clinical care at a healthy facility my mother had to place him after he couldn't be cared for properly at home). Her brother, unfortunately, wasn't very fortuitous when it came to his personal life. (Fortunately, the judge in that case saw through his ex-wife and son's libelous self-victimization efforts, and that all they were really after was money and property)

      Aydın *dayım* was always like a father-figure to me. Not just from the time after my birth one, Zafer, had left to when my mother remarried and I was lucky to get a kind-hearted stepdad, but also whenever I'd visit Turkey throughout my life. When I was working by myself in Istanbul, he was living at the time with
his wife and son in a nearby home in Istanbul, and every day after work he'd make sure to ask me too whether I needed anything to be dropped off. (He drove where I didn't, so he could, for example, stock my fridge with heavy bags of fruits and vegetables that I couldn't really be expected to carry from the supermarket).

      He also taught me the definition of the word 'sacrifice'. Not on the same level as my grandparents (who worked hard upon their migration to Turkey and saved enough to buy homes to leave to their two children- my mother and her brother), but on a personal-sacrifice form of attaining 'happiness' through making others happy, in order to keep a peaceful atmosphere at home. I knew that his wife and him had married young and had spent most of it fighting - the details of which I will not share here, as it is personal to them. All I know growing up was- he would meet with his sister (my mother) and I, and 'cry it out.' He would make 'Top 20' pop-music cassettes for me on my summer visits, upon my Turkish music-loving request. (He had also bought me my first 'Sony Walkman' when I was 6 years old). We would sometimes listen to them all together on a drive, and I'd always see his eyes well up with tears at the songs.

"Don't be emotional, like your *dayı*," my mom would often warn. "Use your head over your heart. Look how his life turned out when he pitied everyone around him except himself…"

Using 'logic' in matters of the heart was accepted, like when having to say painful goodbyes to 'culturally' or 'financially' inappropriate-deemed boyfriends I'd genuinely liked. Yet my 'heart' was expected to take precedence every time I was to react 'softly' and 'respectfully' to harsh criticisms and insults for my own life's choices. Another instance where my lovely mother preached me individualism and feminist ideals, without actually accepting my choices. Her dichotomy, after all, was also full of, therefore, irony. Despite either her mind or heart undoubtedly telling her what she was preaching to me, the other would always march to the beat of its own drum- anchored fixed to its own truth.

From my mother, I learned 'personal sacrifice' in terms of parenting. She, after all, left beyond socially-active jobs in Istanbul as well as her family to marry my new 'father' here in the United States- mostly for me to experience as 'normal' a family as possible

From my uncle Aydın, who too was expected to react 'softly' each time his feelings had been hurt (perhaps this was something they had witnessed as 'the norm' from their mutual upbringing as siblings), I learned about the habitual self-sacrifice of one's pride and ego.

I can never forget his empathetic way of buying me a golden necklace and earring set during the brief time when I was living on my own in my mother's Istanbul home and paying the bills teaching English. "Your stepfather is a great man, but I want to be able to provide you with something in case of an emergency as well, since you're like a daughter to me," he had said while giving it. My physical 'inheritance' from him. It's kept in a safe, I believe, which I haven't even peeked at for a long time. It doesn't even matter.

His real gift to me is in my memory rather than any palpable inheritance- and that's worth more than any cash I could trade in the jewelry for.

Nature versus Nurture

Speaking of my mother's own dichotomous struggles and their effects on me, I would now like to talk about Mert: the Turkish-American man she remarried, whose location in New York City 'catalyzed' my coming to the United States as a little girl. Mert had come to this country himself as a child, and this is where many similarities him and I have- despite not sharing a bloodline- would begin.

He has been the sunshine to my mother's raindrops. The eternal optimist who's worked hard and long hours, with ever positive thinking and prayer, and in his 60's perhaps even 'manifested' finally owning his first beautiful home in this country.

He's been the history buff and reader to my mother's easily-bored, soap-opera lover. The scientifically-inclined engineer and HVAC specialist following magazines about space to her modern and trendy one with years in advertising and Turkish-American civil society, flipping through celebrity and fashion ones. The funny to her serious. No need to elaborate any further: he's been the yin to her yang, and I believe that this too contributed to my attempt at dichotomous harmony, aside from being reared bi-culturally.

Growing up, unless they were family friends who knew our histories, people who met us never even questioned whether or not he'd been my real father. He was always, God bless him, that much warm with me- but, also, we were also that much similar in personality. He too had grown up in New York with a dominant Turkish mother and learned early on the need to laugh some things off on the outside while burying the hurt deep inside.

You know, dear reader: it occurred to me not too long ago that I've never called a man *baba*. Try to imagine a baby's classic first words. What have we often been told they could be? Most frequently they're either 'ma-ma' or 'da-da', in one form or another, depending on the language. In Turkish it's 'anne' and 'baba'.

I suppose as a toddler beginning to speak, I must have muttered 'baba' to my birth father on occasion, though I can't recall since I haven't seen him after age 5. I could never quite feel 'right' about calling my now dad 'baba'. Not out of coldness towards him. In fact, I would witness several American friends calling their stepparents by their names, and would think it weird and 'disrespectful' somehow. 'Baba' or even 'father/dad' always sounded too official to me. So, in my own 'centered' way as a child, I reconciled 'daddy' as being 'in the middle': somewhere between 'baba' and his name, 'Mert' or even 'Mert *Abi*' ('*older brother* Mert' in Turkish- a popular way of addressing people among Turks). From my 'daddy', I learned 'personal sacrifice' in regards to blood, sweat, and tear 'drops' of hard work in order to provide for your loved ones and leave behind a family legacy.

In my debut novel *The Catalyst*, I created a book trailer with a voiceover that included themes from the story. My voiceover ended with the following:

Nature, can heal
Nature, can destroy
Nature, can *catalyze*

Now, dear reader, you may or may not have read the book, but I believe it should nonetheless be clear at this point that I purposely chose this as a 'play-on-words' and used 'nature' to refer both to environmental factors like weather and plantation, but also to our *own* natures as living beings (whether human or not: hint, read *The Catalyst* to find out more). I'd like to take the opportunity to elaborate on that with this collection, and share my belief that it is not only the world around us and our own genetic inclinations which can ultimately 'catalyze' change, but the 'natures' of others too can certainly become catalysts for our various evolutions in life.

If I had never had half of my parental upbringing occur through a Turkish American man, for instance- who's to say I would have been able to feel the courage (and perhaps even 'freedom') to express my open-minded ideas and bold creativity?

Thank you, daddy, always, for being in my corner. Thank you, God and the Universe, for perhaps taking some things from me- yes- but providing so much more magic in return.

> *imagine your life*
> *in the way in which your soul would feel at home*
> *not only in the big moments, but even on its daily roam*
> *where you wouldn't be a second option*
> *or second-guessed*
> *but rather, for someone- the best*
> *visualize your daily tasks*
> *earning you both financial freedom*
> *as well as a spiritual kingdom*
> *thanking the Creator*
> *can reward every endeavor*
> *not on your hypothesized time, maybe*
> *but at the ideal time, certainly*
> *imagine: daily, deeply, truly*
> *accompanied then by the work and chores*
> *and, when bred by Gratitude:*
> *Poof!*
> *here it is- it's Yours!*

SECTIONAL ANECDOTES

(As a teacher, it's become habitual of me to want to do regular reviews of 'takeaways' at the ends of sections and sometimes even include 'interesting facts' or observations related to each section)

Growing up bicultural has meant...

- *feeling dichotomized between a culture dominated by 'instant wealth through inheritance' dependance and the community's prioritization over the individual in one culture, and individuality alongside of success through hard work in the other*

- *most relatives and friends 'back in the homeland' assuming you are somehow 'wealthier' than them, as you are physically living in what they deem a 'brand' name- the United States of America. Even if they're property-owners while you're renting and taking out credit/loans.*

- *being the envy of your circle during summer vacation visits, who often 'order' various brand names for you to bring for them on your flight. 'You must have so many Abercrombie jeans you can afford there,' they'd say, while I'd never even heard of the brand name growing up in NYC- the dorky me who was happy with whatever brand looked nice and felt comfortable during my minimal shopping trips.*

THE SOUL'S REQUEST

her soul is akin to these woods
not as frequented
and hence often misunderstood

her eyes are gazed upon,
smile lingers in their memory
causing them to return from the vortex
of their 'freedom'
eventually

her hands are often cold
despite warmth from fingers or a glove,
with the spirit's satisfaction often disregarded
they're not the only ones that mistake convenience
for 'love'

she haunts like the woods,
yet is haunted herself by the cry of her own soul
pleading to be loved for its candor,
no other delights have made it feel whole

SET FREE YOUR FLOW

THE MAGNET IN THE WIND

she parts her lips to swallow air
and fills her lungs with the current's beauty
to ease inner despair

she then throws back her hair
her flow is attached to the wind
a magnetic force clings
them in unison
following one's own path isn't treason

she's attached only to the unattached
the magnet repels and attracts , like ancient artifacts
she detaches when they've latched
feigned devotion only distracts
her naivete: long ago snatched

affections have departed, more bitter than broken-hearted
they'll deny her lasting breeze only if they dare…
she's left her mark,
She was there

SECTION II:
Flowing Through Relationships

IMPERFECT EMPATH

SET FREE YOUR FLOW

NAPOLEON

being the object of your affection
was torture
both mental and moral

I cried my biographical pain out onto you
as a notepad of comfort
yet could never quite avoid a quarrel

by my tears, you weren't affected
thought you deserved obedience
from a sought gem

from a sought gem
you made to feel rejected

each time it refused to be what you greedily expected

I empathized with your struggle
whilst you could not even sympathize with mine

you talked the talk of an emperor
yet walked the walk of a bear without a spine

you sacrificed and let me be
since you couldn't set your ugly truths free

if one cannot value the jewel
they don't deserve showing it off as jewelry

…for the one without chivalry

THE CAPTIVATING CAPTIVE

removed from the bustle
of busy city sidewalks,
perched on a bench stone,
the captive now inhales maneuver
and freshly-cut grass after the rain
rather than the stench of gasoline

the ears have seagulls for company
rather than police sirens
or drivers speeding by with words obscene

the seldom nature walk has now become daily routine
the busyness of the captive's mind
has become less actual business
and simpler in pleasure,
more serene

regardless,
the pearl still isn't free to roam outside its shell
a captivating captive can get captivated, yes,
while remaining captured
as well

My Assumption About Assumptions

Okay, I know what you're thinking. "This is the 'relationships' portion of her writing, and she's just described her troubled/non-existent relationship with her absentee father before his death. So, she's going to now talk about all the romantic heartbreak she lived through and blame it on her childhood…" Am I right? Or did I just assume again? Yeah, I've been told I do tend to assume too quickly sometimes. It's one of my bad habits. But I honestly feel I do that at times as a preemptive defense mechanism, I suppose.

Maybe I've grown so accustomed to people assuming things about me- mostly wrongfully so- by just looking at me, that I've unintentionally nurtured that same habit as well. Furthermore, I can also at times literally and 'empathetically' sense someone's energy by how they react to something I share with them.

In this case, dear reader, I'm writing these words before you naturally get to read them- and I am no 'Baba Venga' (the late, blind psychic lady from Bulgaria: the same land of pretty much both my sets of grandparents).

But, regardless of what you may or may not have thought, don't worry (or perhaps even- sorry to disappoint): this will not, and cannot, be a romantic 'tell-all'.

True to my main purpose for writing this poetic essay collection: I will genuinely touch on all the bi-cultural dilemmas I've lived through from the perspective of dating, relationships, and even marriage, and allow them to 'flow' through me cathartically. And, yes, one such dilemma is of course precisely the reason *why* I *can't* publish some tell-all book. For if I do so, it could be deemed 'dishonorable,' if I'm not ruffling some feathers already just by all that I've written thus far. (Also, of course, I'm no famous celebrity or anyone of that sort to truly gather such intrigue in my personal life anyway, so I'm purposely limiting my biographical musings only to the most relevant ones for my artistic point as a writer in this collection).

I'm no love expert, and in no way do I attempt to be. But from my experiences, dear reader, I've come to believe that in order for a relationship to best maintain harmony, there needs to be a voluntary acceptance of dual roles in a particular dynamic. In other words, there must be an acceptance of one partner's dominance and need for control as well as of the other's passivity and relaxed attitude.

From the perspective of our main theme of dual backgrounds explored, I believe that a dynamic of duality can best prolong a relationship in the most functional way. If people are both comfortable- outwardly and inwardly- with the 'traditional' role of the male as the breadwinner and the female as the homemaker, another couple where the roles are reversed should also be both respected and accepted. An entire Asian-rooted belief system, after all, similarly has praised the 'yin/yang' concept of the harmony between opposites for years, and it is not my place to go into that. The book I-Ching (I own the one translated from Chinese by Richard Wilhelm and Cary F. Baynes) describes the ridgepole (line), for instance, to describe *"...oneness' (where) duality comes into the world, for the line at the same time posits an above and a below, a right and left, front and back- in a word, the world of the opposites..."*

I can simply tell my story and share my experiences vis à vis a dualistic view situated right on that 'center' ridgepole/line.

In a lot of cultures, for example (not just Turkish, of course)- a man (whether or not he is outwardly seen as the 'masculine' and the 'breadwinner') would likely be ridiculed for showing 'obedience' to his wife and her stereotypically 'controlling' ways, especially around the house.

Let me go into another mini sketch (I dabbled in some theater as a student, so kindly bear with me here).

Wife: **Take off those shoes closer by the door! You're bringing outside germs too far inside the house.**
Husband: **Yes, dear. What's for dinner?**
Wife: **Whatever you find left over from yesterday in the fridge. I've been busy all day. If you don't like it, you can order some takeout.**
Husband: **Leftovers are fine, dear. Here are those plum tomatoes you asked for.**

Yeah, I know what you must be thinking. "She should have been a playwright. This is some astounding dialogue" (insert laughter here). Did I also mention I love employing *sarcasm* in my daily life? Interestingly, many Turks I've met don't really use or grasp sarcasm, so I feel this is the 'American' side of me.

In any random comedy show in Turkey, the dialogue I just conjured up would typically be accompanied by some machine-laughs. Culturally, it would be considered 'funny' for a man to be so 'passive' as to do what his wife asks without questioning her or 'putting her in her place'.

Yes. What I've just said is harsh. But unfortunately, this is the sad reality of the expectations amongst many in machoistic societies. The idea that maybe, just maybe, a husband figure may actually be satisfied in such a dynamic (based on harmonious duality with his wife) is as foreign as the crater of the moon for many people. Perhaps such a man could have been raised by a domineering mother himself or have had dating experiences throughout his life that may have triggered a subconscious need for his partner to be in control of daily routines. We simply do not know.

Maybe it is none of the above. Maybe such a man simply feels comfortable giving his life partner the reins in general: where doing so doesn't make him feel weakened, but rather empowered by the relative relaxation of having to make less of the decisions himself. It's no one's business but their own what works for them- any couple in a healthy, functional relationship.

We should never assume we know what goes on behind closed doors for anyone- and yes, in my plea for people to never do this to me, I also tell this to myself. Assuming is as part of human nature, unfortunately, as jealousy or rivalry. Yet assumptions were a major component of what I've experienced as a Turkish-American growing up in New York City, and vacationing during the summertime in Turkey.

Here in the US, some assumed, for instance, that my slight accent was a result of being educated in Turkey (I never went to school in Turkey beyond 2nd grade but spoke Turkish frequently at home due to my mother's insistence). There, in Turkey, meanwhile, they assumed I spoke English at every opportunity due to arrogance: not realizing for me it was a matter simply of comfort and natural expression.

Here, they assumed I wasn't a particularly affectionate person because outwardly I couldn't express myself as freely as my American friends could- in fear of societal judgement and familial chastisement. There, they assumed I must have 'done wild drugs at wild orgies' since I lived on campus in college (the answer is a resounding 'no' to both).

Back to my personal 'centered view.' I know some people who may be reading this can relate to my musings, even having had experienced just one dominant culture growing up. I have friends in Istanbul, for example, who say they also feel 'too Western' in their ways of thinking compared to their more traditional families- despite never having set foot outside of the country.

Regardless, from personal experience, I would still say that more Turkish-Americans struggle with this in comparison. I would even go so far as to claim that there is most certainly a Turkishness-based disease of constantly worrying about what others think rather than prioritizing individual happiness: particularly when living outside of Turkey. Was it because many of us were struggling to 'fit in' here in Western society, while simultaneously grappling to be accepted by our own social circles? Was this parallel struggle somehow making it easier for us to judge and categorize one another abroad, since our decisions were doubled in difficulty due to the additional realm in which we felt the pressure to conform?

I've seen men peer-pressured, for instance, to 'cheat on their wives' just because, as the man, they 'could' and 'should'. I've also seen women peer-pressured to 'accept' a cheating (or even violent) spouse: as long as they had a roof over their head and could maintain the social illusion of being in a 'happy marriage'! It was just 'dirt on a man's hand' (*elinin kiri*), as the Turkish expression goes, that the man could just 'wash off'. I've even met a young man who had to lie to his mother that his boyfriend was a woman, and who later had to get married to reproduce children- where he had to lead his 'secret life' as a gay man behind closed doors.

Turkey- my homeland of many ironies- tends to condemn homosexuality as a 'disease' that can be solved by religion, while publicly celebrating many transgender singers and celebrities over many decades.

As a child vacationing in Turkey, I would see more transgender prostitutes than women waiting on street corners at night- even in traditionally conservative neighborhoods. Sexual identity is merely one example of irony in Turkey; I will not even go into how covered and uncovered women have been made to stand against one another for decades by men, or how pedophiles have been excused by clergy misusing religious text in different contexts to normalize their crimes.

How the globally-renowned, Turkish-origin founders of the Pfizer/BioNTech coronavirus vaccine in Germany have not been as celebrated by many Turks due to their 'Alevi' faith (a different sect of Islam than the popular Sunni one of Turkey). Or even how the talented Elif Shafak- a world-famous Turkish writer (who writes in English as well) suddenly stopped being pointed out as a role model for my writing amongst some in my circle the moment she recently came out as bisexual.

(Yes. There. I 'went into it.' I know. But I've kept it as brief as I can. It was simply unavoidable).

I've seen parents advocate 'bad in private/ good on paper' dates to their children as potential spouses- not just out of potential financial desperation, but also a social one. And I've heard first-hand of girls engaging in Islamically-taboo anal sex: not by choice, but in order to avoid the even bigger 'taboo' of not being discovered to be 'virgins' on their wedding nights.

Speaking of sex... Let us *flow* right into our next section.

Darn You Arianna Grande & Bruno Mars

"So, what you doin' tonight?" "I'm gonna leave the door open...tell me that you're coming through..."

Lyrics like these from so many artists frequently played on the radio, are NOT lyrics that this bi-cultural girl has ever able to listen to lightly. We can love them and their songs as artists (love you Arianna and Bruno), but nonetheless feel immense frustration every time their lyrics indirectly remind us of our internal struggles.

When you've got Turkish parents, even if you're 18, there's no way any significant other is going to be able to casually 'come over' to your place (if you're actually living on your own at that point as Turkish-American youth, you're a rarity). Nor can you ever go over to theirs, unless you've created about 3 separate scenarios (in case one falls through) that you can lie about and which mostly involve hanging out with your girlfriends in one way or another.

Now, in no way do I condone lying to parents. Especially my younger readers; as much as it may hurt sometimes to potentially be yelled at, risking meeting a stranger somewhere unsafe is never a good idea, so at the very least always make sure SOMEONE you trust knows where you really are at all times.

So why then, if I don't advocate lying, am I writing about it? Because no Turkish-American friend I've met has ever NOT had to do it, due to at times unrealistic and grandiose parental expectations of absolute *holy* behavior from their children.

Whether myself or my friends 'lost' our 'virginities' before marriage or not isn't the issue here, nor is it anyone's business, so I will now diplomatically step aside from addressing that. Rather, my point is as follows.

The concept of even 'casually' hanging out with anyone of the opposite gender was always so 'grand' for our parents that they only really saw doing so as 'black and white': either to potentially spend time to 'get to know' someone 'marriage material' on a 'serious, clean date', OR, to spend platonic time in a GROUP setting (preferably with friends familiar to them there with us as well).

Let's now cue a Tik Tok-like, exemplary sketch.

A.
The Parent: "Where have you been!?"

Their child: "Oh you know, with (insert familiar friend's name here) **at** (insert 'safe' location here)"

The Parent: "Hmm, was there anyone else with you all?"

Their child: "Oh, just some other friends they know. (Immediately add an attempt to switch the conversation) **The food/view was great! Oh my God, we have to go there as a family sometime…"**

The Parent: "Hmm…I see. Was there anyone interesting in particular?"

OR,

B. *(after a bad date with someone your parents tried to set you up with)*
The Parent: "How was dinner, honey?"

The Child: "Oh, it was okay. I'm going up to my room. I still have some work…"

The Parent: "What did you guys eat? What did you talk about? Did you find out his/her car/job/parents' job (insert whatever status icon you can think of here)**?**

The Child: "Not really. It wasn't anything special. We'll talk later...You know, you never asked these questions last week when I had a great time with my friend... (insert name of someone you actually like that they don't approve of)."

In parental defense, especially as I am one now: I am increasingly aware with each passing day that this is – in a parent's mind at least- ultimately to 'help' us 'be happy in the long run' with someone deemed 'suitable' for us. The sad reality, however, is that there's never any 'magic formula', in my experience, when it comes to matters of the heart.

I've witnessed dates between two people 'good' for each other 'on paper' that never went anywhere- despite physical attractiveness. I've witnessed dates between people that went quite well-much to many people's surprise, since at first glance no one would have paired the two of them together for whatever 'logical' reasoning (mainly involving credentials).

However, to be fair, I've also seen dating situations where a child didn't heed his or her parents' warnings about someone, and it turned out that the parent was right- that person really turned out to be a heartbreaker.

So, what is any bicultural child to do? One walking on eggshells to both exert his/her 'individual' choice to follow his/her 'dreams' in a way continuously advocated by Western culture AND simultaneously 'honor' their family and traditions as well?

A girl in love with someone she 'shouldn't' be? A boy who wants to go into the music industry rather than take over his father's architectural business? What is the best course of action for such youth?

I wish I could insert here some pearl of wisdom that I've finally learned after all my trials and tribulations. And, certainly, the Lord knows there are enough such self-help works out there published by people who I'm sure have done research on the issue much lengthier than I ever could.

But, alas, my only formula would be, in all honesty: trial and error, vis-à-vis *surrendering to the flow of life*.

SET FREE YOUR FLOW

That's right.

Aside from the implication of finding your own unique cultural-combination path in life, my implication for the title of this poetic collection itself is to surrender to the 'catalyst' winds directing you towards the most ideal path for you. These currents tend to flow from your inner voice when you meditate or pray in quiet, your instincts, repeated experiences which cannot be coincidences but rather celestial attempts to teach you a lesson, and- finally- universal signs.

Let's consider my 'mate selection', as an example, alongside my 'surrendering' to certain 'signs' that I noticed in my life. The same father who'd left both my mother and myself in my native Istanbul to form another family abroad, was of the astrological sign of Scorpio. Heeding my mother's warnings throughout my dating years, I never even ended up dating any Scorpio- until I married one at age 27! My mother was no astrological expert, but I grew up continuously being warned to 'stay away' from Scorpio men. As fellow Leo women, they weren't 'compatible' with us, she said, and the union would only 'result in disaster'.

Life is said to be what happens when you're busy making other plans, however, and it turned out that Kemal, my daughter's currently innocently-imprisoned father, is not only a Scorpio- but also happens to have a birthday that falls one day before my late father's (albeit in a different year, of course). Here's another, seemingly smaller one: my father was also, I've been told, an avid *Beşiktaş* fan, and I never dated one until- you guessed it- I married Kemal in all his Beşiktaş-admiring glory.

My mother was so traumatized by having 'given her all' to her first 'major love' as a young adult (they'd both gotten married at age 21, and from my current view as an adult, it seems to me they were both practically kids) and then subsequently having been betrayed, that she repeatedly warned me of men similar to my father in any way or fashion- most prominently, their astrological sign.

Ironically, however, she would also tell me stories of how 'blissfully happy' the two of them had been- until he'd met 'that other woman' at his workplace. It's also interesting to me that my Scorpio father ended up marrying a Pisces woman, whereas my Scorpio husband Kemal's first wife- from whom he'd gotten divorced when we were introduced- was also a Pisces. That's one Scorpio-Pisces couple that stood the test of time and another that didn't (so much for astrological signs as reliable predictors of marriage compatibility).

"This is the way things are in life…." It's what many of us often heard growing up. "It's our job to be realistic for your own good." This always seemed to me to be a core component of Turkish culture- especially among families trying to 'keep it alive' abroad, like mine. Family rules were never supposed to make sense, I realize now in retrospect. Just respected. And unquestioned. "Why?" we would ask. "Because we are the parents. We have the experience. Respecting your parents is in the Koran, as well. No one wants the best for you except your parents." That's what I- and many friends in similar bi-cultural households- grew up hearing.

Chastisement of offspring- particularly daughters, in fact- is such an inherent part of Turkish culture that there's a proverb that roughly translates to, "…those who do not discipline their daughters are doomed to beat their own selves up…" I won't even go into the obvious controversial nature of this seemingly violence-supporting proverb, dear reader, as it is not my point here. What I've always had the most trouble with has been the *double standards* placed on young Turkish girls- especially those raised abroad like myself or at least in 'western/secular' parts of Turkish society despite more traditional familial backgrounds.

Had I subconsciously married a Scorpio to 'spite' my mother? I doubt it. I'd dated far more controversial and 'out there' guys before my husband, after all, whom she didn't approve of for reasons beyond relatively more innocent qualities such as their 'incompatible' birthdays. No. In fact, when I was first introduced to my husband by our relatives attempting 'matchmaking'- I'd always thought we'd just be friends, and I kept my distance romantically for a good two years or so. (Frankly, I'd found the military lifestyle- unfamiliar to my upbringing- rather 'boring')

That is exactly why I believe that, in a way, it was also 'fate' that I would end up attracting something to myself I'd most 'thought about' to actually please my mother: 'Avoid Scorpio men at all costs'.

Perhaps we end up living out what we most try to avoid. Perhaps the reason we even end up trying to avoid that 'thing,' in fact, is it could possibly even be a part of our soul's flow- and our focus on it has always been a 'sign' from the universe after all, one which we must eventually face.

Come to think of it, I see now through living with my mother back in New York (while Kemal remains politically imprisoned), in fact, that my mother has a lot in common with him! Could Sigmund Freud have been right? Do we all subconsciously 'flow' and gravitate toward people who remind us of the familiarity of our childhoods- whether or not that familiarity is a warm or toxic one? We can never know all the answers for certain. I'll leave that philosophical question be for now, and continue with my next sub-section.

So, speaking of double standards, let's turn the page to explore it further, ladies and gents.

Women as 'Prey' and Men as the 'Predators'

"Hey, let's go on a weekend getaway to somewhere near the water (summer time), or, some cabin to ski (winter time)…" And CUT! The Hollywood-fantasy daydream would certainly end there for many Turkish-American youth- especially girls. For, of course, 'staying the night' anywhere but in a home environment 'protected' by elders implies the possibility at least of some 'men' sniffing women out as 'prey.' The possibility of luring us into their hotel rooms, or finding some way to manage themselves into ours.

This is but one scenario out of many, of course. And, yes, I'm aware that- as with every cultural group- exceptions exist. Had I heard of Turkish-American girls being able to go on weekend getaways with a mixed-gender group of friends? Absolutely, although these exceptions too were almost always able to exist precisely on the condition that the exact list of people who'd be with them was made known (preferably youth whose families the parents knew and trusted). Frequent phone check-ins were also conducted, with photographed proof that the traveler hadn't actually ventured off with some lover somewhere.

Now, I have to insert here- in fairness to my parents- that I was, on a couple of occasions, able to travel and spend the night without them somewhere (having fulfilled the unspoken-contractual 'conditions' I've outlined above).

However, and this is why I even mention this example in this portion of the book: there was one eventful incident where I spent one evening in another US city while traveling with a female friend (hence, my parents had allowed it). We'd had an unspoken male friend accompanying us: a known diplomat representing Turkey at the United Nations at the time. He was single and friendly, and, despite his older age: we'd trusted him. In our *naïveté* – we'd viewed him as an 'older brother figure'. Did he proceed to hit on me that evening and make me uncomfortable throughout our journey? You bet your bottom dollar he did.

Okay, dear reader, I promised I wouldn't give 'the juice' too much, since I do not intend for my poetic and cultural essay collection to turn into some 'tell-all', if you recall, so I will cut that part of my story there. His identity isn't relevant here. But what I ponder often- as well as what I feel becomes especially difficult growing up bicultural- is the following. In hindsight, I can now, in my 30's, reflect back on my experiences and wonder what the 'other' sides must have thought- with many having been conditioned with the 'machoism' of Turkish culture. Now, in no way do I wish to generalize about Turkish men or insult anyone except the outlying exceptions I've experienced (who should indeed be ashamed of themselves if they ever come across these words).

Like the well-known politician in Turkey also, for example, who lifted my skirt and massaged my shoulders suggestively when I'd visited his office as a family friend, trusting him to give me- as a recent political scientist graduate- professional advice.

I'd gone to him to check out my CV, rather than my legs. He undoubtedly searched for any 'welcoming' hints from me that would have otherwise possibly caused him to go further- which also suggested to me that this was likely not his first attempt to cross the line, nor would it be his last. What did I do? I froze. And I vaguely recall afterward pretending it didn't happen, wiggling away from his touch and taking my CV in my hand to change the topic, both in shock and denial in that moment.

So, technically- no, I was never violated by any Turkish man. I was, however, forcibly kissed despite saying 'no' and 'stop' to two *non-Turkish* men while I was living on campus in college in Long Island. Even younger- when I was a junior high school student riding the Queens city bus to my school- I was harassed by a straphanger man of a different ethnicity. He'd sneered suggestively as he inched his organ close to my frozen-in-fear face until I'd run out of the bus one stop early in tears: running to school so that he wouldn't follow me.

Indeed, a harassing-temperament doesn't discriminate based on background. What goes through the mind of any sexual predator is a topic too huge for me to explore. So, rather, the culturally relevant and specific dilemma I presently intend to explore is this: *what had made the Turkish men in particular- with their positions of power- feel they could do what they did, and get away with it?* I opine that, assured silence- unfortunately and undoubtedly- would likely come at the top of the list, right before their sense of 'entitlement.' They knew that I wouldn't say anything to my parents- who knew them- because I'd feel embarrassed in our mutual social circles. They knew my mother especially wanted them to help me, as 'older brother figures', to 'land a good job'.

That possibility of 'a good job' with their 'connections' was always dangled in front of me like a toy to a cat. A promise that never materialized. A promise they treated like a bribe- as if I were somehow expected to render some 'service' in exchange for a 'good job' in their circle- despite my qualifications sincerely fulfilling the requirements of such positions in the first place.

Dear reader…You can imagine, as someone especially with these experiences, that I've rejoiced the recent empowerment of the Me-Too movement. I always aim to have 'a view from the middle,' however, and gender happens to be one of them. I always try to be fair. Just as I have mentioned agreeing with 'the other' political party on certain issues, there were one or two testimonies from a couple of publicized statements where it honestly felt to me like the man being accused was more of a victim than the woman.

Regardless, those instances were few and far in between. Many of those women displayed tremendous courage to be able to speak out, and I am so proud of the moment overall. I was seldom one to ask, 'why did they wait so long?' For I know, from firsthand experience, that sometimes you just can't speak out. For me, the reason included my aforementioned cultural reasons: fear of professional setbacks, bringing shame- or worse- threats to my family's name, embarrassment, etc.

Perhaps those women had tried to move on from their experiences, until hearing about other women's accusations 'catalyzed' them to finally feel empowered enough to speak out later on through the support of numbers. In my case, for example, I know for sure I'm not the only young woman that particular man hit on in Turkey. In fact, I had a good platonic guy friend in Turkey for many years from the politician's very circle who warned me against both him as well as a couple of his other known colleagues in Ankara (the country's capital). "Don't go on that job interview there," he'd warn. "We all know about (his) come-ons to young women. You're a good person. I don't want you to go through that".

Needless to say- especially after my skirt-lifting experience at this point- I heeded my friend's advice, and never went on that particular interview. What would have happened if I had? The AK Party in power in Turkey had seriously wanted me to get involved with them politically, I can tell you that much. Most recently before my relocation to Norway as a married woman in 2012 (in 2011, in fact) they'd offered me to join their 'Youth' organization in the secularized and trendy 'Kadıköy' district of Istanbul where I'd been living. They said they could 'use' more women without headscarves on their team to show their 'inclusivity.'

Would I have been able to spare myself from the affections of that politician with the 'roving-eye' in Ankara had I met him? Would I have been able to genuinely obtain an influential-enough post within the political party to somehow now been able to get my innocently imprisoned husband out of prison? Or, would they have faultily accused me of being a member of their contemporary choice as 'the other' in Turkey: FETO- and have sacked me (or, worse, imprisoned) before I could do so? (FETO is the name given to alleged members of the Gülenist movement the Erdoğan government accuses of having plotted a coup attempt in order to topple him).

I will never know.

I did, in fact, contact that platonic friend in AK party to relay my husband's genuine innocence and asked if they could help him. "There are so many like him. We cannot help them either. Sorry. We are afraid, too, and are powerless in this situation…" was his response.

What can I say? I can only continue to pray and advocate on behalf of justice for the innocently-accused since 2016: sharing my truths, as everyone who knows me and my family can testify that I am not, never will be nor have ever been associated with Gülen in any shape or form, and neither has my husband. If he had been, I could never have gotten married to someone with such different ideologies from mine.

I do not wish to digress further into politics, so I will now return to my main theme for this subheading, dear reader. *Women as 'prey', men as 'predators'*. There are so many subcomponents to this that it's difficult to choose just one to narrow in on for the purpose of my poetic essay collection here.

Shall I explore that curious acceptance of many transgendered people as singers and celebrities in Turkey for decades- while casting stones (only proverbial ones, as Turkey is still luckily secular country as I write this collection) on gay couples (no publicly 'out' couples can be seen in the Turkish media)? Or perhaps go into the sad dogma still followed by many traditional mindsets that women are 'secondary' to men in 'worth' and should therefore be acceptant of being 'disciplined' physically or cheated on by their husbands? How various forms of abuse tend not to be interfered in- due to them being an *aile meselesi* (a 'family issue') that authorities do not want to get involved in?

What about the cultural disregard for a woman actually desiring someone and going after them- despite sexuality being natural for both genders, and a premarital sin being a 'sin' (according to the Koran) for both women *and* men? I've literally heard Turkish-American parents warn their daughters against men as the 'big bad wolves' that could entice them in bars or clubs for physical intimacy. They'd be told to 'guard' themselves- as the 'sheep'- against the 'barbaric desires of men': ignoring that attraction and desire could at times be consensual and mutual. Such warnings occur in Turkey as well- of course- yet abroad, there tends to be a larger assumption that non-Turkish men will somehow not 'respect' our 'virtue' as much. Personally, I feel that if someone is a predator, they're a predator everywhere. They'll just use different tactics, i.e. false promises of love in one and further false promises of marriage in another.

I will not, dear reader. For these are universal issues that perhaps I am only partial to exploring due to the intensity of femicides being covered on Turkish news; so much so that a black and white image-sharing of international women in support occurred during the summer of 2020 on social media. Though it occurs everywhere and certainly so here in the United States as well: in Turkey, femicide feels comparatively grander in scale, due to the geographically smaller size of the nation.

I will further explore, instead, that I was targeted and 'coincidentally' approached by the 'Adnan Oktar' cult in Istanbul. For decades, they were known to brainwash young, educated people (especially women they found to be attractive and later attempted to fit into a certain voluptuous-look through plastic surgery) with promises of 'good jobs' and an affluent lifestyle. Many of its members have recently been imprisoned, and, especially due to my sensitivity for imprisonment in general, I will not say anything about that here. All I will say is that I was spared and lucky to have been able to 'get out' before I was ever 'initiated' by the grace of God. But anyone curious about that brief chapter of my life has to look no further than the way I have symbolically and indirectly portrayed them in my novel, *'The Catalyst'* (as well as in its sequel, *'The Penance'*). That is all I will say about them.

So why mention them at all? Surely cults- especially those luring young women to carry out their perverse fantasies and 'missions'- have been around for centuries and in many cultures around the world (including ones with celebrities, as seen recently on the news right here in the United States). However, once again, vis-à-vis Turkish culture in general: I have to think of what this means on a broader, sociological scale.

Allow me to assume once again, dear reader, before I go any further. Perhaps you are now asking- *okay, but, umm, Selin, wasn't this meant to be an exploration of setting free your true self despite the difficulties of growing up as a bicultural person, and not a sole study of Turkish culture in general?*

Absolutely.

I mention the Oktar cult specifically for this reason; they aimed to mostly target women who spoke English, to be used as 'honey traps' (espionage using attractive promises of relations) to lure affluent businesspeople and politicians and obtain government information. One of their many controversial components was the sexualized-look of their 'disciples' on Oktar's television channel. A look of *décolletage* and miniskirts (often showing these women dancing seductively around him like some stereotypical Sultan) that contrasted directly with the principle of *modesty* in Islam. They claimed to want to 'ameliorate' the 'bad reputation' of Islam in the world, referring to many still unfortunately linking the peaceful religion with terrorism and extremism in various ways.

Their religion-based discussions were extremely 'Eastern' while their look was extremely of the 'West.' I would love to eventually hear interviews with some of the young women in that cult to find out how-on the inside- they dealt with being dichotomous in such an ostentatious way on the outside.

Finally, I will conclude this section by saying the

following. In no way do I mean to express any antagonist views against people (Turkish, American, Turkish-American, or of any cultural category) who genuinely for themselves and religious reasons wish to be/marry an 'honorable bride' (or groom! You have to be fair!). Rather, I express sadness at the lack of ease in obtaining such an ideal in our modern society. My commentary is not merely about virginity or lack thereof. It is merely about the pure difficulty of finding someone you can spiritually, emotionally, mentally and physically feel connected with in our day and age without being faced with various *double standards* and *hypocritical customs.*

Things are rough enough as they are with the additional temptations of social media which did not exist during the time of our 'forefathers' and grandmothers.

If a young man and woman can still marry today- either for love, or for familial support/ respect that can grow into love- and grow old together…that's amazing! I would love it if such rare couples of our modern era could share more of their stories to give all of us hope! But let's try to take an honest look all around us. All we hear about are romantic failures- either due to various infidelities or economic/socio-cultural woes.

How can a woman be expected to have restrained from any form of physical affection with the opposite gender up until age 25- the average age when modern girls are encouraged to get married in our circles, after having obtained higher education and 'some job experience for social standing' (and, of course, for meeting eligible men)?

How can a man be expected to have- on his own (not just borrowing heavily from his father's pockets or 'inheriting' professional influence)- be able to have accumulated enough status and money to be deemed ready for marriage?

What ends up happening, then? Very often I've heard around me of a young man and woman falling in love, for example, and having to date secretly from the girl's parents. Only to eventually (and heartbreakingly) break up because they would realize their feelings getting deeper as time (and youthful opportunities) would be 'fleeting' by. 'Why', they'd ask themselves, should they 'continue the relationship if the possibility for a socially acceptable marriage doesn't exist' for them?

Very often, social/regional discrepancies are used as excuses for young couples not to get married among Turks ("You can't marry him- his family consists of villagers from the East!" or "You can't marry her- she's not from the Black Sea region like us!"). The twosome, then, realize their families will never support them- and, often needing their support mostly financially- they end up parting ways in tears, listening to popular Turkish 'blues' music called 'Arabesk' and other similarly sad songs.

They tend to watch the gazillions of globally-trendy Turkish soap operas- *diziler*- which then capitalize on such storylines, and air nightly/weekly for three hours (longer than most Hollywood movies) to distract the public from the tragedy of domestic news. Yet, of course, this social unacceptance very often does not mean their love wasn't real- so, very often, by this point they'll have had gotten intimate with one another, as God created our natures to express. Ideally- in a marriage- sure.

Dear reader. I'm a firm believer that the Koran was meant to strengthen out faiths and 'guide us' with maxims for 'optimal happiness' in our lives over the long-run- not as some set of rigid rules deserving 'punishment' upon the slightest disobedience. But what if society- for the various economic and socio-cultural reasons mentioned- doesn't allow for such a marriage to be supported? Hence, the aforementioned scenario is merely one out of many in which couples end up being intimate- often for the right reasons of love, too- and yet cannot get married due mostly to familial interference.

Sexuality. The ever taboo. Especially for dichotomously-torn Turks. The unmentioned, yet certainly noticed, proverbial elephant in any Turkish-American room. As human beings, it is an inherent and undeniable force within all of us- with its seeds and urges budding since childhood- and simply has to be addressed. Perhaps it'll be befitting, dear reader, to end this section- which I started with song lyrics- with a reference to another set of popular lyrics. Namely, the one of 'Let It Go' from the Disney animated feature, 'Frozen'.

"Be the good girl you always have to be…conceal, don't feel …. don't let them know… well, now they know…let the storm rage on…" Thank you, Elsa (of, 'coincidentally', beautiful Norway that catalyzed me to write 'The Catalyst'). I'm allowing my inner 'flow' to 'blow' strongly enough to create a literary 'current' and counteract any culturally-expectant and 'raging storm' they can hurl toward me.

SET FREE YOUR FLOW

SECTIONAL ANECDOTES

Growing up bicultural has meant:

- having to keep quiet about influential family acquaintances- such as an older 'family man' and politician you'd trusted for professional advice and internship opportunities, only to have him 'test the waters' with you through a lifting of your skirt and an invasion of your personal space with an unsolicited neck massage

- feigning that you're not interested in anyone outside of someone good on paper/on a path to marriage: because- as a woman- why would you have interest in anything other than becoming an 'honorable' and 'beautiful' bride, on a path to eventually become a mother? *It is*, they'd claim, after all, *the men with the animalistic need*: where the sex they desire and have can be 'washed off' like 'dirt off a hand', while the same 'dirt' would haunt a girl's reputation. That's why all those precious/ over-exaggerated golden jewels are placed on a bride (she must be the 'virgin prize'), alongside of a red ribbon around the waist of her wedding gown to symbolize the virginal 'blood' traditionally required to be 'spilled' that night.

- being told, growing up, to not let men 'use and discard you like a napkin'- even when the closeness may have been consensual. Where you cannot admit- sometimes even to yourself (unless you're 'a bad woman')- that those feelings were indeed mutual.

BIRDS

the fumbling chick, awkward still in flight
flutters before us, naïve to the potential danger
of a malevolent human's might

unlike its momma sparrow- who is, nonetheless,
risking her life to ensure her offspring can survive another day
for her to feed, nest and caress

one's adventure and experience
is the other's protective bravery
we're oblivious to which role we ourselves fulfill
fluttering about until intervened by destiny

we linger
like nestlings
with inadequate wings

SET FREE YOUR FLOW

OUCH

the narcissist wonders why the
empath has finally
had enough
and in typical fashion,
quite possibly
even suspects the empath of having allowed for another's seduction

yes, the empath has finally severed ties
cutting them off with a proverbial blade
though never sharper than the always brutal, painful cut of the
narcissist's cyclical words

only this time, not on purpose
through the way of tears
or some forced 'silent treatment' game

the cut has simply developed naturally
indifference and neutrality:
reaction from a soul weary
of having been mistreated for so long

the empath has been rescued by another love, indeed
the unmistakable, incomparable and whole love she's found
within her whole self

and by doing so- she's being loved by the universe in return

the narcissist cannot compete
and has thus become obsolete

SECTION III:
Flowing Through Socialization

EXTRAVERTED INTROVERT

SET FREE YOUR FLOW

EYES IN BLOOM

is it the birds chirping
that sets my heart audibly beating?
and my heart blooming?
or
 is it the revival of hope and life
that the pending spring tends to bring?

each month leading up to this one
has catalyzed in me
an awakening:
sometimes rude,
sometimes enlightening

in attempting authenticity
I put my bare soul forth
in its entirety
only to have it be rejected
for minor parts being different
as if that were a calamity

I welcome the birds and spring
and in turn, they welcome me

                                      nature can be a better friend
                                  than wolves in sheep's clothing
                                at least you can see what's coming

                                                        I now see

FELICITOUS SIMPLICITY

not everyone whose attention you desire
can handle your fire
avoid such a situation: the one so dire
your dignity is not for hire

a curious satisfaction feels attached to my current age
so, not with time rewound
but just for a brief moment I'd want again to be *fifteen*

where a simple look,
a word
smile on the face,
or an awkward, blushing embrace

it was everything

it still is…

                        we just forget it with all the social ambition… *in between*

'A Homemaker is Already a Teacher AND Nurse to Her Kids'

It's true, dear reader. No, not necessarily the title of this section in its entirety. Rather, I quote this because I was indeed told this by that AK Party-member guy friend of mine. The one of a traditional mindset in Turkey whom I mentioned in the previous Section.

Upon being unable to find paid, local work out of graduate school in 2008 (right at the onset of the financial crash which affected New York City immensely), I obtained certification in T.E.S.O.L (Teaching English to Speakers of Other Languages). Subsequently, I went to my birth city of Istanbul to teach- thinking I'd be more successful with it there. I would often discuss my 'grandiose' dreams of eventually becoming a college instructor and writer with my friend.

He would tell me I was working 'too hard' for 'nothing'. That I was 'attractive,' and hence did not 'have to' do so. That I could meet someone who would be the main breadwinner so I could then use my 'hobbies' of teaching and writing with my future children- as my 'purpose' in life, having been born a woman. Although I would roll my eyes and downplay such thinking as 'outdated' because he would never 'lived abroad' to have his vision 'broadened' enough, privately his words had gotten to me more than I would ever care to admit.

"Why am I going on all these unfruitful job interviews, feeling depleted- when I see scantily clad women with rich husbands at restaurants, whom I know aren't working full-time?" I would ponder to myself. "Maybe my friend is right. Maybe I really do have to dress either like those women, or cover-up as a fashionable 'hijabi' to 'land' a wealthy, government-supported *husband, and spend my weekends organizing fancy dinners rather than pulling my hair out over a laptop..."*

I can go into the next 'catalyst' sequences of events and details of my life that led me to eventually giving another long-term guy friend a romantic 'chance'- namely my daughter's father, Kemal, and marry him to live with him in Norway where I would then spend most of my time writing my first novel. But, alas, you can read between the lines anyway, dear reader. Besides, this is not a general autobiography. I'm no famous celebrity to need one, and nor do I aspire to be. If I can continue to inspire and entertain readers, that's enough for me.

Yet I mention it because that era in my life (my mid-twenties) was an eye-opening symbol for something I'd come across several times in my life: triggers for change. Rejection causing redirection. Poor timing becoming a catalyst in changing my plans. Heartbreaks and disappointments causing me to close those 'doors' and open others to new professional opportunities and romantic chances.

Needless to say, I never ended up being like any of the aforementioned group of women, and certainly did not marry a necessarily 'wealthy' husband. But Kemal, God bless him, was more 'abundant' in love and character than any men I'd met, and I'll always be thankful for our union and, of course, its fruit- our daughter.

There's always a certain excitement in youth over 'future possibilities', isn't there? Who will you marry? What will your career consist of? How will your children be, if you even have any? And then, you grow up. You get the answers to those things. And then come your mid 30's- hitting you hard. You're faced with the inevitability of aging and less enthusiasm, despite a wiser and more self-appreciating soul. 'Ironic' was always my least favorite Morisette song, and 'Catch 22' my most feared Joseph Heller novel.

Speaking of ironies, let's examine the following. I've always been a creative soul inhabiting a body born into a realism-inclined, fixed-mindset family (if you've never checked out Carol S. Dweck's book *Mindset*, I use it in one of the Business English courses I teach and would definitely recommend it). My choice of major in Political Science in college was mainly to please my parents- especially my mom, who warned me not only that there wouldn't be 'money' for me to make in creative endeavors, but that I'd end up meeting 'predator' men in such fields.

As you've read, dear reader- I, of course, ended up meeting more 'predators' during my daily school life and political internships than in creative fields. I ended up never earning a dime off of politics- instead, making a living off of creative writing and- randomly- teaching. I studied Politics for 6 years- graduate studies included- never to work in it, but 'ironically' to have my marriage fall victim to it after the events of July 15, 2016, in Turkey.

I have to give it to my mother though- when she is on point, she's on point. As aforementioned: she, too, like many among her generation growing up in Istanbul, had struggled with dichotomies. She knew I enjoyed performing theatrical monologues in school and would often tell me that 'politics' was 'similar to acting' since it too would put people in 'public positions' and required 'charisma'. (Yeah- she's had her occasional 'creativity-supporting' moments, in hindsight).

When I mainly ended up teaching language for a living- working as such for over a decade now- I gave her another analogy, instead. "Not politics, mom, but, rather- *teaching* has become 'like acting' for me," I told her. "For not only can I 'perform' in front of a classroom as my 'stage' to make lessons more interesting for students- but I could thus also be able to inspire people in general, just as actors do."

My epiphany ended up being this: I'd originally warmed up to politics (and even had inspired to go into acting) for the deeper purpose and calling I ultimately ended up finding in teaching and writing. Namely, the one of *inspiring people*.

It took me over a decade to arrive here at the point I'm at now. I'm certainly not famous, but I do feel somewhat influential- especially after having received so much heartwarming feedback on my writing from readers, as well as on my teaching skills from anonymous student surveys. Life truly became what ended up happening when I'd been 'busy making other (academic and professional) plans', indeed, as that saying goes.

Yet, strangely, I wouldn't have had it any other way. Like an actress, in a way, I got the chance to play various 'roles' in life and feel fulfilled having had no regrets and 'what ifs'. I felt like a diplomat interning at the United Nations, and like a politician while running for my local Democratic primary race. I felt like an actress during acting classes as well as in front of my classrooms at times with certain livelier lessons. I felt like a 'fancy' lady who 'lunches' during various charity events with my mother in her Turkish-American civil society circle, as well as during my role as a military wife- attending fancy balls and tea parties both in NATO surroundings in Europe as well as in Turkey.

The one thing I never would have wanted to become, of course, was my current role as a 'prison wife.' Being that Kemal is a political victim who is imprisoned along with thousands in Turkey without a crime, the term was initially bothersome to me. Yet I've since come to not only accept it, but also appreciate the fact that it's allowed me to empathize with numerous women across the world (and even here in the United States) who also believe fully in the innocence of their incarcerated loved ones and wait for them while struggling to work, go on and remain strong for their children.

Such women and I can add one another on social media and support one another, for example, without ever having met. Knowing we 'get it'- even if we never privately message one another or even engage in any dialogue to do so. Our paths may have never physically crossed, nor our ideologies or backgrounds, but in that realm of being fellow facers of injustice: we become allies, sisters. Even men who have met my husband at one point in their lives have become my virtual brothers- expressing their positive memories with him as well as faith in his innocence. In fact, I have faced more kindness from strangers than some of my so-called friends during this time. At a time when my faith in my home country had started declining, my faith in humanity pulled me back up to the light of human oneness. No matter what happens after this point in our political and legal struggles, I hope to never lose that.

This brings me to another irony. I had spent most of my 20's trying to avoid becoming an 'ordinary' homemaker of a woman- mostly to make my family and circle 'proud' somehow- only to now be working from home and being just that for the most part. The coronavirus pandemic exacerbated that too, of course. And I am aware that I wasn't the only 'professional' woman to suddenly have had to become everything to their kids at home. So, had my friend had a point after all? I was, if you think about it, now the owner of high-level diplomas whilst literally being a 'teacher and nurse' to my child at home.

I was also being both a mother and a father to Dalya. I was talking to her mostly in English (since I didn't want her to be confused in school) and it is also the language I express myself best in, while her grandmother was trying to exert more Turkish influence. I had the additional responsibility on my shoulders of being the main decision maker in her life. I was always juggling. And- perhaps the most ironic of all- I was doing all of this alone, as a single parent, despite technically being married.

Perhaps if we had still been keeping in touch, that guy friend (who has since gotten married himself) may have said: "See, I told you. You tried so hard to climb the professional ladder, only to end up being at home again." And, interestingly enough, I enjoy it! I've never enjoyed cooking this much in my 20's and even as a newlywed (sorry Kemal). So, perhaps it was the quarantine. Or perhaps it was maturity and motherhood that 'domesticated' me, more than family or any man could. Maybe this, maybe that. I'm content still in knowing I have obtained various accolades as *ends* in themselves- not necessarily just as *means* to some 'promised destination' of financial abundance that tends to be culturally-pledged for 'successful business women' in Western societies. I'm content in being an example for my daughter and all youth in general. For me, hence, the struggle has been *worth it*.

The *joy of being in that 'flow' and of doing* the studying, applying, networking...sometimes even sacrificing sleep all night in front of a computer. Without any immediate payment or professional success of any kind. I can still be content in knowing that I've been in the 'flow' of laboring purely for the sake of a *struggle*. A struggle that strangely provides joy, in the knowledge that creating is something I love doing. Even if that struggle only rewards me one day out of 29 others in a given month- the immense and pure joy I'd feel in that one day would somehow always be worth it.

I had tried. I had worked hard to improve myself, if for nothing else- *for* myself. For the mere satisfaction of knowing I tried. Like a recipe one can never quite get just right the first time they use it to bake something- but the end result eventually ends up being absolutely delicious, sometimes even when least expected.

When the struggle has become habit- so routine that one random day, success surprises you. The pride you feel in yourself becomes worth every drop of blood, sweat, and tears. You've *experienced*. You've *transformed*. You've *inspired*. You've attuned yourself with your inherent *flow:* whether it be the genetic flow of characteristics acquired from your familial/ethnic bloodline, or the one of your soul obtained from your environment and upbringing. You haven't merely survived on earth another day. You've *lived*.

Self-Identity: As the 'Other' in Various Settings

In my poetry, as well as my semi-autobiographical novels, I've noticed that I often somehow end up talking about *duality*. Now, mind you, I didn't always feel as clearly-torn between dual cultures-50/50- as I currently do. I want to say that from the age of around 8 years old- when I first arrived in the US- until my teen years, I somehow felt 'more Turkish' than I did during my high school years. That becoming a teenager later 'Americanized' me, with various trends that all teenagers tend to stereotypically be influenced by. But I can't do so. I cannot be wholly honest with myself or with you, dear reader, if I simplify things as clear-cut as that.

The truth is- when I'd arrived here, I was a blank slate. I'd had no real 'strong' sense of 'Turkishness' instilled in me as a child in Istanbul. Instead, family drama following my father's departure from the house and my parents' ensuing divorce had taken precedence over cultural celebrations that would have possibly deepened my identity as 'Turkish' in my early childhood.

Ironically, in fact, I never quite even felt 'Turkish' until this fact was pointed out to me by all the other immigrants and 'Americans' in NY. Just as a child really has no racially 'different' concept of skin color until society and life experiences show them the sad dichotomy (I've seen firsthand how my daughter- who equally plays with a variety of dolls- treats skin color simply as the difference between one classmate, for example, having blue eyes while another has brown). I too had no sense of 'Turkishness' until I was 'gobble gobble' teased in elementary school. I had also not celebrated 'Turkishness' in any way until my teen years found me being 'Miss Turkey' twice in annual parades, and hosting shows my mother's women's organization would organize to raise money for a weekend Turkish school (Turkish Women's League of America and its *Ataturk/ Cumhuriyet* school branches, respectively).

Yet on some days, it got (and still does) harder than others. The earliest memory I have, in fact, of my being 'different' is from what must have been around 4th grade- one year after I had emigrated here with my mother. In Turkish culture, we customarily kiss friends and family members on both cheeks to say *hello, goodbye*, or even as an affectionate and non-verbal way of saying 'cheer up'. The latter is exactly what I tried to do when I noticed that one of the first friends I had made in school- an Asian girl named Anna (who had language issues as well, so we got along in class)- was sad one day during our cafeteria lunch at P.S. 13 in Queens. I'd asked her what was wrong (or I thought I did, with my limited English at the time), and she just continued to shed some tears. And so, as her classmate and friend, I tried to make her feel better in the 'Turkish' way I then knew how: I gave her a kiss on both cheeks. (Oh, the post-Covid world horror of this if it were to happen now!).

She was stunned, but more so by what ensued almost immediately after I had done so. I'm not sure how those mere fourth graders had heard of the term- and why they were using it as something derogatory- but suddenly one boy yelled 'lesbian!'. Subsequently, almost the entire table was laughing at me. I, of course, had never heard of the term and had no idea what it'd meant- and neither did most of those other children who were laughing, I imagine. But this one boy was- I guess, in retrospect- the 'popular guy' in the class, and I'm sure they must have supposed that if he were teasing someone regarding something, it must indeed have been something *tease-worthy*. And so- they laughed along with him.

Imagine the horror of my mother and stepfather when I returned home that day (I'll now refer to them as my 'parents', as my biological father ceased being one to me along with the divorce when I was 5, though he was alive on this planet until I was nearly 25 years old). "What is a *lesbian,* daddy?" I asked my stepdad, as he was, naturally, the one with the English skills, having grown up in the US himself. I don't recall exactly what he responded, but I remember a lot of curious questions. *Where did you hear that? Who said that?*

Anna, needless to say, felt shy to talk to me following that incident: likely fearing being teased for a mysterious reason for both of us. I was lucky to then develop a friendship with a more outgoing ELL student (English Language Learner in academic terms) named Nicole, of Chilean origin. In Junior High School, it would often follow in this same pattern: I tended to develop friendships with ELL students more than 'American' students, although, to be fair, there were also a lot of 'immigrant' students in the Queens public schools I attended!

The only other Turkish student I ever met was '*Özlem*' in junior high school, and we ended up having a tumultuous on again/off again friendship right through our college years. I only mention her here for this following purpose: I learned that meeting other 'Turks' in a 'foreign' city didn't equate to automatically-close friendships. (Interestingly, neither did meeting a couple of other 'Americans' I met in Istanbul when I lived there as a single woman to teach English).

And yet I'd often mistakenly think they would. In my contemporary musings about the woes of social categorizations, I find that, in retrospect, I'd been so conditioned to them that not only was I a victim of categorizations, but also a perpetrator myself in terms of my expectations.

I wasn't the only one. Over the years I met many Turks living in New York who told my family and I the same thing. How they'd end up creating 'smoke breaks' and 'car rides' and basically any opportunity just to talk to someone in Turkish for socialization-even people they'd never previously see themselves chatting up due to differences in lifestyles.

Turkish or not, I tended to get along with male friends better growing up and had trouble with female friendships lasting beyond the periodic commonalities I referred to earlier. Furthermore, I also ended up hurt by friends of my own cultural background more frequently: with some sort of dramatic fall-out playing out, in contrast to a subtle fading of non-Turkic friendships.

Aside from personality clashes and losing the test of time (surely experienced across the world): I would, in hindsight, attribute my particular friendships woes to unclear categorizations. I loved to dance in clubs, for example, but had to watch the way I dressed and return home by a certain time. My lack of freedom with my time availabilities and lifestyle choices in general tended to irritate non-Turkish friends who didn't face the same intensity of possessiveness ('protection') from their families. I was neither 'the prude Turkish girl' nor the quintessential 'American party girl.' I was often made to feel, in fact, that I wasn't 'cool' enough to for the cooler parties, yet also not the favorite among more traditional Turkish friends to hang out with (especially with their boyfriends around the same social settings as us). The idea that I genuinely loved dancing and music- and that I honestly was not looking to flirt with anyone- would never occur to them. A girl enjoying dancing for the art of it- after all- is a more 'American' thing. I'd feel extremely misunderstood and misjudged, and this hurt me more than by any non-Turkish friend doing so; the shock felt double-fold, somehow.

I also acquired my sense of being not only Turkish or American, but by that point equally *Turkish-American* in my college years, as I experienced stigmas attached to 'Turkishness' with regards to controversial historic events. From Armenian-American protesters at the annual Turkish parade (to whom I'd wave conciliatorily as the parade 'queen'), I heard of the term 'genocide' for the first time, and genuinely wondered *"...why do they hate us when we don't hate them?"* From my stepdad's professional circle of Greek-American colleagues and friends, I heard of the term (with their half- jokes and possessive sentiments about modern-day city of Istanbul) 'Constantinople' for the first time.

From college friendships in general, I only heard 'stereotypes' against which I'd continuously need to battle and defend. "No, camels aren't common in Turkey: we're *not* an Arabic nation made of deserts". "No, women *can* walk outside at night, and are not forced to cover their hair". "No, we cannot be labeled as a third-world country- we have the second largest military in NATO, don't you know!?"

Finally, I must include the following addendums to the issue of friendships resulting from periodic commonalities- for they often tend to be pronounced with Turkish friendships in particular. Commiserating and nosiness.

MINI-SCENARIO

Friend A: **Hey,** *canım* (Turkish equivalent of 'honey'). **Oh my God,** (insert name of some 'heartbreaker') **didn't take me out again this weekend. I definitely think he's seeing someone. How about** (insert the name of the other friend's heartbreaker)**? Has he finally been attentive to you this weekend?**

Friend B: Aww, I'm sorry to hear that, canım. I was just about to call you! (no, they weren't). **Well, yes, actually. He surprised me with flowers and took me to a nice dinner.**

Friend A: Oh. Oh, nice. Happy for you. That's great! (::disappointed sigh:)

Misery indeed can love company as part of human nature across all nationalities, yes, but only Turkish-American friends in particularly would make me feel guilty somehow if I suddenly became happy when they were still sad. Or, adversely, turn their backs on me when my luck in life appeared to take a turn for the worse at a particular time. Coldness flourished as text messages diminished. I deemed myself a friend for people to share despair- a *'kötu gün dostu'* in Turkish. They didn't seem to want or be able to handle me when I was doing well, nor wanted to make the effort for me anymore when they themselves were. To those fair-weather acquaintances I'd mistakenly called friends: I'm letting them go with love. They can rob another person's aura without paying with genuine friendship.

Didn't anyone tell them we were all on the same roller coaster in life- that there is never some underlying competition? Didn't anyone tell them, just as importantly, that just because I was going through a rougher period in my life than they were, and needed to vent, I was never going to stay in the 'dumps' for long- and that they didn't need to lose their faith in my value as a person to somehow be effort-worthy enough to keep in their lives? Would they have been so fickle had they been true friends? All I know is, I've been hurt just as much by platonic friendships in my life as romantic ones. And my cultural duality, for my aforementioned reasons, definitely often felt like it had
played a major part in it.

As for nosiness- I think the term speaks for itself. I never experienced a string of questions that my American side would deem 'intrusive' as frequently as I have by Turks. *'How much?' 'Why? What's the size? What's the label? What's his salary? Which school? Which restaurant/hotel- how many stars?'*. There's almost no question too 'personal' in general in Turkish culture (under the guise, of course, of 'making friendly conversation').

Yet, once again, I've come to witness how bicultural Turkish-Americans like myself have tended to be this way more than others. After I was interviewed by a Turkish-American online news website about my premier novel, for instance, I noticed how- aside from a couple of genuinely warm and congratulatory social

media comments- the rest ended up indeed being judgmentally intrusive ones by fellow Turks residing in the US. *"What's the name of her publishing company- is it one of the mainstream ones?"* ("What does it matter?" I wanted to respond, but didn't.) This nosiness- tinged with a touch of both arrogance and pressure of putting on 'appearances'- has, in my opinion, had a detrimental effect on Turkish-American lobby groups not being as politically effective as the ones of other cultural minorities in the US (whose groups don't focus on the 'categorizations' of their various organizations, uniting instead
for a common cause for their people's benefit).

In *The Catalyst,* I intrinsically found myself gravitating toward the theme of environmental friendships as well. In case you haven't read my romantic suspense novel yet (what are you waiting for?), here is a brief summary of one of the underlying themes as it pertains to this particular section. Kaitlin Maverick, the female protagonist of the story, feels so alone and desperate for friendships in a new land she's traveled to through marriage, she signs up for social activities she's not even interested in just to have human company (other than sales associates on various shopping outings to pass the time while her husband is at work). Was this portion taken from my direct life experience? You can bet it most certainly was.

Subsequently, the reader ultimately sees how everyone Kaitlin has met crossed paths with her for a reason- as 'catalysts' to motivate her to take a certain step in her life she otherwise wouldn't have. Her feelings of jealousy over a friendly female colleague of her husband, for example, incites her to join a social club- where she meets a Turkish woman named Sibel, who herself turns out to be a 'catalyst' for her of another kind.

Situational and environmental friendships of convenience may have been just for that, in retrospect, for many of us: for catalysis to make certain changes in our lives or open our minds to some things we otherwise never would have.

That annoying colleague who convinced you to quit a steady job on Wall Street? You may have gotten angry with her- but ultimately you may have henceforth redirected your life in another professional direction more suited for you (autobiographical, yes). That frenemy with whom you were seemingly 'close' one week and distant the next? Think about it. Did they incite a recognition in you- even if it was ultimately self-recognition or truth-facing you otherwise may have been too scared to admit even to yourself? Yup. You've guessed it. They were catalysts for your life.

Am I saying that literally everyone we meet is for some grand reason? That random parent, for instance, with whom you conversed about the weather while waiting to pick up your kids from their pre-K class? No. Not at all. However, if the same parent did happen to mention- even if casually so during the few conversations you may have had- that their kid was enjoying a certain ballet class, for example, which made you realize your own daughter was inclined to do the same? Exactly- they could have been catalysts.

The Reclusive Open-Book

My general shyness growing up wasn't really any more noteworthy than the shyness, I'm sure, employed by millions of people around the world. Perhaps that number is even smaller in scale if I were to include myself in a group of those who were shy children due to an absentee parent. Adding the final characteristic of shyness due to having emigrated into a whole new country as a child with your mother and her new husband? Now we may be getting somewhere: I may truly be in a smaller category of people with similar experiences (if you, dear reader, are one such person- kindly contact me to briefly share your story as well. I'm genuinely curious).

Not only had I never been able to ride a bike (perhaps for psychological reasons, due to the story I shared in Section 1) but I barely remember having done many other typically 'childish' things either. I was already an only child. I never remember uttering the word for 'father' in my first language of Turkish- 'baba'. I never grew up playing various games with any cousins. With various lingual barriers here in New York on top of that, I felt so lonely at one point, in fact, that I remember having told the 2,3 friends I was able to make in grade school that I had a mysterious brother and sister (no, not imaginary friends, as I was well aware I was technically lying). I had no idea really why I felt I had to do so, either. I even remember inviting some over for Halloween trick-or-treating in my apartment. When they'd asked about the whereabouts of my so-called 'siblings', I had to tell them one was 'away in college' while another was 'off somewhere shooting hoops'.

Ironically, life would show me perhaps I was already embodying what my subconscious already knew I was- an older sister to a half-brother being raised across the pond in England, also without knowing about me, and also sour about the man who'd fathered us both.

That's right, dear reader. I hope you can tell by this point that- with that kind of an imagination- I could have either gone on to develop serious mental issues, or turn to art as survival. Luckily, I found solace ultimately in writing, and chose the latter.

There I was. Shy to say 'hi' to people I knew on the street sometimes, yet completely 'at home' whenever an opportunity to 'prove myself' presented itself as a schoolgirl- especially in the form of creativity. A school play? The school Chorus? The spelling bee? A poetry contest? I was there.

"Damn girl," I remember one particular high school classmate telling me after one of our senior play rehearsals. "You dance well and you're not shy at all! I wasn't expecting that from you! It's always the shy ones, isn't it…"? Surprising people who would later express that they'd initially expected me to be shy or aloof (or even sometimes 'snobby' and- gulp- 'bitchy') would always motivate me.

I had to not only overcome the loneliness I felt in my family life and cultural duality, but also this 'false' image I quickly became aware that I was displaying to people. In retrospect, even in photographs I see that I barely smiled as a schoolgirl- even though I'm pretty sure I thought I was doing so.

Subsequently in my life, I felt so afraid of being misunderstood among both Turks and Westerners ("I can't stay out late, but I still love to party"/ "I physically can't handle fasting during Ramadan but I'm still very spiritual and believe in our prayers and alms-giving") that I decided somewhere along the line to be an *open-book*.

Despite my overprotective mother always warning me against my tendency to overshare every detail of my life with friends and acquaintances- being anything other than an open book eventually became difficult. If I didn't overshare, I'd feel 'mistakenly categorized'. And despite Western self-help quotes everywhere telling us, 'don't care what others think'- I did. I cared what they thought- not because I wanted to mold my life choices in accordance with others' opinions, but rather to balance my idealist individuality with a dose of such 'realism'.

Did *The Catalyst*, for instance, require its subtly-erotic scene toward the end? Artistically- for the storyline- it absolutely did. Could I have described it with longer, more evocative wording than the sentence or two I ended up using to describe it? Not if I didn't want to completely ostracize Turkish readers (and my own family) whom I knew would be reading it.

You can sell hundreds of books and even thousands. You can be complimented on just about every part of your being you can imagine. You can physically be in a glorious space in a glorious town, with glorious belongings. You can receive 50 likes or 500 on social media. Ultimately it all comes down to this: are you smiling as you fall asleep? If you are unable to maintain meaningful connections in this life, you're lonely even if not alone. Period.

With my daughter Dalya, it has been really fascinating to watch her grow up in the United States, from a younger age than I did. Watching her daily struggles with shyness in greeting new people that belie the artistic and 'outgoing-with-familiar-people' side of her, it feels like watching a movie clip of my own life: right before my very eyes. It is as if God is giving me a second chance in life. A do-over of my childhood, through my daughter. Not for her to 'accomplish what I couldn't', as that parental cliché goes, but rather to purposely view the world through a child's excited eyes- more than I was able to as a child.

which of your shadows represents your true essence best
as you stride?

are you able to swim and ride the waves of the highest tide
you experience inside?
you're still that young girl with the messy handwriting
pretending
in mock interviews that she's already written the books she's
discussing
you're still the hider of the most precious jewels lurking in your
imagination
while also the writer whose low mood rises
when it can motivate another:
an over-sharer
no need to have all the answers
or feign divinity
no need to be anything other than humanly free
imperfectly perfect
just BE

    Many of my English students share that one of the most surprising facets of Americans according to them has been rhetorical questions. "Americans ask how everyone is doing without really expecting an answer," they say. It's true. But I could never become 'that' American. If someone asks me 'how are you?'- I pretty much verbally-vomit various details of my day. And I truly believe that I've been doing so- now in both hindsight as well as self-reflection- in order to wholly be myself. So that I can increase the chance of somehow being recognized by my 'soul tribe'- friends that would find my 'weirdness' and 'quirkiness' compatible with their own. No matter which socio-cultural 'categorization' we were boxed in. No matter which 'group' we belonged to.

    As Marilyn Monroe is attributed as once upon a time saying: "I knew I belonged to the world, not because I was very talented or even beautiful, but because I never belonged anywhere else." *Belonging.* Can someone missing a parent growing up ever truly feel like they belong somewhere? Could I have made wiser dating choices- and perhaps better friendships- if my birth father had validated me? I will never know.

> *"why did you leave me?"*
> *a tearful voice asked through the phone receiver*
> *there would never be an answer*
> *he hadn't just left her mother*
> *so the girl would always ponder*
> *and never ask the same to another*
> *she can finally understand*
> *now that she's older*
> *and with that answer*
> *will feel broken again by a man*
> *no longer*

"I miss you, baba," my daughter now says into the phone receiver. Except this time, unlike me in my own childhood- she isn't speaking into the void. Even if- for over 5 years- it has only been through letters and the occasional/brief telephone message rather than in-person: she knows she has a father somewhere in the world who's dying to hear her voice.

And with even just that, if nothing else, I can get some closure for my own childhood. I can make peace with my own experience: know that my daughter is accepted, in a way I was never able to feel. I hope this ultimately can lead to an increased sense of both self-acceptance and self-confidence in her later years growing up, with her friendships and all relationships as well. Sometimes, I feel I even went through these things so I can be there for my daughter in a more understanding and helpful way when she goes through similar things in her life.

SET FREE YOUR FLOW

purity is enough
your peace of mind
is enough
to not only accept being alone
but actually relish it
treasure it
make the most of it
never lonely, even when alone
much lovelier now, than with any fake clone
of the lost that had been- and could only be
the only one to really feel like home
we can become grown
better on our own

little one

remember your wings are not meant to carry and hold
the burdensome weight of ungrateful, additional load

if you give them the flashlight to use on a whim
to create shine around their dark souls
to use and dispose
who is going to help you when you need your own light
back to carry you through?
when you were counting on them to shine for you too

wisdom, I'm afraid, only pays a visit
when you've had enough, reached your limit

SECTIONAL ANECDOTES

Growing up bi-culturally has meant:

- choosing a Major based on an 'ideal' profession it could lead to, deemed as such by your social-circle. Where the question of 'what job would make you happy?' is an absurd and almost unheard one. *"Her daughter will be studying Business? Good money. Oh, teacher? Nice- men like feminine jobs like teachers and nurses. Teachers also have more days off to rear children easier. MY niece is studying Art. Argh! She'll never land a good job, nor a wealthy and respectable man..."*

-being told to come out of your comfort zone and 'go say hi' to potential 'friends' or 'professional contacts' deemed appropriate by one's circle. My mother once convinced me to approach Rahmi Koç on a Turkish Airlines flight, to let him know I 'idolized his company' (I didn't even know what they did) and that I'd been looking for a job fresh out of graduate school (that part was true). He gave me his card to e-mail my CV, saying he appreciated my 'go-getter' attitude. I did land a fancy interview in Istanbul 2 weeks after that- one that, of course, went nowhere.

- expressing 'extroverted' qualities most comfortably through *art*. A microphone or social platform allowed me to make myself 'heard'- and feel accepted- despite nervousness

SET FREE YOUR FLOW

THE WARRIOR

you carry the sword
to fight uphill battles
of injustice
both real and imaginary

the burden is heavy
generational responsibility

break the proverbial curse
free the repressed verse

write out your world into existence
protagonist of your own art: fight and employ persistence

slay the dragon
of fearing what others think

don't forget that your sword
is the one that bleeds ink

SET FREE YOUR FLOW

GAMBIT

they copy you
but it's not the same
no room for a princess
in this game

I've got Knights and Bishops
on my side
you've only got insufficient Pawns
and your pride

a spiritless face falls flat on a screen
it's obvious who's the original Queen
the previous efforts: I appreciate
but it's history now: I won't take the bait

Checkmate

DO BEFORE DONE

flutter off
before discovering your plight
you've been set free
before prepared for flight

remember you're a butterfly
not a used kite

Section IV:
Flowing Through Parenting

POETIC POLITICS
(STUDENTS OF POLITICS BECOME ITS VICTIMS)

SET FREE YOUR FLOW

THE MENDING OF UNBANDAGED WOUNDS

a man
politically-imprisoned
kept away from his wife, his child, his home, his human dignity
crime-free
he's joined by many
similar victims of circumstance
for company

he'll soon be set free, they say
we live in a democracy…it can't forever be this way

is the path toward mending a probability or simply a distant possibility?
to repair the shattered backbone of a nation once promising the ideal
regional stability and legality
when many have bent their backbones cramped into caged-spaces meant
for few, not twenty

is there a path to ameliorate and heal families back together up ahead?
following tears of widowed wives and orphaned children, not of ghosts, but
of the living dead? Every evening, for all of them, filled with excruciating
dread?

animals can lick their wounds in place of bandages…
what can separated families do
when faced with human savages?

SET FREE YOUR FLOW

TWO LITTLE GIRLS

I wish I could tell her it all gets better,
when you love yourself enough to better yourself
through any weather

wish I could tell her - if they step on you to rise
or play you for a fool, leaving you misled
you'll be the one in the end more wise
and you'll always be one step ahead

don't wrap your entire life
around being someone's wife
anything can end
always need an alternate plan

ours was torn by our birth state
some other marriages are slashed by hate
or losing the one the other cannot appreciate

wish I could tell her … you'll rise through the tears
you're more than your fears…wise beyond your years

to the little girl

both the pure one I see by me
and the one I see still in the mirror

T.A.M (Turkish-American Mothering)

It's largely universal (though there are certainly refreshing stories of exceptions) for parents to 'disapprove' of their offsprings' professional pursuits. It's another thing, unfortunately, for Turkish-American ones (or perhaps bicultural parents in general) to do so. Because when they do, they not only point to the usual and universal parental 'concerns' over one's ability to earn enough to make a living or the potential dangers associated with a certain job, but rather also tend to lead to quarrelsome and judgmental accusations.

Imagine someone that can list an entire set of 'terrible' things about your choices- but then back off into a safety net of *"...but it's only because I think you deserve better"* or, *"I'm not saying to leave them/change your mind. I won't take that responsibility. I'm just saying...It's up to you."* That's likely a Turkish-American parent. Refer to this following sketch for my case and point.

Mother: **What are you doing?**

The son/daughter: **I'm painting, mom.**

Mother: **Don't you have real work to do? Why don't you look for some real work online? You're wasting too much time on your hobbies. Look at ......** (insert name of random family acquaintance's son or daughter)

The son/daughter: **But, mom, this is my dream and I can actually make a living with this as well. Be a little more open-minded, please. This makes me happy.**

Mother: **Will you be happy when you're a bum on the street, unable to pay your rent and bills? What will everyone say? You must take after your** (insert 'black sheep' family member's name here). **Why did we work so hard to get you through college? For this? Are you trying to give us a heart attack?**

The son/daughter: **No need to be paranoid just yet, please! I'll always regret it if I don't at least try. Everyone else sees that and supports me on this, I don't understand how you...**

Mother: **...This is for your good! Your friends aren't going to be honest and warn because they want the best for you. They see you as a rival- of course they don't want you to become more successful than them.**

The son/daughter: **...Right. And just what is your definition of 'success'?**

Mother: **...That's enough. Just wrap it up quick- you still have to help me out with these boxes.**

End scene.

Allow me to share an even more subjective and concrete example from my own personal experience, dear reader. Though my mother likes to refute it to this day, she's the reason I chose Political Science as my college major: a major which hasn't helped me professionally thus far in any way, shape or form.

Now, fair is fair. She *does* have a point when she says that, yes, at 18-19 I could have indeed taken responsibility for my decision, I suppose (in retrospect). And, I do. Yes: I made the decision to major in Political Science. Yet it was done so with so much maternal influence exerted that I cannot tell where the line of 'interference' ended and my 'personal decision-making' began. An influence that externally gazed upon my physical presence amongst Turkish-American civil society- and likened my presence as 'belonging' in that company- without actually asking me if I was enjoying diplomatic discussions over weekend-cocktails at the Embassy building, munching on little meatballs on toothpicks being passed around by caterers.

I also never realized I could have even *had* a 'personal choice' to take on such a responsibility; I was expected to be 'Americanized' and 'individualistic' when it suited the flow of events, whereas mostly I was otherwise expected to be as 'Turkish' and 'family-centric' as possible.

Before starting to write *The Catalyst* in Norway- I had actually started a blog named 'The Musings of a Reluctant Housewife' soon after I'd gotten married and literally had become one (namely, a 'reluctantly' domesticated 'housewife'). *The Catalyst* itself, in fact, had initially had the working title of *Scandal-avia*. (Cheesy, I'm aware, but, hey, in my defense it *does* involve a culturally 'scandalous' plotline taking place in Scandinavia, and I love a good play on words, so…)

On that blog, I'd added some pretty pictures of Norway alongside my first attempts at baking brownies and trying horseback riding; all up until I lost interest as soon as the then newly-rising Instagram proved more 'instantly' satisfying.

Now interestingly enough, even prior to that blog, I used to have another blog named 'T.A.P', which stood for 'Turkish-American Princess'. (I suppose blogging was there for lonely creatives like me before social media really blew up like it has now). I had been chosen twice as the 'Turkish-American princess' in annual parades held in Manhattan- mostly because I was seen as the *hanım hanımcık* ('lady-like') daughter of my Turkish-American non-profit community 'notable' of a mother, and had hence thought that title to be *cute*.

Today, I stand here (well I'm technically sitting and typing these words as I watch the raindrops from my suburban window, dear reader) as a politically-single mother. Trying to 'write out' my 'drops' and creative 'flow' of consciousness in various states of exhaustion. Just like I've been doing whenever I found the chance to type them out after my toddler managed to fall asleep only around midnight. Mostly munching on sour-candy to stay awake (sorry, wisdom teeth).

No 'Musings'. No 'T.A.P'. Perhaps if I didn't go into becoming an author, I could have dabbled in this latest stage in my life using some variation or play on words relevant to my contemporary struggles ('PSM and PMS', perhaps? Get It? *Politically-Single Mother* and…yeah. You get the drift).

What would I have done if Instagram hadn't been there to distract me from delving into typing out all the trauma in the form of blogging, by making me turn to artistic expression as catharsis instead? Symbolic photography and stories (which I've called 'visual storytelling') juxtaposed with political/ human rights related hashtags and captions just may have saved me at the time. Particularly during those 4-months when I'd been bound to Istanbul, due to a travel ban placed following my naval officer husband's incarceration. A ban I was only made aware of *after* I was stopped from boarding my flight to the US by officers leading me to the questioning room. My then two-year-old in my arms. Everyone on the line behind me looking at my being prevented from traveling as
if I were some criminal on the run.

"I'm an American citizen," I told them politely. "I should be able to travel, regardless of my husband's local case." The clerk had smirked at me. "It doesn't matter if you're also the citizen of Sweden, lady. This is Turkey- and you have Turkish citizenship, too. Only Turkish laws apply here!" (He wasn't kidding. The American embassy of Istanbul I subsequently called told me the same. It was the first time in my life I'd felt the relative powerlessness of my American citizenship abroad, though up to that point I'd witnessed countless people risking everything for such a citizenship).

We'd just paid a 2017 visit to her father in jail. At the time, I had taken that risk, completely comfortable in knowing I'd never gotten myself involved in anything that could be deemed controversial by the state. Just the opposite, in fact. Remember those Turkish-embassy civil society events I mentioned a bit earlier? The ones with the little meatballs being served on toothpicks? Erdoğan, his wife, and countless other AK Party members would frequent them as well (I even have a photograph with Emine Erdoğan , Abdullah Gül, and countless others. I admit that I-*gulp*- even voted for AKP at one time).

Sigh. Back to 'motherhood'.

"Write to Emine Erdoğan," my mother suggested, referring to the authoritarian president's wife. "She's a mother too. I've seen her cry for those Palestinian children on TV. She may sympathize with your story as well."

"She's not going to be given some random personal mail among countless others, I'm sure, mom," I'd responded, rolling my eyes. So, I went to the 'official' website the state had created for 'legal complaints'. CIMER. And I wrote. To Emine Erdoğan. To Erdoğan himself. And- yes- out of desperation for my crimeless husband to be released, I wrote even to *him*: the womanizing, skirt-lifting minister himself.

I swallowed my pride as a young woman after the humiliation in his office I'd chosen to ignore, and asked him to help my innocent husband. "Write *him*, too" my mother had further suggested, after all. I didn't tell her. Just like he knew I wouldn't. His position of power and closeness to Erdoğan having given him some sort of protective shield he's since been able to use to overcome various other controversies in the country as well (hushed quickly in the state-influenced media).

I didn't want my mother to become further disappointed with one more 'civil society/political star' amongst our Turkish-American circle. I couldn't do that to her. I had to let her think her social circle still could have some soft power to 'save the day'. Once again: my Turkishness, encouraged by my mother and observation of similar mothers of friends I was witnessing around me, was whispering into my consciousness that influential contacts could 'save the day' in a time of need. My American side had learned by then that that was all BS- and that we can only ultimately really save ourselves. The only thing 'they' were able to 'influence' and 'save' for me had been business-class seats on Turkish Airlines flights and popular concert tickets in Istanbul (That's right. More things of only showiness value).

Now let's move on to: *'Catalysis'*.

Yes, I've mentioned my mother's at times overbearing influence- but I've also learned not to blame her. Especially since the birth of my own catalyst: my daughter.

It's easy for a mother of any background to unknowingly 'cross the line' of interfering in a child's life due to a self-made mission of lifetime 'protection'. But Turkish-American mothering tends to be unique with its involvement of the social circle and the child's 'placement' in it. Ranging from: *"They won't invite you without your husband to accompany you- you'll be deemed a threat for their relationships, being a woman alone"* to *"What will they think if Dalya can't speak two languages fluently when many of their kids are bilingual already?"* And, of course, the ever-dreaded, *"Who will want you now for marriage? They'll only be after your body as a woman- or after your citizenship."*

Yes, dear reader. From a young Turkish-American 'princess' blogger to a 'reluctant housewife' musing in Norway: I have now become a T.A.P.S.M ('Turkish-American Politically-Single Mom'). Blogger turned Instagrammer.

But- let's remember- *Catalysis*.

I have also been able to evolve myself beyond my mother's imagination for my social-placement predictions. Through going on- despite everything- for Dalya: I have also gone from dreamer to *author*. A Dreamer to Doer. Pursuer of spontaneous nonchalance to meticulous planner and manifester.

I am not a 'princess' or 'queen'- my life certainly has not become what fairy tales are made of (neither Turkish, or any American ones I've heard of, anyway). That is for sure. Yet- I do have a story. A story of my own. A story with my new partner in life: my daughter. She's been left fatherless and I- husbandless- by the Turkish state. Yet we put on smiles on social media and in real life for memories. For inspiration. For each other. I am a Turkish-American mother, too, now. Imperfect in my own ways. But I am my own. And I aim to inspire my daughter and others like her to have the courage to be able to find their 'own' inherent flow and mission, as well.

Before I verbally give the proverbial 'floor' to my politically-jailed husband in the next sub-section, I want to continue this 'parenting' section on a lighter topic, dear reader, to ease into the increasingly more emotional subject matter. As we all know, after all, motherhood is such an easy breezy task to discuss by itself, isn't it? (Cue in the American sarcasm punch line). But, just for a little fun, let's now explore a relatively more humorous aspect of daily parenting life. *Food.* Let's hit it. Bon appétit/ *Afiyet olsun.*

Sincerely,

T.A.P.S.M.A

(Turkish-American Politically-Single Mom, and Author)

SET FREE YOUR FLOW

Pekmez versus Avocadoes

In Turkey, there's a saying: '*Anasına bak, kızını al*', which roughly translates to 'look at the mother when buying the daughter'…since of course, in many Eastern traditions, brides are still thought of as being 'bought' into the grooms' families like pieces of furniture. There's also another saying that goes '*Armut dibine düşer*'. This is a more culturally neutral one since there's a similar one in English about the apple not falling too far from the tree (Well, except, of course for the Turkish version mentioning pears instead of apples. Perhaps because more Turkish women have pear-shaped bodies like mine? Who knows? I smile. I digress). Why is this relevant, you may ask? (No. Not the 'pear' joke). Well, it is precisely so since I will now elaborate on the more traditional 'mothering' ways of the generations before mine, in comparison to the newer generations' relatively more 'modernized' practices.

I'm pretty sure there were no avocadoes sold in Turkey when I was being brought up as a baby, but my daughter has sure loved eating them for breakfast ever since I first started giving her solids at around 5 months. 'Avocadoes are packed with just as much nutrition as eggs', numerous parenting blogs and news articles- both Turkish and American- were screaming at me.

Up until becoming a mom, I'd enjoyed avocadoes only as the main ingredients in guacamole: found in numerous diners and Mexican restaurants in New York City. Having tried the fruit itself and gotten no taste- I never thought that something other than the onion-tomatoes-spices combination used to make a good dip for my favorite Tostitos chips could be created for a baby- until the day I came up with one. My then barely 6-month-old baby was deemed to be 'slightly underweight' after my 'breastfeeding' was apparently no longer enough. I was told by her doctor to 'start introducing solid foods earlier than the typical 6-month mark'. In desperation, I began experimenting with different combinations; Dalya ended up loving the taste of avocadoes sweetened with shredded pears, which I combined with shredded walnuts and sometimes almonds (for the extra brain power boost which I'd also read about).

Now, this is not an article on 'Nutrition for your Child'- I would love to be able to write one, but there are already many such wonderful articles written in that subject by mothers and experts more talented in that area than I. So, what's my reason for bringing up avocadoes? Why, no one in Turkey seemed to get me when they'd heard that that's what I'd been giving my baby for breakfast, of course!

Immediately, I received such remarks as, *"...That's nice, but you already give eggs: why the avocado?"*, *"Isn't avocado something that should be given as a fruit snack in between meals rather than for breakfast?"*, and, of course, my favorite- *"Why don't you give her a traditional breakfast of tomatoes and white cheese with olives so she can get used to it? Our classically-Turkish 'Tahin and pekmez'* (tahini and grape molasses) *is better than peanut butter and jelly or jam, you know: and much more filling..."*

There it was: the top three ingredients of a 'typical' Turkish breakfast, thrown in my face. I could have tried to explain as much as I could that my daughter tried but didn't like eating raw tomatoes yet, and that she spit out white cheese and olives each time. I could have even fallen back on my typical 'social commentary loving' self and stated, *"Who's to say what a 'typical' breakfast 'should' be like? It's different all around the world."* But, alas, I just took a deep breath, smiled and said (I still do): *"I tried it all, but this is how my girl likes it, and I'm the only one who can get her to eat* (yes, they had all tried)."

Period. End of discussion.

People ranging from my mother-in-law (with whom I had to live during those entrapped months waiting for either my husband to come home *or* be able to fly back to New York to my family home again- whichever happened first) to neighbors, friends and my own family members. They all judged me slightly in my 'non-traditional' choices for my child in this respect.

What it all comes down to is- what's 'right' is what works for you and your child. You could take a little bit of the East and a little bit of the West, and create a formulaic soup in life that works best for you; no one else has to drink it if they don't like. A little bit of *traditional* choices with a little bit of more *modern* ones- and combining them all to you and your little ones' content. And no one should be able to judge you, since they're neither the ones living your life, nor the ones possibly offering to help in any way (except by offering unsolicited advice). Well-intentioned or not, such interference only tends to contribute mental stress to a mother who is already under tremendous pressure to raise her child as best as she can.

It's not just avocadoes, of course. I also tried to have my daughter be raised with being accustomed to having both the 'American' peanut butter-and-jam combination and the 'Turkish' tahin/pekmez combination on her morning bread slices. I had an Asian neighbor back in New York City tell me her toddler daughter only ate plain rice with fruit juice in the mornings! 'Good for her!'… I'd exclaimed at the time. Who was I to offer any further opinions to a mother who volunteered on her own that she had 'tried everything' but that her daughter had 'refused to eat much of anything else'? As for me? I replaced the 'jam' with 'honey' in the classically-American PB&J combo, The inclusion of 'honey' satisfied 'them', whilst my insistence on the peanut butter 'for protein' satisfied me *and* my delighted daughter, who luckily continues to enjoy this unique combination to this day.

Added to all this has been the stigma that came with the fact that my daughter was, and still is, very attached to me (I breastfed her until, *gulp*, well into her pre-K years, upon her insistence: I believe she insisted for the extra comfort since her dad couldn't be around). This is a girl, if you recall, who doesn't eat white cheese, either. What else could I do? Well, I got her to eat yogurt to compensate for the possible calcium loss, and luckily, she still likes yogurt- so that has worked out okay. I hope.

Being a parent has meant an increase in humility. On your absolute worst day- when you're sleep-deprived, down in the dumps with intrusive, depressive thoughts about yourself and your life- there they are. Adorably innocent and in need of you to be stronger in order to serve and help them in some way. You're 'needed'. And in that depressive moment- you hence feel 'relevant' for a bigger purpose on this earth than making sure your ego feels victorious and accomplished.

Allow me to reference once again, dear reader, the Turkish proverb about the pear. 'Armut dibine düşer'. My mother was wronged by my birth father, and I was 'fatherless' for the couple of years between their divorce and her remarriage.

I wonder now how my daughter will reference her own childhood. Will she focus on her own upbringing by a lone mother? Or will she focus on the difference between the way that that happened as such? Namely, will she dedicate her life to political and legal justice for those wronged like her father was, whereas I have dedicated mine to using creativity to heal my abandonment issues and life experiences?

I wonder if my daughter will *write out* her angst against injustice- witnessing the political and legal one inflicted on her father. Here, dear reader, is the poem 'Blue' in full: written by *my* teenager self. The same one I referenced in my poem 'Innocence Lost' in *Write Out Your Drops*

SET FREE YOUR FLOW

Blue

I'm blue

there's no end in sight
my mind keeps wandering off to the different possibilities that seems so far away
and unattainable
Blue
I'm like a satellite, roaming around space slow at times and fast at others; yet I'm
all alone in the vast universe
I can see the planets and other formations but they are so distant
I'm stuck floating around this miniscule space called earth
Blue
I'm the frosted flake you're encircling with your spoon,
drowning me inside
this sour milk
and I can't escape for I am lifeless- merely grain
I can't protest
Blue
I'm the other side of you
the side that reveals itself when there is fear, embarrassment or anger
the world is baby pink then beige and it seems purple like scars, then red, black,
and red again...but it is never white
for the only thing pure in life is death, and this has become my motto
Blue
I'm stuck on this shadow of breaths and motions, senses and emotions

Like Glue

Addendum:

General Things I Would Tell the Little Girl Now

First, if someone has chosen another in your place, avoid losing yourself in the paranoia that they're continuously idealizing that person at your expense and relative detriment. Their choice may have been a logical one for societal support and ease, rather than one based on intense attraction or an emotional connection as deep as yours.

Better to be 'the one that got away' and 'what if' rather than 'good riddance'. Accept all 'goodbyes' with grace…for even if it was none of the above (and the new couple is genuinely in love), be sincerely happy for them. Better they met their 'one' now rather than later down the road when it would have been harder for you and have caused you to lose time. Better to be free to find your 'one'- starting with intensifying love and prioritization for yourself.

Second: beautiful and attractive are different things, the latter being subjective. A 'beautiful' person may subliminally be attracted to someone that may be attractive to *them* more than others' eyes can see. Childhood experiences, familial reminders, deeply-buried hobbies and fantasies may be triggered, which may be activated by someone not conventionally considered 'beautiful' or 'handsome'. Thus, 'tis truly best to be your authentic self. For you never know who will be attracted to all the beautiful quirks hidden deep beneath your surface.

Third: Your emotions- just like your individual experiences- are valid. Don't let anyone underestimate what you've been through as "…*oh, you're not the only one…get over it"*. Only you- and God above- can truly know what you've experienced behind closed doors.

If you loved someone, for instance: own it. Don't deny it. That love exists – like an offspring formed from love. It's been birthed, and cannot be taken back into the womb. Take the love, even after a relationship is over. Place it upon yourself. Upon your art. Upon someone or some form that deserves it. Use it. Be catalyzed by it. *Write it out. Set it free.* Don't curse it.

Fourth. We live in a world where one's idea of *sin-* obtained from a personal understanding of a particular religion's holy book, and something sacred between the individual and God- will most likely be different than the dogmatic ones more audibly promoted. Among many Islamic societies in particular: one that unnecessarily highlights punishment in the afterlife rather than the Koran-written clemency of God provided through true repentance.

Though it may at times be difficult to do so, we must make an effort not to categorize anyone with automatically-assumed 'labels' or 'traits'. I have encountered genuinely devout Muslim women (whom the world would never deem as such based on their uncovered appearance) commit more charitable acts and pray daily when compared to some of their more 'covered' counterparts. I have also encountered numerous open-minded women in headscarves with higher levels of both education and freedom in their social powers compared to my own self.

Forgive your curious and imaginative mind while keeping your intentions and actions as pure as you can. Do the best you can to be a good, grateful person for this precious life we've been given- and your flow can only be your compass toward a beautiful life experience (where you can enrich others' lives and in turn, enrich your own).

Fifth: my generation growing up didn't have all the tools of the internet and terms for various neuroses as the current one. Beware of *narcissists*, for they can be anywhere and in all forms, sometimes covertly so. You'll surely fall for the hauntingly beautiful Turkish songs on vacations: focus more on their melodies, for most contain 'love-bombing' lyrics that will allow you to believe someone confessing 'love' too early on without it being genuine. Whereas, in the US, such lyrics are so rare that they become controversial (sorry Bruno Mars, to 'ring your ears' once again, as the Turkish saying goes, but I'm thinking of your controversial hit 'Grenade' here).

Equally beware, however, of the American boys who will tell you that you are 'an independent individual capable of making your own decisions…' (true), and that you '…should enjoy being young with rampantly free sexual exploration' (not so true). Being a woman is a beautiful blessing in many ways, yes, but this does not mean that you must be a 'gift' for many (most who will prove to be undeserving) at the expense of your own dignity and the gradual degradation of your soul in the process.

Finally, you'll realize it's only when you've let go of a dependence on someone that a more genuine connection between the two of you actually develops. When you can pray for their happiness, even if this has to occur without you or your current status quo. Human beings inherently value genuineness and kindness more than any other qualities.

Dear *yıldız çiçeğim* ('star flower') ... My Dalya.

May you hopefully be able to discover your calling earlier on in life- enough to focus more intensely on one or two interests that can lead to a lifetime of both professional success as well as personal fulfilment. Elders tell us not to place 'all our eggs' into 'one basket'. That is real, but remember: so is suffering from a lifetime of indecision and vacillating between various options.

May you figure out early on how to differentiate between your ego and self-preservation. When you react negatively to something, ask yourself: is it instinctual protection, or at times natural-occurring human selfishness? If it's the latter, like one of the poems in my first poetry book says, *"Tame your ego, not your hopes"*. You could very well be hoping for more attention from someone, for instance: yet someone's genuine and momentary focus on their work or other people in their lives may not always mean they don't value you in your own special way. Including overworking mommy, who apologizes for all the times she's been glued to her laptop- writing away- when you'd been craving more play time =)

I could not always love you perfectly, or have been able to express it as often as you deserved (not just for being my daughter, but for being the amazingly kind human you are in general) but believe me: I've always loved you whole-heartedly.

Your *'momma cici'**

* ('sweet' mommy in Turk-lish. Half Turkish, Half English. Your first words were bi-culturally dichotomous as well. Coincidence? I think not)

When You Become What You've Read About: the Atypical Mama and Papa Bears

When my house was raided by police after my husband was politically imprisoned and I was left alone with a 7-month-old baby in my hands- I put on a smiling face despite my rapid heartbeat, and even offered them tea. Putting on appearances of being 'okay', even whilst crying inside, was in my blood after all. When a preordered cake was on my table- two days after July 15th, and invitations and party favor gifts had already been prepared; I gave them out to the would-be-attendees anyway after each event-cancellation phone call. I took pictures with my daughter- so she could have that memory immortalized (if she ever develops into a nostalgic/ photography-loving teenager as her mommy was).

When the wife of the admiral, who had just been posing for pictures while holding our baby mere weeks ago, suddenly didn't have anything to say on the phone in response to me crying to her. "My husband would never betray his country! There's got to have been a mistake." She remained silent.

When you're prevented from boarding your flight back to the United States after paying a visit to your politically-imprisoned husband to show him your baby daughter, and everyone looks at you like a criminal as you're escorted to the police area to discuss your surprising, uncompensated 'travel ban' and flight cancellations (and have to from thenceforth continuously frequent police stations for paperwork and legal requests).

When you've faced all of the above and countless other similarly movie-like, dramatic moments: your life flashes before your eyes like a television series, and you can only hope for the quintessentially-Hollywood 'happy ending' of justice and reunion.

I've already mentioned, dear reader, the irony I feel in my having studied politics in college and graduate school, only to later

become a victim of it rather than a professional politician. My husband himself was also a 'student of politics' in a way, I suppose. As a naval officer who had to attend military school- often on campus and away from his family- since the age of 13, he had to study a lot about domestic and global politics in order to be able to best 'defend' the country in case
of an attack.

Could he ever have foreseen that such an 'attack' would be an internal one? Not only at the state level, but professional backstabbing by his own military colleagues whom he'd seen as 'friends', while they'd apparently been viewing him as 'competition' to get rid of through unproveable slander?

I'd known politics, dear reader, but not a single thing about 'the military' until I met Kemal in 2009. He'd worn all white to our coffee date- 'Ak' in color (*white*), coincidentally like his conscience of any 'wrongdoing' that'd warrant any type of arrest (alluding here to my YouTube documentary on the events, entitled 'Alnım Ak').

Cut to: Summer of 2011. By that point we'd grown closer than 'just friends', and I'd told my mother he was serious about me. I remember sunbathing on one of the Princess' Islands off of Istanbul with her, and the newspaper headline was about the imprisonment of then General İlker Başbuğ. The phone rang just then, and it was Kemal: a military officer, and my mother's Spidey-sense tingled. "Be careful," she began. "Look at these headlines arresting military officers. What if you marry him and they arrest him too? It's a dangerous occupation."

"I doubt it, mom," I'd always say. "Kemal has an 'Atatürkçü' lifestyle and ideals simultaneous with his religious faith. The government will like a multi-faceted soldier like him."

How naïve I was. My husband was never a member of the Gülenist organization. No substantial 'FETO' evidence was ever found on him anyway, and it was never the reason given for his imprisonment. Kemal was imprisoned, rather, for being 'in the middle'.

One of his closest so-called friends, in fact (a man whose wife had befriended me in the last port-town we'd been stationed in before his arrest- Foça- and told me our baby daughters would 'play and grow up together') not only didn't defend him, but actually testified that Kemal had remained 'suspiciously neutral' during the evening of the coup attempt (That's right: picture Sweden facing sanctions for its neutrality during the world war).

From what I know of Kemal, he's someone who's always wanted to please everyone. To make sure all our guests at home, or both sides of our families, were always satisfied and treated equally with respect and gifts, etc. If he bought his mother a bag, he'd want to buy my mother one too. If we ended up going out drinking one night, he'd also want to make sure he'd fulfill his Islamic obligations of fasting and giving alms. He was both 'West' and 'East' as well- albeit in a different way from myself. His unwillingness to 'choose' one side over the other, however, tragically cost him his freedom in a nation and profession that always forces one to choose.

When we were dating and sightseeing around touristic spots in Istanbul, for instance, Kemal had once stopped me from taking a selfie of us in front of the popular Blue Mosque. He'd cited that as someone in the military, if someone saw him posing in photos with 'religious symbols'- it could cost him his position. Such severity in misapplied forms of 'secularism' have unfortunately caused the reactionary, misapplied form of 'democracy' in modern Turkey; where those in power, purely because they were elected, feel they can imprison innocent people based on hearsay 'opposition' and weak 'evidence'.

Are you a man who drinks? You must automatically be a 'bad Muslim'. Why people can become so concerned with others' 'sins' (as long as they're not hurtful) if they're not the ones who will be 'burning in hellfire', as they believe, for their 'wrong-doings' (though God is also written as the *great forgiver*) is beyond me. Are you a woman who likes to dress conservatively and cover her hair? You must automatically devalue higher education and prefer being a docile wife to your husband with 'at least three kids' (as Erdoğan advocates). You don't support Erdoğan ? You must automatically support 'FETO' and deserve being labeled a 'terrorist'- being purged from your job or imprisoned, with a severity that does not allow being able to be close to your spouse and children once again in privacy.

I've already spoken at length about myself and what I've faced since 2016, dear reader. I would like to now give the remainder of this Section to my husband, Kemal. A voice from inside the political bars of Turkey. The most patriotic and law-abiding man I've ever met, who would even feel 'bad' for taking extra napkins from a restaurant. A man who hasn't been able to see his baby daughter grow up or be there for any of her birthdays or milestones. A man who, nonetheless, has supported my being here in the United States with my family for the safety and future of our daughter and family unit as a whole, since we had this blessed dual citizenship opportunity that many dream of.

I now give my 'ink' over to Kemal Akın, the 'captain' of my poems. A student and victim of politics himself. A dichotomous struggler. A decent man who, along with countless other innocently-imprisoned people like him, will one day leave those bars with their dignities intact and heads held up high. Before I do so, I will include some personal poetry relevant to this sub-section.

I hope Kemal gets to read this collection, too, where he is, just as he's supportively done so with *The Catalyst* and *Write Out Your Drops*. In the next sub-section with his name, I'm including poetry he's written from prison to his daughter, as well as an essay he wrote specifically for this collection (encouraged by myself over the weekly telephone call I had to stay up until 4 am for, since he is not allowed to call at will).

I wanted to be his voice- both of the personal ramifications of this injustice to be on record for the world, and for his daughter to treasure as a keepsake in printed form. He is one of many- and I wish I could be able to give a voice to many such victims. I figure, if Kemal is innocent (as I know in my heart, as well as looking at the particulars of his case, he is), though I don't know many of the others' specific cases: the odds are high that they are filled with innocents as well. Kemal and I feel grateful even just to be alive, as many have even lost spouses during these historic years. I cannot print each wronged voice (especially since those in Turkey are afraid to speak out, understandably so). But with Kemal's own *drop*- just one- I hope they can know that their suffering will have created a river already. Hopefully they can all *flow* into the global oceans and be free to roam the world as dignified citizens soon enough.

a newly-arrived immigrant girl
self-taught in her accented English
filling her loneliness with academic ambition
has managed to rise to the top 3
in her 4th grade Spelling Bee
…wanted to prove herself: as her own competition
*   she's spelled the word correctly*
*   she's sure- the boy next to her spells the same word in the same way*
*   he wins, while she's eliminated*
*   in shock, she remains quiet, but jaded*
'…they must have misheard through my accent'
since then, few people have understood things she's meant
the outcome: not just, and not fair
she'd won that spelling bee: fair and square
*   injustice has always catalyzed her*
*   she fights now against others that occur*
*   helping ease the pain others too may incur*

THE CATALYZING SCORPION

the scavenger hunt for belonging
led her to Stavanger, among modern Vikings
her parental-caused avoidance of Scorpios halted
when she married one
he'd glued her when she'd come undone:
by the scorpion, she was stung
we can ultimately attract, what we purposely ignore
we can foolishly think: there will be more
only to end up catalyzed by the one
we'd once deemed a 'bore'

'BABA'

'wherefore art thou?'
she yelled
'father, oh father

                                      why when I try to get closer
                            you pull yourself farther and farther?'

'father, are you even alive?'
her offspring now cries
'I hear your voice,
but I don't know your face or touch.
are they lying to me?
I'm not being told much'

                            one was a prisoner of his ambition
                              the other- a prisoner of politics
                      both affected deeply their vulnerable nestlings
                 cross-generational pain, tugs at the heartstrings

SET FREE YOUR FLOW

KEMAL 'AK' AKIN'S Ode to the 'Little Mermaid'

Dalya is a very lovely girl.
she's our diamond, and she's our pearl

since you've been away, my head is in a painful whirl

you're our life's miracle…pinnacle
rainbows have pink, orange and purple.
I yearn to see them reflect in your eyes' twinkle
in our nest, I dream of D sleeping on her daddy's chest
and all this mess coming to a rest:
our prayers will not go to waste

for her happiness, I will do my best

we will make up for losses of the past
in the ocean, my ship is sailing from east to west
your captain can see the land from the ship's mast
soon we'll get rid of the pest
and our happiness will forever last

away from you, I'm adrift
for me, your existence is a gift
when my ship comes to port, will you give me a lift?

though I'm not a good poet
our future will be marvelous, I bet

from now on, don't ever be sad
I know, no matter what, I'm the luckiest dad

June 2021

My darling daughter,

How I wish I could have been able to hug you tight and say these following verses while looking into your hazel eyes in real life, rather than to the photograph of you I've attached to my magnetic cupboard here in this prison cell.

Just as our eyes locked miraculously in that moment right after you were born, how I wish I could do so every night while telling you 'goodnight', every morning while telling you 'good morning my sweet girl'. Though I can't do so, know that you are my last thought every night before I go to sleep, and my first one every morning after I open my eyes: God is my witness.

I remember a saying I'd once heard about how a father can 'sell the world in exchange for a *smile* from his daughter,' while I can only do so with the memory of yours- which I've engraved into every cell in my being. And I'm thankful even for that- and my heart and my thoughts are with you and your lovely mom, my mermaids.

I envision the moment when I can finally be free to come to you in person and hug you so tightly that it can feel almost as if time is able to stand still.

In a movie we watched here, there was a saying that fathers fight for their children and live for their promises to them- and I promise to fight for your future to the best of my ability, despite these unjust conditions. I promise you that, God-willing, everything is going to beautiful: for where there's hope, there can be miracles.

I heard from your mother than your first tooth fell- the same one I'd been the first to see appear when you were about five or six months old. It was symbolic of the tragedy that the time we've been apart is now longer than the lifetime of a tooth.

We were so excited that we wanted to throw you a little *'Diş buğdayı'* party to celebrate it, as Turkish tradition beholds. We had ordered the decorations, cake, as well as the invitations which had already gone out to the neighbors for July 17th. It was to be a Sunday, and your mother said more people could be free on that day to attend.

Remembering those days takes me back to when I couldn't stand being away from you for too long and would drop by our *'lojman'* military-housing during my lunch breaks from work, just to breathe in your heavenly smell. It pains and surprises me, thus, to think of how I've now managed to be able to be away from you for this long: 1,800 days and counting.

I thank God for giving me the strength to be able to go on despite this heavy pain- especially after knowing that that baby is now an almost six-year-old angelic child who wishes for her 'baba's return' with every shooting star, angel-number 11:11 on the clock her mom points out, every candle ever blown and every night before bed.

My dearest one. You were only about seven-months-old when they separated us, leaving you fatherless and your mother husbandless. You hadn't even begun to crawl yet- I can still remember your efforts to do so on your stomach as you laid on the carpet.

In the first 3 months of our separation, they didn't even allow me to have any picture of you, let alone any prison visits. The first time I was allowed to finally see you was through the picture of you your mom thought of to print on an allowed t-shirt to send in to me. And yet, I had been waiting a very long time to finally meet you, my child- 44 years, in fact, to become a father. Even a picture of you had been deemed too much by them.

I couldn't witness anything. Not your tooth party, your first or any subsequent birthday parties, your first time crawling and later taking your first steps, your first sentences, your first songs. I couldn't see your beautiful face and hear your angelic voice for years. I couldn't hold your hand as you walked to school, when you received your first diploma as a preschooler, when you first did your homework or drew your first pictures (I'm sure you wouldn't like my own drawings too much).

I couldn't prepare toast to send you off to school, and later pick you up from school- proudly witnessing you pointing me out to your friends as 'my dad'.

I couldn't be there to embrace you when you were sick or sad- when you needed both of your parents. I couldn't help to brush your hair or calm you when you were afraid of thunder. I couldn't take you to the park and point you out proudly as 'my daughter'.

I couldn't be there to teach you how to ride a bicycle, fly a kite, or run in the fields. We've also missed the seasons, darling daughter. We couldn't watch falling snow together, couldn't throw snowballs to one another, or go sledding. I couldn't warm your fingers cold from the snow with my breath.

We couldn't smell spring's first flowers together, couldn't chase butterflies together, couldn't roll in the grass or share excitement over rainbows. In the summer, we couldn't make sandcastles, go swimming, or make wishes on shooting stars together. We couldn't walk on the crunchy leaves of autumn together or enjoy beautiful foliage views in our mutual birthday month of November.

I couldn't, with the responsibility of a father, teach you about life and spirituality- our faith, religious holidays, morality and our prayers. We couldn't watch cartoons or go to the movies together. I couldn't play your favorite game of 'Hide-and-Seek' with you or witness you performing the steps you learned in your ballet classes and school/summer shows.

We couldn't celebrate Mother's and Father's Day together- couldn't get a gift for your mom doing both parenting jobs together, or for your grandma and grandpa there in the US who've sacrificed so much for all of us during this difficult time.

I couldn't share your various joys and excitements, encourage you during your hesitations, guide you when you needed courage and ease your concerns.

I couldn't be your childhood 'hero'. I couldn't be an actual father for you. What would otherwise be daily, 'routine' things for many fathers and their children are for us now so monumental- because we were not allowed to experience them.

I tried to find consolation in your pictures and drawings for me- sometimes falling asleep with them in my hand. Because of the terrible timing of my allotted family-call-time due to our geographical time difference, I couldn't even hear your speak to me for years: never live, anyway, just through recorded little message clips your mom would play for me.

"I drew cats for you, baba. Will you come to my birthday party?" I still get a lump in my throat each time I recall your voice in such messages. And, of course, "I love you, baba."

I couldn't do anything for you and your mom from here. My physical inability to be there for you handicapped me from this prison and I did what I could do- pray for you and dream about a beautiful future together. I never, ever lost my hope or vision. Even though I only had mere and brief memories to hang on to.

Those moments when we were finally able to get you to fall asleep as a baby, when we played on the bed while mommy was busy and I lifted you up in my arms and said 'let's fly to....'and you giggled each time I named various cities around the world as I lifted you. I remember the stressful times (I regret now being too much of a worrywart over things like water temperature) of bath time, your lovely babble when we first went in the sea together and you were able to sit up on the sandy shore. When I proudly carried you on my chest around town in a baby carrier.

Every day, through my brief, caged view of the sky: I tell airplanes, clouds and seagulls to always carry my *'selam'* and my love-filled greetings to you, my darling daughter with a heart as beautiful as she is.

As a part of our faith, *babacım,* know that we will be rewarded for this injustice and we will make up for these days to the best of our abilities. The vision of you- and my innocence- keeps me standing and enables me to go on living. You have to believe too, *babacım.* During this roughest time in my life, I have learned the value of being grateful for everyone and every little joy in one's daily life, as well as of being patient.

I learned that, even if you are right, it is never worth it to hurt the heart of someone you love. As I read here in 'Don Coyote' (I hope to read it with you soon), we always have a lot of friends in our 'good days' who can suddenly leave us alone when the weather gets cloudy. I realized how I had collected such friends and relatives over the years, who've shown their true colors during this time by not extending their support to us. This reminds me of another saying, one by Martin Luther King Jr: *the ultimate measure of a man is not where he stands in moments of comfort but where he stands at times of challenge and controversy.* We will hopefully evaluate such 'unnecessary' fair-weather acquaintances in our new lives after this nightmare ends.

I've learned and felt to my very core the immense magnitude of everyday joys that the average person going through their daily lives can take for granted: walking and sitting on grass, watching the sun rise and set, walking on the beach or taking a boat ride while inhaling the sea, listening to the sounds of the birds and trees, taking long walks in all kinds of weather without doing anything else but simply strolling along, lying on the knees of someone you love or on the sand together, driving accompanied to music, buying gifts for those you care about, being able to look someone in the eyes and telling them you love them, dancing to a song you love together, being able to watch your favorite shows whenever you want, sleeping in a quiet and peaceful environment without the snoring sounds of a dozen other people with you, and countless others.

SET FREE YOUR FLOW

Babacım, I call my world here, the world of 'small forms of happiness'. And because we're not allowed much in our prison cells (not even scissors/glue, so I have to cut out cartoons and designs for you from newspapers to add to my letters through the use of a nail clipper and chewing gum) we've come to truly appreciate joys from even the smallest things and to not take anything for granted. To not waste anything in extravagance, not even toilet paper. Most of all- to appreciate the joy upon hearing even routine 'good news' from loved ones' lives outside of here. When we manage to have a decent meal to eat, when we're able to get hot water for a warm shower, a rare occasion where we don't have to wait a long time for using the bathroom, being able to have an unshared bed of our own to sleep on, etc.

But my darling daughter- most of all I've come to appreciate what I still have in you and for our health. For I've met people here far less fortunate. I've met men who never even got to see their children being born, men who lost their loved ones while they were locked up, men who went through divorces and the pain of finding out their children and wives got cancer, men whose family members too are jailed, and even those who don't even have anyone to call or write to them.

My little mermaid. I couldn't be there for your mommy mermaid- who I found in the rough oceans- when she had to be both a father and mother to you, when she had to handle so many things (with both the bad days and good days) for which I couldn't accompany her (including having her book publishing dreams coming true). I never got to tell her everything I realized the value of more now that I've been here, and tell her in her eyes that my love and appreciation for her only grew more each day. But you are both in my dreams and prayers every morning and night, and I know that rainbows will appear at the end of this storm. I thank God every day for having experienced both of you in my life- for you having been the peak of my life's happiness in my memories.

My Dalya: when you were born, life and all the flowers in it grew more colorful, the sun shone brighter, my world grew lovelier and everything took on more meaning. Please never forget this: for me, one smile from you is worth a lifetime.

My smart, sensitive and kind daughter. From what you've been told (for your young psychology), you knew your dad to be 'a captain on a long ship voyage'- and I actually have come to feel that way too, along with you. I feel in my heart this ship is finally nearing the harbor and, when it does, I will hug you both very tightly and never let go in our new life together.

The apple of my eye, sweetest part of my soul, my heartbeat: they say life is what we make of the challenges we're faced with. Life is also said to be 'trouble' while only death is not. But we must not grow gloomy and lose hope that our story will have a happy ending, no matter what hand we've been dealt so far. What doesn't kill us truly can make us stronger, and I believe with all my heart that at the end of this arduous path we will all triumph and prevail. I know in my heart we will be able to laugh about these days one day, and this forced, political separation too will come to an end.

We will sing, dance, fly kites, ride bikes, and travel together; just like the way I'd lift you up in the air as a baby and say, 'let's go to...' and list various places...only this time, we'll actually go to them.

I will do my best always to be there for you through both your joyful as well as saddest moments, and will only continue to be proud of you always.

My mermaids- you are my prayers and dreams having have come true in this lifetime and I am always grateful. I am comforted knowing that God is watching you both- *Allaha emanetsiniz*.

I wish I could hang on to the wind, jump on a cloud, and come beside you...I wish I could frequent you through a butterfly in your garden...wave 'hello' at my little mermaid in the form of a lightning bolt through her bedroom window.

SET FREE YOUR FLOW

grateful to have a daughter I adore
every day I only miss you more and more

our precious- I promise you, all the truth will one day come to light
I will then spend the rest of my days as my Princess' Knight

my Dalya, you are the prettiest flower
how marvelous to have you as my daughter

nothing can compare to being your father
longing for time spent together,
know your daddy will be loving you forever

**With love always,
your 'captain' baba**

Dear reader… It is impossible for me (Selin) to speak on behalf of all the political prisoners of Turkey since the 2016 coup attempt. I have no idea what their 'crimes' and case folders consist of. I particularly cannot fathom, for instance, how mothers imprisoned (some with their children) could possibly be so dangerous to the 'state'- especially at a time in Turkey when many actual criminals and murderers of women have controversially been released.

There are just so many stories. Stories like the 45-year-old wife and mother who succumbed to cancer and ultimately death after her military pilot officer husband was imprisoned- and he couldn't attend her funeral even handcuffed due to 'coronavirus restrictions'. I was told by Kemal that he was since able to briefly visit their two surviving children for a couple of hours, before being taken back to the prison for solitary confinement to 'quarantine' for 2 weeks. I can't even imagine what that man must have been running through his head during those additional 2 weeks of isolated torture after such a tragedy.

As I've said: I can only be a voice for one 'drop'- Kemal- and vicariously through him, all the innocently-imprisoned ones like him. The man who'd once responded to someone over dinner (after the person had casually and jokingly said *'you guys are the military- you can always do a coup and get rid of leaders if things get bad in Turkey'*): "Military coups have always taken this country backwards- don't even joke of such a thing". A man whose only 'crime' on that night of July 15th was choosing his professional duty (befitting his high rank) to stay in his office to guard the premises until the morning (when they took him in) instead of saying "…*to hell with this: I'm going back home to my wife and baby daughter"*.

A man whom I know was raised by dichotomous struggles of the *traditional* and the *liberal* of his own. A man who was the traditional 'Paul' to my liberal 'Kaitlin' in *The Catalyst*. A man I'm sure is crimsoning as he (hopefully) reads these lines too, as he told me he'd blushed while reading the novel. If so? *Sorry, honey. But what can I say? I write freely. It's our true story, and it can hopefully help to inspire others. You did choose to marry an outspoken and American-raised feminist, after all :)*

THE REBUILDER

there's a guest in the garden: a bumble bee
buzzing intensely…searching
beautifully chubby, circling
wildly foraging
(I'm pretty sure it's a *she*)
in and out of the remaining twigs
dashing about repeatedly in frustration
a mother scorned, we hypothesize in exasperation
her nest is now gone
following the landscaping
she's relentless: her vengeance, through rebuilding
she accepts what is gone…eventually
whether the first disappointment, or the tenth
her pain and loss, add to her strength

WRECKAGE

words of sympathy, aiming affinity are easy to express: kind in tone,
but depth-wise empty
when you're not the one who's faced a national tragedy
one's family could have faced affliction, political displacement and
separation
disillusionment of an entire nation
another's can involve untimely death- heartbreaking catastrophe
or being fired from their livelihood- economic adversity
or perhaps immigration: causing ridiculed accents and frizzy hair
an ever-nomadic situation: never belonging here, there, or anywhere
allow the cursed to cry it out… let them express their gloom, healing
away the doom
freedom of speech shouldn't be deemed treason…
don't judge someone's words without considering their reason
empathize with facers of misfortune- keep your judgement in check
for at any given moment- your life, too, can become a wreck

SECTIONAL ANECDOTES

Growing up bi-cultural has meant:

-Realizing everything they told you about Istanbul being 'special' was a one-sided exaggeration. It turns out, for instance, that, no: the Bosphorus is not the only lovely strait in the world (just symbolic to be situated in both Asia and Europe). And, no: it is not logical to call anyone a 'traitor' every time they critique their homeland. We can't truly be loving what we automatically approve blindly, without the acceptance of all its admitted faults.

-Western education teaching you to be inquisitive and open-minded, while 'religious' Turks claim it's 'sacrilegious' to have questions and want to do research before blind acceptance (meanwhile, critical-thinking is actually encouraged in the Koran). For example: when you call the Prophet's beloved wife until her death- Khadija- the first Islamic 'feminist' (a twice-widowed businesswoman, 15 years his senior, who also proposed to him).

- Recognition that most of the so-called 'close people' in your circle have only loved you conditionally: *"You'll be inviting them for dinner- we need them to be our friends"/ "You're going to dress appropriately, smile, and politely greet everyone- you're representing us."/"He dumped me. I'm sad. Let's meet."*

Section V
Flowing Through Creating

LION IN THE CAT'S REFLECTION

SET FREE YOUR FLOW

EVOLVE

each time life threw me a curveball-
I learned to pitch it on my own,
and hit home runs for survival

I saw the lion in the cat's reflection
the potential
before disappointments
threatened to make that little girl believe she was unworthy
of dreaming, or of compliments

I held on to that image during the moments
when the cat couldn't even affect a mouse

hidden behind the mane

finally
I roared
I soared

DESPOSING OF DESPONDENCE

vulnerability
eats away
through our shields
our skin
you hold your head high
noticing their gaze
like a freshly cut rose
showcased in a vase

only to wilt when alone
no water, light, or attention
that temporarily feel like home
words are empty promises
when merely uttered
without their definitions shown

I decide, hence, to hold on to the unreliability
and allow change to be my constant
life is rarely an offspring of excitement and safety
can't have it all, though acceptance is new layer of skin

no need to be despondent

What the Leo Mane Hides

Another lifetime 'struggle' for me (aside from the cultural, generational, and political ones I've gone into) has most certainly been: self-image. My attitude towards confidence.

Those who've heard of my books through my usage of social media promotions will certainly have seen the visual-storyteller side of me: I adore poetic book trailers and voiceovers. With each photo shoot I took part in to use in such visuals and my 'Author' profiles: I had to quiet my own impostor syndrome alongside my fears over what 'people' must 'certainly be thinking' (some based on actual life experience).

"Why is a Turkish, Muslim woman posing for artistic pictures? And she's a mother. And she's not model-thin. And she's married..." That list accumulated from voices in my head- some imagined, some from memory- can go on and on.

Meanwhile, how many times had I met someone hurtful 'behind the scenes'- who put on 'appearances' of being the 'ideal' friend, spouse, student, professional, devout person, while committing hurtful acts in private? As I've grown self-acceptant, if I were to be confronted by such people I'd now confidently be able to say:

"Thanks for your unsolicited opinion, but we're obviously at different frequencies. Did you experience the things I've experienced? Have you faced the same situations I've faced, and in my shoes? No. My daughter is proud of me. My family is proud of me. I am proud of me. You should be proud of you, and mind your own business..."

However, I believe I'm now also 'centered' and aware enough to the fact that I even have such self-accepting (yet, at their core, defensive) thoughts is precisely because of all the dichotomous

Turkish-American struggles I've written about here. Many American friends would tell me throughout the years, the now cliché: *"Who cares what they think? It's your life, and you're not hurting anyone!"* The Turks care. Especially the bi-cultural ones. They care. For various reasons, but they care. Regardless of their particular reasons, they mainly care because they have the inherent need to compare.

Have you gotten a better job than them? A showier partner or spouse? A better house? A better car? A later version of the 'it' smartphone of the year?

The list goes on and on, only with this addendum: *how has it been received by our circle? Has his/ her new* (*insert name of positive development in life here*) *gotten him/her more likes? More followers? More friends? More customers? More sales?* You become their experiment. Their litmus test. *"If he/she's done it, and it's been accepted, I can do it, too. Maybe even better".*

If you have tried, and you haven't had success? The same people can be one of the first ones, unfortunately, to cast the 'stone'; as if they hadn't been the one to secretly wish to try the same.

That is why, I've come to accept the unreliability in life, while still maintaining the Turkish/Muslim part at the core of my identity that believes in '*hayırlısı* (for the best)'.

I don't necessarily believe in- however- the Turkish adage on '*kismet*', or pre-destined fate. In my humble, and dichotomous, Turkish-American opinion: I believe God and the Universe present certain (yes, predetermined) options in our paths, yet after a certain age it is up to our own free-will and choices that determines which path we go on to experience in life.

After all, without free-will: where would the celestial test of our spiritual faith be? Nonetheless, despite our at times mistaken choices, I always try my best to maintain the belief that God is on our side; like the ideal parent who may disapprove, but always loves.

that offer you'd been counting on-
wasn't truly a lifetime gem, like you'd sought
heed the Creator's warning-
they weren't for you, despite what you may have thought
accept your exception
believe in redirection
reject undeserved rejection

'Art Doesn't Pay'

Art. Why art? Why *not* art? I believe creativity to be a human need: for variety, for purpose, for sanity, for beauty, for hope. Creativity exists inside all of us. Even if, dear reader, you've never picked up a pen to write or draw, or held a microphone or instrument to create music- you employ creativity more than you realize.

God, too, is *creative*, after all. One only has to gaze at the stars and look at the meticulous plan and symmetrical beauty of nature and the seasons all around us. So, too, are we as His creations.

When you're cooking soup and you want to 'mix it up' that week to try something a little differently, with a novel ingredient? You're *creative*. When you're washing your car or mowing the lawn and do so whistling a tune to make the routine go faster? You're *creative*. When you're signing your name somewhere and you want to use a special pen because it will 'look nicer'? That's right. You're *creative*.

Yet- as with money or a joyful life- creativity, too, can sometimes be conditioned and instilled in us as something 'shameful' or 'excessive' among some circles. As if a largely ascetic life, deprived of pleasure, could somehow by itself make one 'moral' and heaven-worthy; without regarding the irony of why the loving God we believe in would want us to refrain from joy in life, only to prepare us for an afterlife in which we are promised to be able to do so.

Growing up among my two cultures has meant the desire to create art, but not knowing how much of your soul you can 'set free' without your family feeling 'shamed'. You're told, in fact, it isn't even 'relevant' to set your soul free with art in order to cure boredom and purposelessness. That it's a waste of time that could be spent on other 'more valuable' things, like baking spinach pies or dusting the house décor- shining yet more things meant to appease others rather than your own self.

But I've written this collection, dear reader, to take that chance. To take that risk. So that if there is ever a young child- or soul young at heart- reading these verses somehow and they are going through a similar inner struggle, they can know that it can be done. It can, and perhaps even *must* be done.

I sincerely hope from the bottom of my heart and very soul that you've been enjoying my musings, dear reader. But, no matter what. As I sit here typing these last lines, I can attest it sure feels damn good for me to have expressed them. To have gotten it out 'there', wherever 'there' may have been. ('Getting it out' of people- to appease their psyches and souls by talking out their issues- is one of the main functions, after all, of a psychotherapist as well, isn't it?)

For most of us- especially independent ('indie') ones not represented by a well-known publishing company or agent- art may not pay much in dollars. But it surely does so in life-purpose identification and spiritual satisfaction. We persist not to be done favors (the social-media prominent 'like for a like' or 'review for a review', for example) but be given an equal chance to share our art- the quality of which we believe in. To start out on equal footing as the institutionalized, establishment-represented artists.

We believe in the fruit of our sacrifice and labor, which simply couldn't wait any further and needed to be birthed without the hierarchy of the literary world. We have a story, a message, a beacon of inspiration that's been brewing inside of us so poignantly that it's palpable enough to hurt when not birthed. A beacon of hope for at least someone out there who needs precisely to hear our tale at a particular time. Our art can come at a time where it may be the only way some messages- otherwise curtailed by politics or socio-cultural limitations, could be gotten across. Our art, then, becomes a bridge. A messenger of healing- of telling others "…you are not alone, fellow drop in the ocean."

Dear reader... I mentioned my newfound empathy with a large group of new women around the world- namely, prison wives. I've experienced the humiliation of being searched down to your underwear during each visit, including your toddler daughter's diaper. I know the pain of being on the other side of that glass, talking to a prisoner via a now ancient-looking telephone receiver. I know the pain of not knowing what to write in their long-awaited letter from you. Shared experiences make women allies- if not quite friends- as I've mentioned before. With this experience more women have a friend in me than perhaps they even know, and vice versa. Friends are, after all, said to simply be strangers we haven't met yet.   Let's take a certain fellow instructor at one of the colleges I work at, for instance. Eileen Merwin. We were virtually introduced during the pandemic by our supervisor as fellow authors, for a school event. Yet the moment I heard that her partner was once wrongfully-incarcerated right here in the US for many years- in a realm, it felt like we were now allies for life, if not yet friends since we hadn't met in person yet. She bought my book and I hers- and we genuinely enjoyed each other's work (genuineness is something no one can fake) and provided feedback. Our art had become cathartic for not only both of us- but for our loved ones as well. Her partner now lives with her and is free- I'm manifesting the same hopefully for my husband, of course. He's an artist with various paintings that she said helped him hold on to life while in prison, and she herself helped to write a theatrical sketch, in fact, about the prison experience.

Was it 'coincidence' that I'd met another partner of a wrongfully-imprisoned man, who was also both an author and an instructor at the same college where I work? Had I subconsciously wanted to feel a bit less alone in my 'unique' status- and attracted such a meeting?

There's been an undeniably increasing 'manifestation' trend lately. YouTubers are going viral through various 'Law of Attraction' videos giving advice on how to attract abundance and happiness into your life through affirmative thinking. Many times, such manifesting includes gratitude to the 'universe' for allowing the manifester's dreams to come to being, and this term also tends to vary from 'ancestors' and 'angels' and 'mother nature' and- finally, and in my view, above all- God.

Prayers to God in general have now become trendy under this overall 'manifestation' trend. Yet it is not the only way in which I feel the 'traditional' has become 'trendy' again with the 'current'. I had conversations with Turkish-American friends about how, in fact, yoga, in some ways, was similar to the Islamic daily prayers: physical movements varying between prostrating on the ground and standing up with different arm positions, for instance. 'Meditation' being akin to 'prayers' in a sense.

In a way, with such open-minded thinking- we'd exemplified a cultural synthesis, so to speak. A 'gray' hypothesis from the middle of two different spiritual practices- finding synergic commonalities to both. After all, whatever we believe or don't- we are all a part of this world. A part of this universe. What I call God/Allah- you may choose to call something else. But we all have our humanity in common.

the universe flows through you, as a vessel with a creation
when you are its storyteller- you can catalyze folks into action
heed to the call, to the flow, and the Universe will thank you
with your contentment

SET FREE YOUR FLOW

Dear reader,

I've never enjoyed the company of narrow-minded people: people who practice one-way thinking without consideration for any alternative opinions or possibilities. I don't always agree with 'new age' folks- to be honest- and believe in some things more conservatively than they do.

But that's the rare beauty of my dichotomy: I may not agree with them, but because I've grown up facing lifestyle choices from both liberal and conservative expectations- I don't, and cannot, judge them.

Spending your time and energy on art just for the joy of living and breathing that art- being in the flow of the creative process through which your soul feels most *purpose*... is enigmatic to people in our lives with such closed visions. Not only can they never fathom 'the point' vis-à-vis the lack of immediate or routine/ 'paycheck style' financial rewards, they also can't comprehend an alternative purpose of 'success' when it doesn't come in a form they associate with that word.

Your books aren't bestsellers? They'll assume they're 'not on par' to those that are- not gripping the powers often of publicity and the right connections for some to achieve such statuses. Your songs aren't on the radio? Same... Your paintings aren't displayed at a trendy place? Ditto...Little do they know: just one person appreciating our art sincerely is worth an eternity of strenuous labor for it.

be the flower growing through the concrete
flow like a moderate breeze- no frost, no heat

Write Out Your Drops AND Set Free Your Flow

I've written extensively on contributing our unique stories and experiences artistically onto the world 'stage' of collective/human 'oceans'- where we could all learn from one another and feel less lonely in our individual struggles in life. In this collection- I've taken it one step further in suggesting that our cultural identity and various struggles we may have faced in them by nature (both genetic and environmental) precisely provides us with a unique imprint in our fluid souls. One that we need to take a step back and listen to once in a while, despite the rising sound of technology and globalization pressures.

Our eccentricities can become what ultimately attracts people to us the most, and the inner struggles we face in blossoming our culturally-influenced personalities can ultimately provide clues to our missions on earth. I've been attempting to bring forth a voice to injustice through creativity- making, literally, 'art' out of activism through love and not 'war'. No derogatory insults hurled at political figures- no matter how much some may deserve it, it'd achieve nothing.

I also have a deepfelt connection and love toward the land of my birth, despite my cultural and political heartbreak. I miss eating *simit* on the ferry boats of Istanbul. I miss the Aegean coast- where Dalya first experienced the sea. And I miss waking up every morning to the mystifying call of *ezan*. I realized I could not turn my back on my Turkish-American pride simply because the Türkiye-half had currently (socio-politically) turned its back on me and my core family.

"Writing makes me feel more relevant as a human being- to connect my one drop of contribution to the entire ocean of humanity in the world..."

SET FREE YOUR FLOW

The quote above is included in a section on my website entitled 'Author's Writing Process'- taken from one of my first literary interviews. In it I highlight how- once I'd taught myself English- I enjoyed taking it one step further and combining my love of words with my love of music: namely through writing 'lyrics' to 'melodies' I'd create in my head. These later became poems to describe moments in my life. Simply writing daily journal notes or 'dear diary' entries wouldn't satisfy my need for creativity after some point, and over the years, my academic research writing didn't satisfy my soul either. (I wish, in retrospect, I would have majored in English Literature or something of that sort). I wanted to take a brief excerpt from the interview, for I believe it sums up my artistic 'flow' perfectly for the sake of this collection:

"...As an only child, I remember having had an overactive imagination, sometimes even pretending to be 'interviewed' on the radio about some book series (!) I'd had. I've always been a pondering wonderer, preferring to reflect on my thoughts alone rather than feel lost in noisy crowds. Hence, writing in general has always felt both natural and like 'home' for me...Like the female lead in the novel, I too had to initially cope with becoming a 'bored housewife' immediately into my marriage- as I also had to relocate to a foreign land and grapple with solitude, like Kaitlin Maverick. Despite the beauty of Stavanger, Norway, the slower tempo of life (in comparison to my native NYC) was difficult for me to adapt to- especially as, I later realized, I'd always idealized a marriage or live-in relationship to be full of more 'romantic adventures' than domestic docility.

I refused to allow myself into a depression, however, and knew my need for productivity to maintain my self-esteem; hence, the 'catalyst' for my starting to work on my lifelong dream of writing a novel began...In the 7-8 years in total it took me to complete the novel: life happened. I was a military wife in Norway and the novel took a halt at various points due to relocating, my pregnancy, my husband's politically-motivated (sans any 'criminal' action or evidence) incarceration in Turkey, and my moving back to my childhood home in NYC to adjust to a new life with my parents and my toddler daughter (in that order). I also knew I had to make ends meet, and so took on a lot of classes teaching international students.

After all of the struggles I went through raising my daughter, I felt like maybe everything had happened so that I could finally release it when I was more ready to- at the 'right' time. It wasn't easy- and the story had to be edited and re-edited about 3 times before it could be published (and during a rough time too at that, with COVID-19). I still believe in my story so much, however, and believe everything truly does happen for a reason. I know somehow- perhaps slowly but surely- this cumulation of my hard-work and sleepless hours will reach the right hands at the right time and 'catalyze' whoever needs to read a story like 'The Catalyst' at this particular time in history..."

Writing makes us all legendary. All of our experiences- no matter how seemingly trivial, controversial, or even grand and dramatic- through writing them out, will have a purpose.... To be able to affect, and perhaps even catalyze...through our verses, even long after our bodies are gone.

THE PAIN OF FREE WILL

I simply want to express
my current state of distress
I can't have it all- we must admit when we fall
I can't triumph professionally and feel happy emotionally
I can't be the perfect mother and also make time for another
I can't maintain my socio-cultural duties and also prioritize my own wants and needs
                sometimes-I simply can't be both the East and the West
          and I wish I had a compass that could decide for me- less stress

LIONESS

      they hunt for the kill whilst you do to defend and survive
you're not the darkness of their hatred- let them eat themselves up
                                while you thrive
    you affect beyond what meets the eye, delicately-strong butterfly
          you are feared, yet tireless…worn but mighty, dear lioness

IGNITERS

summer nights and summer days, facing sunsets in a haze
our lives have become a maze…pain we mistake for excitement
who can share our atonement? lighten our burdens… exorcise our demons…we had set their souls ablaze…we were never a passing phase
being without our deep love of legends is their punishment:
                    living out their days faking fulfillment

THE MASTER'S MUSE

     the lady's broken smile curved higher after she'd left this earth
           her absence added to her now legendary worth
didn't anyone tell her, back then, that maybe she was never broken…
   and that she never had to suppress fully expressed joy, with words unspoken?
        we only seem flawed to hearts of a different style
      we will be shown effort by the *true* ones worth the while

AFTERWORD

As the founder of the creative term 'flow', psychologist Mihaly Csikszentmihalyi would hopefully agree with me when I say the following: I've been bleeding out my art and writing out my drops. And, with my writing: setting free the natural *flow* of my bicultural soul despite socio-cultural 'taboos' and hindrances.

I've been doing so purely for the sake of doing so; not to obtain some end result that is out of my control. The only thing I can control is my conscious concentration on my art, which gives me joy during otherwise difficult times. The art of storytelling- both autobiographical here and fantastical with my fiction novels- merely for my joy in the creation of it. To be able to joyfully create art out of having been collateral damage of dichotomous social pressures- as well as much drama in life overall- provides me a sense of fairness and healing.

Regardless of how pessimistic my outlook may have appeared in this collection about my duality- to be crystal clear: I am now wholly acceptant and even celebratory of it. I love being an offspring of the cultural legacy of the Ottoman Empire, as well as forebearer of the secular (which I do not believe was ever intended to be anti-religion), socio-intellectual remnants of the world-renowned Atat*ü*rk. His lingering resonance among the youth of Turkey- despite all the politics of the past decade- fills me with hope that my birth country will, too, somehow be able to recover from its dichotomous neuroses, and come out of everything much stronger. United. Not divided.

I love having experienced first-hand the value of true democracy and freedom in the United States- more palpable since my 2017 return here after my airport trauma in Turkey.

I love being able to connect with the great variety of beautiful music in Turkey (often beautiful dichotomous fusions themselves), where reggaeton/pop sounds can be found intertwined with belly-dance rhythms and Turkish instruments like *ney* and *saz*.

Following my nearly decade-long process publishing *The Catalyst*; I see now it's truly been a 'catalyst' for me as well in its own right. Not only has it improved my writing ability, but it has also given me a fulfilling sense of purpose: enjoying the cathartic process and encouraging others to do the same, rather than writing to employ some mission solely for sales or entertainment.

Regardless of whether your path involves art or not, I know it will somehow involve innovative thinking and creativity-cornerstones in nearly any profession imaginable on this earth, in one form or another. I've discovered my motivation and purpose. I can only hope I have been able to help you get at least one step closer to discovering yours. *Let my storytelling be your 'catalyst' to release your 'flow' and your 'flood of drops'...*

Selin

EARTH UP YOUR ROOTS

WE STUDY THE ROOT OF HUMANITY:

Observing collections of art- visual or literary
yet always extraordinary.

And what about our own?
The source within that's created us
can differ from what is actually shown.

Uncover the depths of your roots for optimal grounding.
Don't deny what's been rotting:
uncared for while in hiding.

Providing it breathing room will keep you away from doom.
Providing it breathing room will allow your soul to bloom.

Earth Up Your Roots. Earth Up Your Essence.

EARTH UP YOUR ROOTS

EARTH UP YOUR ROOTS

Dear fellow seedling of the earth we inhabit,

Do your roots anchor you so tightly you cannot flow free in the wind? Or do they ground you steadily, yet loosely enough to allow swaying toward your own way, instead…?

A plant, if ripped with its roots intact- can be replanted: allowed to flourish elsewhere… Unlike one cut off from its roots completely. Sometimes we must accept and carry along the 'rotting' (or even already 'rotten') portions of the seeds that have formed us through our lineages and early environments.

No culture or family is without flaws- no matter how they may manage to make it appear on the surface. Yet it is with our flaws that we are unique and able to experience life through a unique perspective- ultimately making us more intriguing and fulfilled.

Denial is painful, while acceptance is freedom. We can relocate our 'roots' if we must- in order to possibly avoid toxicity or stagnation, and flourish- but must keep them nonetheless, in order to bloom. And mine?

my roots are Mustafa Kemal Ataturk
my roots are the Balkans
my roots are the Huns, the Hittites…
as well as the Byzantines and Ottomans

my roots are tragedy,
both victory
and controversy

my roots include both the fungi
and the nutrients-
some better to bury
others, shared, like a berry

EARTH UP YOUR ROOTS

the good and the wrong
the silenced and the song
before a microphone

my roots are mistakes
raised steaks
heartbreaks
yet doing whatever it takes
undeniable…uncrushable

In this, my third poetic compilation, I present you, dear reader, with various symbolic short stories from my subconscious, adding to the purely poetic-verse setup of *Write Out Your Drops*, and the memoir alongside the poetry of *Set Free Your Flow*.

'The Rose Moon', for example, presents a forbidden romance between an Armenian boy, Tigran, and a Turkish girl, Gülay- in the backdrop of both the tragic events of 1915 as well as the historically-subsequent expulsion of Turkish Muslims from Bulgaria. This was one of the first stories I had written, having intended to develop the love story into a novel- until 'The Catalyst' storyline took over my mind during my time spent in Norway.

I've comprised the first three sections of this compilation through interweaving two short stories in each one with 'root'-themed poetry. The 4th section, *Upkeep*, has a longer story, 'Ordinary', which was first published in a multiple-author anthology named 'Flash' in 2020 (I'd written it during the Fall of 2019 right before the pandemic) and later in the 'Journal of Academics & Fiction' for New York's *The Media High School* in 2021.

Finally…there's 'Zelle' of the last section: my sole play. Just as the intrigue of Mata Hari herself- the controversial historical figure at once political and representative of dance- holds a special meaning for me, so does this piece as my first attempt at a short play. Few know I was an aspiring actress as a college student and later in my early 20's. I participated in theatrical performances and took various acting classes- including a summer program at the New York Film

Academy. But as so often occurs, *life is said to be what happens when you're busy making other plans*, and I'm so much happier and more creatively-fulfilled writing now. Yet I'd love for someone to play out my stories one day. Life is also said to *imitate art…* as well as at times to *be stranger than fiction.*

> *what's out of control, can control you*
> *what you can't love, can leave you*
> *what your eyes won't see, can seize you*
> *if you don't live life, life can outlive you*

Here's hoping these words will 'root' themselves in your soul after you've read them, and inspire you to 'bloom' your own flowers- all the while as you **Earth Up**[1] **Your Roots.**

PHOTOGRAPHY BY: ENGIN TUFAN SEVIMLI

> we can't expect roots to ground us,
> magnificent birds to surround us
> or flowers to bloom from our deeds
> without first planting the seeds

XOXO,

Selin Senol-Akin

---

[1] *earth up*- **to gather soil around the base of a plant in order to promote protection and growth.**

EARTH UP YOUR ROOTS

I. PLANT

*and sometimes you can feel
like a little puppy
groomed yet doomed
begging in the shop window
for the smiling passerby to adopt you*

EARTH UP YOUR ROOTS

branches-
leafed, visible, mighty
extended creators and majestic figures
on the earth, endurant- with shadows
nifty enough to shade those wishing to inhabit
the green-brown
embrace
for brief
solitude
and contemplation,
the limbs
of nature
mirroring
themselves
across the porous soil-
branching out as a root system
underneath the earth that is
unleafed, invisible, yet even mightier

*Inspired by 'The Oak Tree' by Johnny Ray Ryder Jr

EARTH UP YOUR ROOTS

multiple elements exist
for the hatchling to avoid leaving the nest

                                                        it flies anyway

multiple dawns signify the end
of the most beautiful nights

                                        the sun shines anyway

you, grounded, stay
while they, undecided, stray

despite lingering pain
more loss palpable than gain-

                                          you blossom each day

THE ANT

LATE SUMMER, 2005

"...FOUR...FIVE...SIX! OOH, I BEAT YOU!" Skipping stones across the waves was one of the past times Ömer had missed the most from his childhood home by the Aegean Sea.

He felt grateful that his new buddy in London, Mark, was there with him once again on that cloudy day in September by the River Thames.

"Only because I let you win!" Mark snickered, interrupting Ömer's indulged reverie. His eyes caught something moving farther ahead. "Mate, look at that big ant on the rock over there! Who's going to squish it first?"

"Mark! Did you know that if you kill even a tiny little ant, you will pay the price for it?" Ömer shook his head as he looked at the direction where Mark had been pointing, seeing the tiny, doomed animal flurrying about.

"What?" Mark smirked, fiddling with a smooth pebble. "Oh, please. How many ants have all of us likely killed on a daily basis- without knowing- just walking down the street?"

"And how do you know you haven't paid for it?" Ömer raised his eyebrow.

"What do you mean?"

"Well, let's say everything was going just fine one day, for example, right?" Ömer's eyes were lit up as he responded. "And suddenly you tripped while walking- how do you know that wasn't your punishment?" He flashed an all-knowing smile.

"Punishment?" Mark's mouth was now hanging open.

"My uncle- Mehmet *amca*- told me that life is a test, did you know that?" Ömer's tossed a random pebble out toward the water.

"He's back in Izmir. I miss him. He always says: *if we do good, we get rewarded, and if we do bad, we get punished*. Right here on this earth, he says- even before death and before heaven or hell. That life is like a video game. I mean, you never think about this stuff?"

"I don't know, mate," Mark squirmed his face. "We're twelve, not twenty, or…old- like forty or something!"

"My *amca* says 40 is not old…"

"*Aja*?" Mark snickered. "Oh, you mean your uncle? Sorry, mate, you know I suck with Turkish words you share with me. Well, he must be old to say such a thing! Huh!"

"It's pronounced *am- ja*" Ömer enunciated, rolling his eyes. "And my uncle is not old at all. Plus, he knows things. He reads a lot."

"Oh, yeah?" Mark crossed his arms. "Well, my mom tells me 'dem religious folks peach what they don't do!"

"You mean…*preach*?" Ömer began to laugh so hard he had to hold his jiggling stomach.

"What's so funny?" Mark's face had finally turned serious.

"Nothing mate, sorry," Ömer cleared his throat. "Look…all I know is- from this day on- because now you *know* and can no longer be excused by the ignorance of sin- your punishment will likely be twofold. Now that you *know* you cannot kill even an insect- unless you sense an immediate danger to you and you do so purely in self-defense- you will pay some level of price for it if you do…"

"Ignorance of sin? Okay, mate…" Mark scratched behind his ear. He got up to his feet. "The sun is going down. My mom's expecting me home for dinner."

"It isn't even 16:00, Markie," Ömer checked his watch, puzzled. "The sun won't set until…"

"We eat early…" Mark interrupted.

"Well, um, alright..." Ömer took in a deep breath. "See you at soccer practice tomorrow?"

Ömer watched as Mark threw in a quick smile behind him with a wave as his body sped toward the block of his apartment.

He'd never see the face of his friend again for another ten years.

§

LATE SUMMER, 2015

"Turn the volume up, Zehra," Ömer insisted. His wife was still busy talking on the phone with her mother in Bursa, not allowing for him to hear the BBC news very well. He placed his palm on his forehead and shook his head.

Ömer could envision the two of them as an older couple already- and, unfortunately, it wasn't looking too promising. Beauty, morals, kindness- not to mention great cooking- Ömer loved many of the traits Zehra possessed. Of that, he was sure. But in regards to whether or not she'd actually been his intellectual equal was up for debate, as far as he was concerned.

"Zehra!" Ömer raised his voice with a sterner look in her direction this time, extending his bare feet onto the glass table in the center of the sofas. He exhaled with a satisfied glee, allowing his head to fall back onto the sofa cushion.

Zehra's wooden slippers clicked and clacked their way closer to him. "Momma says hello too, by the way!" she nudged, plopping down adjacent to her husband. She handed Ömer the remote control she'd brought with her from across the room.

"I just talked to *Fatma anne* yesterday!" Ömer protested, scratching his head. "I'm tired!"

He added a smile before Zehra could protest.

"Okay, my lazy love," Zehra rolled her eyes, returning his smile with a wink. "Let's watch the news."

Scrolling down a plethora of talent shows and soap operas listed on the Guide, Ömer had decided on the local news channel. Besides, he knew it'd soon be ending, to be followed by his favorite cop show. He reached his arms across Zehra as the two shared a chuckle over the image of a child making a funny face while hugging a puppy- part of a final commercial before the familiar news anchor continued with a stern face.

"*Yok artık*....!" Ömer got up with a jolt as a photograph of a familiar face flashed across the scene.

"*Aşkım*? What's the matter?"

"The body of Mark Kensington, just 22 years old, was discovered yesterday morning at the construction site," the woman with a well-coiffed blonde bob was saying. "His mother had difficulty identifying him, as his face was gnawed nearly unrecognizable by carpenter ants."

"Ants?" Zehra was shaking her head, turning to lock eyes with her husband. She couldn't, as Ömer's peepers were frozen on the screen. "Who's that? What's going on?"

"That's him," Ömer was mumbling. "I follow him on Facebook."

"The police are still investigating the nature of the case, as it is not clear whether the further damage to the face occurred after his death or not," the presenter continued. "The exact cause of this horrific death is still uncertain at the moment. Authorities are asking anyone with any information to call…"

Ω

THE TREE WOMAN

SPRING, 1912

THE WOMAN'S FRAIL HANDS caressed the callused, strong ones of her fiancée's. "I will always be with you, my beloved." Celeste Frost's amber eyes teared at the sight of Robert Carlisle's strong jawline and baby blues. "I will caress your cheeks with the blowing breeze, keep you warm through rays of the sun directly hitting your arms, tickle your face through a drop of rain when you're feeling dry and parched…."

"Do not speak of these things, my canary," the handsome carpenter before her replied softly. Celeste loved it when Robert would call her that. He knew she adored singing.

"We *will* get married this summer as planned," Robert went on. "You *will* become a beautiful bride, and soon after- a wonderful mother. The mother of a little child who will get to see her survive and be strong for our family. I need you. We will need you. The female bird makes a home."

"And all birds need a nest, Robert," Celeste spoke softly, gazing at the body of water in the near distance. She leaned her body onto the nearest bark. "They need the trees. I think I shall be a part of this tree most of all, Robert. Overlooking New Rochelle Harbor where we both grew up. Providing shade and shelter when you feel unsafe…Promise me, Robert, to never cut it down."

"Rest assured, my darling," Robert tucked a strand of Celeste's raven locks behind her ear. "In the unlikely event that this wicked cancer does beat us, I shall never betray your wishes."

"I wrote a poem, Robert, do you want to hear it?" Celeste forced herself to smile, licking quickly the teardrop that had befallen her cheek.

"Hush, my darling," Robert placed a gentle finger on her blush-pink, pale-leaning lips. "We've conversed long enough. You must save your breath. Your precious lungs…Perhaps we should go inside our chambers and…"

"Robert, please…" Celeste insisted, adding a playful pout. Upon his encouraging smile in return, she started to recite her poem:

> *oh, to be like a tree…*
> *rooted,*
> *yet with branches allowed to sway*
> *shedding old leaves*
> *with multiple chances*
> *to begin anew*
> *and lean a new way*

"That was beautiful, sweetheart," Robert squeezed her cheek with affection. "If not my canary singing around it: then at least you shall be my rooted tree for evermore. Around for many years. You'll see."

§

SPRING, 1913

"Ow!" Lenore exclaimed, looking up as she brushed her golden hair off of her face. "Those branches keep tugging at my hair, Rob. This is the absolute last straw. I'm telling you. Please remove this ugly old tree from our yard at once, Rob. I don't want to see it…"

"But, my dove," Robert took her ivory hands into his own. His new fiancée's fingers were rougher than Celeste's used to be, he noticed. *Rougher around the edges.* Lenore was certainly no fragile flower, but nor was her passion for the faint of heart. And, oh, how Robert was titillated to be wrapped around her finger.

"It provides shade for the delicate flowers, remember? Besides, it's merely a tree. What could it possibly…"

"I don't like it!" Lenore insisted, rolling her eyes toward the clouds.

"It's as simple as that. If you and I are to be married, I shall lay no eyes on this hideous thing blocking my view of the harbor from our bedroom."

"My darling, our bedroom would not even be facing this…"

"I don't wish to hear another word of it!" Lenore folded her arms across her full chest. The pursuant quiet caused her to glance at Robert from the corner of her eye. A change of tactic was called for, she decided, in order to solidify her convincing.

Ever since she'd discovered his ex's little poetry engraved in the thick bark- signed by the initials she'd known to be her sister's- Lenore wished to have no remnant of the shameful past. A past that had caused her to lose a sister, in order to gain a wealthy husband. Desperate financial times upon the family had called for desperate measures.

Lenore raised the pitch of her voice and spoke through a sultry smile. "You do wish to have me happy in the bedroom, the living room, the kitchen, and in all the rooms with all the views we could enjoy each other's company for years to come…don't you, Robbie?"

"Alright, my darling," Robert sighed, clearing his throat. He was blushing, Lenore noticed. "I'll call my men first thing in the morning to take a look. They've got some sturdy axes and…"

He was caught midsentence when a particularly strong wind gust brought down the heavy thick branch atop his head at top speed. It was as if something had hurled it straight onto his skull.

"Rob!" he heard Lenore shriek as she rushed over to him with panic. But he could not even turn to see her beautiful countenance one last time before another woman's image appeared before his mind.

"You win, Celeste," Robert croaked in a whisper, looking up at the tree. Towering mighty before his fallen body. The branch that had just struck him was now raised in its usual position once again.

As his eyes closed to the world, he began regretting it all. The gradual poison he'd fed her nightly to expedite her death- albeit in a covert manner, of course. Had Lenore been worth it? God knew she'd been pressuring him to leave Celeste for the longest time, and he just hadn't had the heart. Robert wasn't a monster. If he'd told Celeste he'd fallen in love with another woman- her very own sister, at that- surely, she would have succumbed to a quicker death through a heart attack, or even a more painful one through an actual cancer of some sort.

No. Robert couldn't allow for Celeste to hate him. It was a wonderful thing to feel- *being loved* by someone as much as she had. Yet what could he have done? He also wanted *to love*. And he simply could not feel any romantic affection toward Celeste. It'd been Lenore who'd stolen his heart. *Perhaps literally so*, was Robert Carlisle's last thought as he closed his eyes to the world.

§

Lenore wiped the single tear off her blushing cheek. Her sharp nails dug into her neighbor Michael's arms before her late fiancé's grave. What a kind neighbor Michael Thompson had been. *A well-off widower*. Lenore gazed into his eyes as the sermon continued, witnessed by several others- the identities of whom she could not quite make out at that moment.

Her and Michael were more appropriate for each other, Lenore supposed. *Perhaps this entire thing could have been destined- kismet- after all.* The thought brought a smile onto her face.

To be fair, Lenore had insisted that her mother-in-law-to-be bury him right by his favorite tree: the one he hadn't wished to cut down. *Poor Robert*. He should have listened to her.

Thank you, Celeste, Lenore thought, taking in a deep breath as she gazed at her late sister's engraving.

You've forgiven me, after all, I suppose, she smiled as the leaves almost whispered a soft agreement with her in the wind. *Causing this occasion by giving Robert what he deserved, I suppose, and allowing me to grow closer to Mr. Thompson.* Lenore glanced at the luscious leaves shining in the sun. *I'll let you remain here after all, in return.*

Ω

EARTH UP YOUR ROOTS

to wake each day on the battlefield
lacking weapons or a shield
against enemies both perceived and real-
both the green-eyed monster they never reveal
and the inner critic you attempt to conceal

no one is without fault
even if they've casted the first stone
discover the solace you seek in nature
discover the solace of what has been sown

                                                  in environments
                                          where authenticity
                              can ignorantly be referred to
                                      as 'mental illness'

                                      an inauthentic self
                        being deemed 'appropriate'- meanwhile
                       can bring about actual mental ailments

                 salvage your psyche: relocation and redirection
                                    can-in one lifetime-
                                    catalyze reincarnation

EARTH UP YOUR ROOTS

slice a poem

you'll find the dirt
underneath the charming verses
the blood
underneath a message that rejoices

the tears contributing to the floods
…and the heavy sighs to the flow
…blooms in secret, not allowed to grow

the silent screams
the hidden dreams

concealed pathways and dark rooms
unawareness of all that looms

slice a poem
and you'll find *reality*

…and there within lies the real beauty

II. BUD

*some bruises
are grapes
that simply cannot be
turned into wine*

*best thriving
left on their vine*

EARTH UP YOUR ROOTS

a lovely home
can hide a million flaws
a beguiling smile
can scratch deeper than claws

some rule emptiness
situated on thrones
throwing only petals
while evading hurled stones

a broken vase
can struggle to keep the rose
sniffed but not rooted
only joy stems from prose

                                        the most beautiful walls can hide
                                        the most heartbreaking tragedies

                                              plaster painted to look sturdy
                                              vines wound to appear pretty

                                all the while with the foundation- shaky-
                                      accruing rooted, lethal maladies

                                                   a façade of dreams
                                                          while
                                      coming apart at the seams

EARTH UP YOUR ROOTS

nature fills our shoes
whilst we're occupied
in our daily ruse

rain waters the seeds
we tend to ignore
in our daily grind
whilst we're stepping on the earth's weeds
tending to man-made deadlines and deeds
paying no mind

climbing the corporate ladder,
or
watching the dandelions scatter?
which one is sadder?
       I prefer the latter

THE RUBY

WITH THE SUNRAYS STINGING HER EYES stronger than usual that early autumn morning, Ruby Sternstein woke up to a curious mix of bird sounds and suburban construction projects in her Smithtown neighborhood.

Her wrinkly hands were adorned with rings. Her usual, even when sleeping. They held on tightly to the edge of the bed, where her silky pajamas had allowed her to slide herself up with ease.

My hair! Her Harold had adored it in curls. Ruby had to ensure they were still intact each and every morning. She squeezed her thighs as a massage- her right leg had particularly weakened over the past four decades. Wobbling toward her wooden vanity table, Ruby situated herself on the velvety-cushioned chair.

What she saw in the mirror nearly took her breath away, and she had to hold on to the corner of her armoire for dear life. So hard, in fact, that her perfectly lined-up row of peach and mauve lipsticks fell down to their sides- with one or two even rolling down to the musky-carpeted floor.

Before her, the silver ringlets on her head were now transformed in time to their once-chestnut hue, silky and gleaming in the sun with life. Ruby's staggering hand caressed her cheek, viewing the reflection display her once supple skin. With cheeks of rose-pink- she appeared to be closer to herself around age 30 rather than the current one of 70.

Her heartbeat grew speedier. What exactly was happening? Ruby closed her eyes and said a little prayer. *Blessed are you, our God, Ruler of the Universe, who is good and causes good. What I see before me- youth- is beautiful, but I am frightened. Please let this go away, please let this vision go away.*

She opened her eyes with hope, only to shut them again at the sight of her younger self reflecting back at her. *If only prayers came true in an instant,* she thought. Ruby had prayed every night for two years- never missing a single day, after Harold's accident- until eventually giving up. The tragic, heartbreaking car crash many of the locals continued to whisper about on the rare occasion they saw her walking about her front lawn. Tending to a random plant still hanging on to vitality, though Ruby and time itself had long given up on tending to them.

Crazy lady, she'd overhear the neighborhood kids say about her with chuckles- undoubtedly overhearing things from their cold-hearted parents. *Children, after all, are never inherently evil,* Ruby knew.

§

"Dylan? Oh, Dylan. My handsome son, I'm so happy you're visiting on this day out of all days?"

"What's the matter, mother?" Dylan pressed both of his firm hands on his mother's shoulders. "Is everything alright? Is it those damn opossums again? Because, you know I've been meaning to call the exterminator this week. Really, I have. But that latest client at the firm has been bugging us constantly about…"

"It isn't the opossums, Dylan," Ruby dismissed. She ran her fingers through his light, sandy hair- wavy like the Atlantic. *My handsome, lawyer son.* Why hadn't he gotten married with that girlfriend of his yet? She was probably delaying it, that foolish girl. Her son was quite the catch, as far as Ruby was concerned.

"Is it the raccoons, then, mother?" Dylan's hands were moving a mile a minute. The rate of his speech- even speedier. "Have they been stealing your gardenias again? Because you know…"

"Come with me upstairs to my bedroom," Ruby interrupted with a smile, linking her arm with that of her son's. "I want to show you something…"

"Ok, hold on tight, mother. Are you sure you don't want the stair-lifts to help you when I'm not around? It can be dangerous, you know, for you to …"

"There are more dangerous things for an old lady living alone than navigating up and down stairs, my Dylan," Ruby went on, her toes inside thin velvet slippers- a shade darker than the color of her name- gripping on to each step for dear life. Her free arm was gliding up the handrail. The tone of her voice dropped. "More disturbing things, such as her foggy mind. Oh, I do hope I'm alright. But I saw it. I saw what I saw…"

"What did you see mother? When? Where?"

Ruby paused before the crème-colored wooded door with the brass doorknob. Her bedroom. She took in a deep breath. "In here…"

Ruby pushed the door slowly and placed a finger onto her lips. As if there were a class in session in the room she did not want them to interrupt. How she missed her teaching days. Harold had advised her against working once she'd become a mother.

She stood before the table with an abrupt halt to her lethargic strutting, pointing. "There!"

"Can you even make out your reflection in this aged thing, mother?" Dylan walked to the table and hunched downward, eyeing the glass with a quizzical countenance. "I'm afraid we might have to replace this..."

"It shows me what I need to see just fine, Dylan!" Ruby raised her voice, albeit it was quivering. She gasped, slowly cupping her hand over her mouth. "Oh, my dear Lord…."

She stared this time to see Harold hugging her from behind, placing a red-jeweled necklace around her neck.

"A ruby for my Ruby…" he was whispering in her ear. Fastening the necklace behind her neck with meticulous attention, he added a soft kiss on her neck in the way she liked- still giving her entire body goosebumps.

"Thank you." Ruby closed her eyes, allowing her smile-ridden face and head to lay backward toward her husband's sturdy chest.

"Mother!" Dylan suddenly called out, coming up behind her. His voice sounded to Ruby as if it could have been coming from the garden outside. "You were almost going to fall!"

"Nonsense, Dylan," Ruby chuckled, blushing as she turned around to face her son. "Your father's a strong man."

"Mother…please lay down. Rest a bit."

"Why didn't you welcome him- your father? Say hello! You certainly have been taught your manners, my boy."

"Who?" Dylan asked with a raised brow. "Mother? You really should sit down, and I'll get you some…"

"You don't see him? Oh, dear." Ruby blinked a couple of times. "Harry?" she whimpered to the mirror, smiling as he slowly returned it, appearing before her again. "There you are…"

"Uh, mother…."

"He's wearing his navy gentleman's suit," Ruby went on, cutting in. "Do you remember it? The one he adored wearing to special dinners. Come to think of it, Dylan- you should wear it. After your father takes it off, that is. You should borrow it. You have your father's build."

"I will," Dylan's voice accepted. He added a heavy sigh.

"Why don't you wear it to your special dinner tonight with Emma, actually?" Ruby threw a mischievous glance at her son from the reflection in the mirror. Her Harold had dissipated, though he could sense him there with his family still. *He must be avoiding calling further attention to himself,* Ruby decided. *We both know there's a more important matter at hand, with regards to our son.*

"My special dinner? Oh, right, right. Emma's birthday," Dylan's voice was lackadaisical.

Could it be that it was her *son* who'd needed more convincing? Could it have been Dylan who was to blame for their cold feet toward marriage, and not Emma's? Ruby rolled her eyes. What fools the couples of this generation were. No one was getting any younger.

§

"Ta da!" Dylan did a little spin for Ruby, throwing in an exaggerated, toothy grin at the end. "How do I look, mother?" He had decided in a manner of minutes to indulge her mother in her little hallucination before the mirror in her room, and had put on the navy suit he'd known his mother to have been referring to earlier. Her favorite one of his late father's. Hanging crease-free on his side of closet.

"It's perfect!" Ruby exclaimed; her palms folded together atop her chest. "We knew you'd be perfect in it!"

"Well, I'm honored papa has allowed me to wear it," he winked, adjusting the collar while caressing his mother's cheek. "I just have to make sure to spray on some cologne before I pick up Emma, though. Smells a bit like mothballs, and there's no time for dry cleaning…what's this?"

Dylan locked eyes with his mother, whom he saw to be smiling wider now as she observed her son placing his hands into the jacket's pockets. His hand gripped something hard, and took it out to see a classic-looking crème box in the left pocket. Dylan shed a tear. *Papa was left-handed, too.*

"What's inside, Dylan?" Ruby's voice quivered, yet Dylan could still glimpse a hint of a smile on her expression rather than shock. She placed her hand on her mouth as he opened the box. "Oh, my Adonai! That is the very red necklace I saw him place around my neck in the mirror!"

"It's…beautiful, mother," Dylan stammered. "This…I…well, why would this be in his pocket? Had he not given this to you?"

"I believe he must have intended to, my boy," Ruby's gaze became lost in the mirror once again. "He whispered to me, as he put it around a young version of myself I saw in the mirror. 'A ruby for my Ruby', he said." Ruby sat down on the foot of her bed, closing her eyes.

"It was lovely to see my younger self in the mirror. Now that I think of it, your Emma sort of resembles my younger self, Dylan…"

"Oh, my," Robert bent down on his knees before Ruby. "Didn't Papa get killed right before your anniversary? Mother, I think he'd been wanting to give you this…."

"Yes," Ruby smiled now through her tears. "But he could have appeared to me for all of these years had he still thought I should own it. I spent other anniversaries without him. So, no. No, that couldn't be it, dear son. I think…I *sense* he wants you to have it- something in addition to that little rock I saw you prepare to propose to Emma…"

"Mother, it was on sale," Dylan was shaking his head. "I was waiting until Christmas. When I knew more for sure whether it would be the right thing…"

"We give you two our blessing," Ruby interrupted. "Harold has always dreamed of growing old together in this house, with the sound of grandchildren, Dylan. Your career will not provide you with any of that coziness. Possessions- present or of the past- will only possess *us* if we hang on to them. The future is more important…"

"It's not just about your blessing, mother," Dylan started to say, only to grow quiet as he saw the suddenly-stern expression on his mother's face. He sighed. Dylan really did want to move into the grand house- with or without Emma. His apartment in the city wasn't doing it for him anymore. And if a marriage was the only way to keep his folks' support…

"Dylan?" Ruby's voice cut into his thoughts.

"I just meant…we couldn't take something so obviously special for you, mother," Dylan cleared his throat.

"You two will have more use for it with your lifestyle than your little old mother, my boy," Ruby chuckled softly.

Was that her late husband shaking his head at her in the mirror? Ruby kept her head held high. So what if she had to get a little creative to convince their son to finally form a family of his own already?

"Don't worry, Harold," Ruby assured the reflection, twirling her silver curls in the mirror. "I'll get it back from that Emma girl. Eventually. Being married to someone of Dylan's status: I'm sure she won't mind. Not at all."

Ω

THERESA

MEETING A SELF-PUBLISHED AUTHOR, deemed notable enough to be a dying young girl's last wish? Had the world turned upside down while she'd been asleep?

"Are you certain I am the author she wishes to see, before she passes on?" Rebecca Thompson had inquired that morning, lowering her voice. "I mean, you know, *if* she passes on, that is. I do certainly hope she will recover, the poor thing...."

"Yes, Ms. Thompson," the man on the other side of the phone had assured her, introducing himself as Brock Richardson from the local chapter of Make-A-Wish Foundation. "We confirmed with young Theresa by showing her your indie-author's page. Quite professional by the way. You did the design all by yourself? I'll have to check out your books myself sometime."

Rebecca had blushed, at once flattered and also relieved. Few people knew of the 'indie author' label for self-published, independent authors such as herself. A route that left her with little financial benefit after all the marketing expenditure she had to make out of her own pocket- uncovered by her actual cut of royalties from sales- yet creatively in control and happy about the entire process nonetheless.

Brock Richardson. The tall man with the slicked back brown hair and wiry glasses was now smiling handsomely before Rebecca. *His name sounds like a character I could use in the next book*, she thought, mirroring him as he eyed her up and down. Taking him up on his invitation from earlier that day hadn't disappointed her thus far.

"I appreciate that, Mr. Richardson," Rebecca went on,

ignoring the burning sensation from the crimsoning of her cheeks. "Please forgive my confusion on the phone earlier. Despite having been fortunate enough to obtain some dedicated readers through my social media presence, I'm not exactly- you know- a J.K Rowling or Stephen King. To be widely-known enough to have been able to reach this young reader. I'm surprised, yes, but don't get me wrong- also incredibly honored!"

"Call me, Brock," the man replied, ushering her to take a seat on the other side of his desk. "Ms. Thompson, I also happen to be Theresa's personal therapist. We've been having a lot of conversations about her need for connections, actually. She wouldn't tell me where she first came across your book- it was in her backpack when her aunt dropped her off here for treatment- but I believe she's connected through the title bearing her own name. Not sure what the plot is about exactly, but I'm sensing some particular affinity with the main character…"

"I suppose that could be it…" Rebecca said, unsure if the smile she'd plastered on her face was capable of disguising her concern. She was hoping that this young leukemia patient, whom she was told was around 14 years old, was not terribly affected by the particular, dark story she'd written.

Rebecca had never considered the impact- positive or negative- any of her writing could have on anyone. She liked to believe she'd been able to formulate an image of an inspiring writer on her social media handle- motivating aspiring writers to write stories of their own, and for readers to merely be intrigued and entertained. She'd always been careful not to include erotic or violent material- Rebecca hated the impact of such material on youth, especially in movies and video games.

But a young teenager - a likely sensitive one at that, with her illness- reading the story about a young girl's self-destruction? And coincidentally sharing her name, at that? What impact was a lesser-known author such as herself possibly having on an impressionable young reader?

"I really do want to read your book, though, Ms. Thompson," Brock cleared his throat. "Especially now that I've met you. I'd love to support you. Is it available for sale online?"

"It sure is, through most online retailers," Rebecca smiled, biting her lip. "And, please, call me Rebecca."

"Will do," Brock smiled, swaying his body back and forth.

"Well?" Rebecca raised her eyebrow. "May I see her now? Theresa is expecting me, is she not? And you do approve of this meeting, I take it, as her therapist?"

"Oh, yes, yes, of course," Brock shook his head rapidly. "Your Covid-test came back negative. As I've stated, we'll keep the meeting to an hour- supervised by myself from the adjacent room to listen for potential emotional triggers for her. However surely unintentional as they may be, you can understand I may- in such a case- need to come in with some excuse and change the topic…"

"Oh, yes, of course, of course," Rebecca nodded. She held up the palms she'd lain on her lap. "I'll do my best to stick to how I developed my love of writing and what kind of things she's liked reading about, as discussed. I know the impact of the human psyche on physiology."

"Thank you," Brock smiled. "Medically, her cancer hasn't gotten worse over the last two months she's been here. The chemotherapy has catalyzed some stability, though we're now seeing that a bone marrow transplant to replenish the damaged stem cells may be in order. A donor with the haploidentical form of an allogeneic transplant- one from a parent- would have been ideal. Sadly, it cannot be the case for Theresa since her aunt's filled us in on how she lost her folks in a tragic crash as a young child."

"I cannot even begin to imagine…" Rebecca folded her arms closer across her chest. Or maybe she could. She closed her eyes a beat longer than intended, nodding as Brock continued to speak.

Tessa.

The name ran across her mind and Rebecca has to fight back tears. The baby daughter she'd had to leave beyond as a young woman studying away from home, having been left pregnant by the bartender that'd crushed her heart and idealistic dreams about love. *How can a young girl grow up not knowing those whose seeds had sprouted her?* The daughter whose name had inspired her naming of her fictional protagonist- not wanting to jinx her life somehow by naming her in the same exact way. The girl she had to give up for adoption to a kind, childless couple in Florida before her parents back up in Boston could ever suspect anything upon her return. Had her adopted mother ever revealed the truth to Tessa? Would she be angry with Rebecca if she knew? Could she understand?

"Her oncologist has actually been thanking me, claiming the stability might be the pleasant byproduct of our uplifting therapy sessions- igniting vitality into her spirits and such. But Rebecca..." Brock leaned in closer to her face, his coffee eyes piercing through her own. He lowered his husky voice even lower.

"I know that deep down- it's somehow your story which has been the catalyst. No siblings or many friends she's ever spoken of. Her aunt concurs my theory with each visit- it's this *story* that she clings to. Your novel has somehow become her lifeline."

Rebecca reminded herself to blink, letting out a deep breath. "Brock...that's a lot for me to take in. A major responsibility. I mean, my book; I'm honestly not sure if it's- I don't know quite how to word this- a *positive* enough influence on such a vulnerable young girl. It's not exactly a self-help book, you know? Nor some inspirational autobiography. It's a psychological thriller of a sort..."

"She reads it over and over," Brock shrugged. "Excitedly so, each time. It makes her smile. And we don't ever want to deny that to our patients. We did read some of the reviews. We were assured there were no horrific scenes, foul language or intense eroticism or anything like that that could potentially jeopardize..."

"Oh, no, no, of course not," Rebecca interrupted, folding her arms across her chest as she leaned back in the black swivel chair. "It's nothing like that. It just describes...well...a broken family, and a young girl's search for herself through her search for them. And now that you've told me a little about her life- I'm a bit concerned."

"Well," Brock stood up silently, eyeing the circular clock on the wall as he patted his palms across the desk. "I understand your concerns, but it will be Theresa's time for dinner soon. The nurses are strict with her schedule, and I don't want to take away from your time with her. You don't want to cancel on her, do you?"

"No, no," Rebecca cleared her throat, sitting up straight in her chair. "Of course not."

"Then let me take you to see her," Brock gently tapped her shoulder two times. "Rest assured that seeing you should only be a good thing for our sweet patient. She's truly a bright girl- an absolute delight to talk to. Just like yourself."

As the two of them walked closer before Room 202, Rebecca shook out her arms and put on a big smile. A melodic, soft voice muttered "Come in," in response to Brock's knocking, and the door opened to reveal a cheerfully-dispositioned girl with a blue beanie covering her bare head, dark eyes striking on her pale skin.

"Rebecca!" she exclaimed, grinning from ear to ear. "Oh, sorry. Ms. Thompson. Come sit, please. Look I'm sitting crisscross apple sauce! There's room for you at the foot of the bed. Can she please sit here, Brock? Please, oh, pretty please?"

Rebecca and Brock exchanged smiling glances. "What a sweetie pie you are, Theresa. It's my pleasure to meet my favorite reader! And of course, you can call me by my first name."

As Brock motioned for her to sit down in deed on her bed's edge, Rebecca did so, folding her hands on her lap.

"I'll be right outside if you girls need me," Brock stated gently, giving Rebecca a wink that felt supportive to her.

"You're finally here!" Theresa was swaying back and forth, her arms hugging a pillow on her legs. "I'm sure Brock's filled you in on how much I love your novel. I've read it three times!"

"Three times?" Rebecca gulped. *So, she has read the ending.* The ending that Rebecca had secretly wished this teenager somehow hadn't gotten up to when she'd decided, merely halfway through the book- perhaps on some youthful whim- that she'd enjoyed enough of the story to request meeting her.

"Yes! May we take a picture together, Rebecca?"

"A picture?" Rebecca stammered. "Oh, of course. I can take it on my phone and send Dr. Richardson. I'm sure he can…"

"They give me a cell phone, you know," Theresa rolled her eyes playfully. "I use it to chat with my support group mostly. Other kids across the country. Three back home in Florida, actually. Come closer please- my arms can only reach so far for the selfie. The cancer is not contagious…"

"Aww, nonsense..." Rebecca dismissed with a nervous chuckle. *Florida.* She tried to push her own trigger words out of her mind, as the name of the state Rebecca herself had grown up in was mentioned. *Tessa.*

"It is not that, dear Theresa," she continued, edging herself closer to the young patient. "On the contrary, it is I who wouldn't to pass germs of any kind from the city life outside of this secluded space you've got out here.…"

"It'll be alright," Theresa's eyes met hers. "Say cheese…"

Isn't this AC turned on a bit high? Rebecca rubbed her hands across her arms following their little photography session. She instinctively found herself reaching for the blanket she spotted hanging off the side of Theresa's bedside chair. "Put this across your shoulders, honey. It's chilly in here, aren't you cold?"

"You're right, I do get cold easier than usual these days," Theresa smiled, allowing Rebecca to place the navy-blue sheet across her shoulders. "Theresa in the book also got cold a lot, didn't she?"

Rebecca's stomach did a little drop. She plastered on a smile. "Yes. Yes, I suppose she did." For a moment, she had to fight the urge to let out a tear, staring there right into this young reader's eyes. *I wonder what it would have been like to raise a daughter.*

"I have a secret…" Theresa whispered, glancing toward the door before cupping her tubed hand around her mouth. "I *am* Theresa. *The* Theresa."

"Hmm?" Rebecca tried nonchalantly, despite a rapidly increasing heart rate. "Sorry, I didn't quite catch that…"

"This story, Ms. Thompson. I mean, Rebecca. This is my life. Well, *almost* to a T…. It's remarkable…"

"*Your* life…?"

"I keep thinking about what will become of me…" Theresa went on with a nod. "Since, so far in my life everything's come about as the chapters had happen to the 'Theresa' character in the book…I mean, except the part about her mother having left her and her dating the wrong crowd. I'm not even fifteen and sixteen yet like those chapters in the book. But I do wonder if I'll end up like the ending?"

"The ending…" Rebecca sighed. She closed her eyes. The character which was based half on her own life…where she'd purposely written in a twisted end for the character's father- literally- to creatively avenge the bartender who'd broken her heart and left her pregnant. The other half of the character had been based on the life of the one person she had long suppressed from her consciousness; how she'd long imagined her Tessa growing up, including a quarter of the details she'd known of or imagined from the daughter she'd given away. *It was for her own good.*

"I like to believe I purposely left the ending a bit open-ended," Rebecca forced herself to smile. "We see the tragic end her father faces, but I've left it up to the reader to decide if Theresa ever gets to meet her mother or not. I wanted to leave some room for hope, I suppose, after the rest of the book. I didn't want to have any regrets with a concrete ending…"

"Do you have any regrets, Rebecca?"

"Not really. I mean, I like to think that I've made the best decisions based on the options I had at a time throughout my life." *The baby I gave up for adoption.* Of course, Rebecca could never share that part with this young fan of hers. She'd certainly view her as a heartless monster, and her fantasy of a favorite author would diminish. Brock would call it a terrible mistake to make in the life of a cancer patient.

"Oh, come on...pleasssse" Theresa insisted in a sing-song voice with a wide-mouthed smile. "Just for cheeseeee."

Rebecca raised a curious eyebrow before breaking out into laughter. The bright young girl before her was still so childlike she could literally feel her heart melt. "Oh, alright. You're adorable. I really do feel chilly in here. So, hmm, a regret? Maybe I would say- not staying in Florida. I was studying at Florida State University in Tallahassee. Fell in love with the warmth and the general vibe of the place. I would have stayed if I could. I returned up here to the Northeast too soon."

"Why?" Theresa made a face of disgust.

"Oh, you know- let's just say it was a romantic heartbreak sort of situation. You'll understand when you're older. And you will, dear Theresa! I spoke with Brock- the doctors are saying you've been making such progress..."

"No," Theresa interrupted. "I meant- why would anyone love Tallahassee that much? I spent my entire life there-until Aunt Lucille took me up here last year for better treatment. It's the most boring..."

Aunt Lucille. As Theresa continued relaying tidbits from the 'boring' activities she took part in during her young life- Rebecca couldn't shake the name she'd just heard out of her mind. *Lucille.* Certainly, it couldn't be Lucille Phelps- wife of William Phelps- the adopted mother who had been staying in contact with her regarding how *her* Tessa was being raised, could it?

Her Tessa was a cheerleader, Lucille had relayed to Rebecca- a lithe athlete, even as a freshman in high school. *Her* Tessa was an avid horseback rider- with long, flowing brown hair in the video clips Lucille had sent her.

"Rebecca?"

"Oh, sorry," Rebecca attempted to return from her reverie and back to the curious-eyed girl before her. "I was just thinking back on a friend I had back in Florida. A woman named Lucille, just like your aunt."

"Where is she now?" Theresa asked.

"My daughter?" Rebecca asked in response.

"Your…who?" Theresa's voice quizzed. "You have a daughter?"

Shit!

"Hmm? Oh…um, Theresa," Rebecca held out an imploring finger, walking toward the door. "Could you excuse me for a moment? I have to have a word with Mr. Richardson- I'll be right back. I promise…"

"I was asking about the friend named Lucille you mentioned. But Rebecca- you have a daughter? That's so cool! I don't remember reading about it in…"

"Just a moment…" Rebecca's quivering hand had to struggle a bit with the door handle, yet she was able to step outside and into the adjacent lobby area where she knew Brock Richardson would be waiting, listening to their recorded session from his smart phone, headphones on.

She spotted him walking toward her. "Brock, I…"

"Ms. Thompson, you mentioned something about a daughter to young Theresa?" Brock's voice was stern. He was shaking his head. "I'm glad you stepped out. I was just thinking of a way to come inside, actually."

"Brock, I…I mean, Mr. Richardson. It was a slip of the tongue. I wanted to ask you, if you don't mind, the patient's aunt's full name, if I may?"

"We are not allowed…" Brock continued. "Ms. Thompson. I'm sorry- I feel we may be in need for a more thorough discussion, perhaps, of young Theresa Phelps' background-but not now. You left her in there before your hour was up. She must be feeling so confused. May I please suggest going back in there and at least rounding up the discussion with something about the writing process or…."

"Phelps?" Rebecca whispered with a crack in her voice, placing her palm across her mouth. "As in Lucille and William Phelps?"

"Rebecca...." Brock placed his arms softly on her shoulders. *He called me Rebecca again.* "My God...Did you do background research on your young reader, after all, or something? How did you know the full names of Theresa's aunt and her husband?"

"Brock..." Rebecca shook her head subtly side to side. "No. I had no idea who this reader was before today. I swear to God. And Lucille and William are the twosome who adopted my daughter from me in Florida, before I went back up to Boston to my family. I was a young woman. After a mistake...and..."

"Theresa's parents- adopted or real- are passed, as far as we know..." Brock shook his head, puzzled.

"No, no! Lucille and William are perfectly alive, and living down in Tallahassee, raising my daughter they adopted when she was a baby..."

"Rebecca...could you kindly tell me more about this daughter of yours?" Brock guided Rebecca's arm downward as they both sat in the lobby chairs. A couple of onlookers shot them dirty looks. "Really briefly and quietly, please. We could discuss this further in my office later, but I don't want to keep Theresa waiting too long..."

"It's a long story. I was too young to raise my Tessa. My parents would have absolutely disowned me had they learned I'd gotten pregnant while living away for college. It was the best I could do..."

"Tessa?" Brock asked loudly. He took a deep breath and lowered his voice. "When was your daughter born?"

"Brock...no...you can't possibly be implying..."

"When was her last birthday, dear author? Just curious? Come on! Indulge me. A parent always knows his or her kid's birthday. I sure as know my own girl's birthday! And, yes, you can bet your bottom dollar I sure as heck am asking because I know certainly when we here at the clinic all celebrated Theresa's birthday last..."

"May..." Theresa, solemn, continued for him.

"May…?" Brock glanced at Rebecca quizzically.

"May 25th!"

Brock stayed silent for an entire hour- at least that's how long around a minute or so felt like for Rebecca.

"Please say something Brock…" she managed to get out through falling tears.

Finally, he spoke. "This 'aunt' that visits Tessa; I don't believe she's been wholly honest with us. Or your daughter's adopted mother with you. I'm beginning to think they may even be the same woman. So much mystery here. About her identity, and the crash, and …heck, now I'm seeing maybe it wasn't coincidence this 'aunt' has given her your book…"

"When is *Theresa's* birthday, Mr. Richardson?" Rebecca asked, enunciating each word. "You called her Tessa just now. I'm sure it was a slip of the tongue…Right? Right?"

"May 25th…" Brock's gaze was fixated on the floor whilst he chewed on his lips. "Theresa was just the nickname she's asked us to call her by. *Tessa* Phelps was born in 2008. Sound familiar?"

"Yes," Rebecca whimpered, eyes closed. *Too familiar.* "When's this *Lucille* coming to see you next? I'd like to be here as well. I'd like to know whose pictures she's been sending me, saying they're of my daughter…"

"Can I see those pictures?" Brock asked, reaching out his hand. "Please?"

"Oh my God…," he continued, after Rebecca had given into his insistence and shown him the photos from her smartphone. "Lucille's been sending you *my* daughter's photos and videos. Mary- my ex…She shares Maddy's photos all the time on social media. I warned her! I always warned her…"

"Brock…" Rebecca interrupted. There was a matter of life and death, she'd realized- more urgent at that moment than unraveling the mystery before them. "If she's really… *my* Tessa in there. Then maybe…there's a chance for her? For that- parent donor you'd lost hope on?"

"Yes" Brock smiled through tears. He took her hands in his. "I'm beginning to see that too, now.

EARTH UP YOUR ROOTS

dependent flora
ornamental
wait for their roots
to be watered-fundamental

to be nourished by nature
if not a human caretaker

they can rot:
they're prepared
for their lot

dependent humans
need nourishment
from one another

a friend, a lover
a sister or brother

must too prepare for their fate
watering may not arrive
at an expected date

what differentiates us
from the plants
is a better ability
to earth up
our own dents

everyone mourns the dead
until they forget…

appreciate-
while alive-
the chances to refresh
you still have, yet

EARTH UP YOUR ROOTS

promises spoken
bad habits unbroken

not recognizing a king or a queen
while so used to the routine

exposing your heart
pain disguised as art

life is already rough
if you're soft while they're tough

my diamond in the rough
say 'enough is enough'

III. REAP

we cannot **BUILD**
with a small 'u' and capital 'I'
or a capital 'U' and small 'i'
as equals
love grows

EARTH UP YOUR ROOTS

you've weathered the storm
surprised to have remained warm
they worshipped tiles and sheltered their hearts
while transparent vulnerability
like glass
was *your* norm

the lightning passed and only remained the showers
your authenticity your umbrella- you didn't know your powers

uproot if you must, but replant immediately
seeds need planting and stability- don't disrespect serenity

nourish your seeds, and soon you'll grow flowers
even if the soil has pebbles, a home empowers

EARTH UP YOUR ROOTS

observe
the tree branches
like those of our lungs

one births sources of oxygen
the other utilizes to enrich lives

like the brain-shaped walnut
good for our thinker

or the eye-shaped carrot
good for our seeker

interdependence
is nature's silent reminder

without one another
living things
could neither blossom nor thunder

THE ROSE MOON

1952

WITH THE BREATHTAKING THRACIAN PLAINS growing more visible by the minute, Mehtap couldn't contain her excitement. "We're lucky, Elmas," she smiled at the young daughter seated beside her, the little hand sticky from clutching her own for over an hour now. Her daughter had just opened her eyes from a lengthy nap. "Your grandmother didn't quite have this comfort when she and her mother were expelled to Türkiye from Filibe[2]."

"When will *anneanne* return from her trip to Bursa?" Elmas inquired, rubbing her eyes- half-shut with the glare from the sunshine. "She'll be meeting up with us once we're in Istanbul, won't she?"

"You want your grandmother to tell you stories from my younger days again, don't you?" Mehtap asked with a mischievous wink. "Or better yet, her own stories…" At 45, she was told she still had looked to be at least ten years younger.

Her husband, Ali, had insisted she make the dangerous journey for the unification of their family. Originally from Sivas, he'd found work in Istanbul. "My people feel more comforted in the blend of this bigger city," he had told her, referring to his status as a minority in the Turkish lands- being a non-Sunni, Alevi Muslim man. "But no place can quite feel like home if you and Elmas cannot be with me. Besides- it seems it is not going to be much safer for you two in Bulgaria."

---

[2] The Turkish name for the city of Plovdiv in Bulgaria

The newly victorious Communist regime had been expulsing as many Muslims as it could in an effort to 'cleanse' the country, and it had only been bringing the tales her mother would tell her from her own youth more vivid in her mind. The tales of similar expulsions and forced conversions to Christianity by a country that had newly acquired its independence from the Ottoman Empire.

"Well, sure," Elmas' expression turned quizzical in an instant. "But I was just wishing she'd bring back more of those candy chestnuts."

"Why you little *kestane şekeri* yourself…" Mehtap tickled, causing both of them nearly lose their balance.

She knew she could have revealed her Christianity to the government in Bulgaria- half of her wasn't Turkish by blood, after all. She would then perhaps have been able to be spared the atrocities she'd begun to hear were being faced by the other Turks back in Bulgaria.

But Mehtap had secretly been glad to be inside Turkish borders again. Perhaps she could arrange to travel to Kars, as her mother had once taken her to as a little girl. Perhaps she could get more answers. Feel more fulfilled. And allow Elmas to meet the land and culture of her grandfather by blood.

§

1905

"*Gülay*," Ceyhun's azure eyes were sparkling in the sun. He held out his hands in a performing fashion. "*Sen güldün, ay güldü. Sen güldün, gönlümün bahçesine güller açtı. Sakın solma…*"

"Oh, Ceyhun, *ilahi*," Gülay blushed, placing her hand over her pink lips with a giggle. She gave him a small round of applause regardless. She'd grown accustomed to the neighbor boy's romantic poetry, using the 'rose' and the 'moon' references of her given name. His pushiness had always made Gülay's eyes roll toward the sky.

They were only fifteen years old. What did Ceyhun- or she, for that matter- know about love?

"I have to go, Ceyhun. I promised *anne* I'll pick up some *kashkaval*[3] for our breakfast tomorrow. But I'll see you for dinner. Mother said we accepted your mother's generous invitation- I can't wait to eat her delicious *yaprak surmise* and *börek*. Mom refuses to accept that hers just aren't as delicious!"

"Oh, we can't wait, Gülay'ım," Ceyhun smiled. "I helped mother wrap those grape leaves with my own fingers- just for you!"

"Görüşürüz"!" Gülay waved him off, walking faster toward the market. Her mother, Ayşe, had indeed sent her to the market- just not for cheese, but rather for Swiss chocolates she insisted they take as a gift to dinner.

There were two markets in town- her mother would always tell her to go to the one owned by 'Ahmet amca', although the other one had been closer to their house. The one owned by a man named 'Hrant' she'd known to be of Armenian origin- mostly from his last name ending with '-yan'. That, and also from the way her mother and their neighbors would always warn her against visiting it, of course.

"What do we have against Armenians, mother?" she'd ask.

"Nothing, my love," Ayşe would answer her. "My favorite jewelry lady is an *Ermeni*, as you know, as is my hairdresser- Anoush. It's not us that has something against them- it's the other way around nowadays!"

"What do you mean?" Gülay had pressed her mother one time when they'd been having tea with Ceyhun and his mother, Sevil. Both of their fathers hadn't been around much, and this had bonded both the children as well as their mothers.

For the life of her, Gülay simply couldn't comprehend why residents of the same region- who'd been getting along well together for as long as she knew- would suddenly not like each other.

"Ever since the Russian uprisings began earlier this year,

---

[3] a yellow cheese common in Balkan communities

hear there has been fighting between Armenians and Tatars over there…"

"So? We're not Tatars, mother," Gülay had shrugged.

"No, but Tatars are of Turkic origin," Ayşe had continued. "And some Armenians have begun to gossip that the Sultan may have been in support of them in Russia too…Mostly Russian-backed gossip, of course."

"That's absurd, *anne*," Gülay had rolled her eyes. "Who cares what some sultan did or thought? *Ermeniler* are our friends and neighbors here. We are all a part of the same empire…"

"A crumbling empire," Sevil had interjected, cutting her *dolma* dish as Ceyhun had returned her smile. "You'd be surprised at the paranoid things people would do and think as loss of power lingers nearer and nearer as a possibility."

Ever since he was a little boy, Ceyhun had been by his mother's side like a little pet. How Gülay had thought it childlike. And to think? Her friend Arzu had suggested he'd wanted to marry her!

The thought made Gülay shake her head- her flowing russet waves appearing almost golden in the glistening, August sunlight. She returned to the present moment, and decided to try to see what the big deal would be if she had decided to go to Hrant amca's bakkal, after all?

§

"*Kimse yok muuuu….?*" Gülay dragged out the end of her question whether or not anyone was there, pushing the creaky wooden door further in.

The market appeared empty of any human inhabitants, yet the plethora of fresh fruits and vegetables in crates were inviting to Gülay. *My mom has got to shop here more,* she thought.

The produce in this novel market smelled better than the weekly street *pazar*[4] they'd often stock up at.

The lights were turned on, and Gülay thought she heard someone or something lurking about in another room behind a door adjacent to the main wooden counter. "Hello? I-um- was just looking for some chocolates, if you have…"

"Only the best ones!" the voice of a young boy around her age- smiling confidently despite his rather disheveled, uncut hair- took Gülay by a surprise. He closed the door behind him. "My father is at church. Sorry- I didn't hear you come in. Chocolates, you said?"

"Oh, alright," Gülay stammered, feeling heat on her cheeks after realizing the boy's eyes were fixated on her. She diverted her gaze to the apples situated before her. "No problem. Um- yes- those famed chocolates from Switzerland. Good ones. If you have. Which you said you did. So, yes. Special ones for guests. I love chocolates, don't you?"

Gülay focused on the boy's eyes again, noting his lingering smile despite his silence. What a fool she was! To ramble on about chocolates like that.

"You can have an *okka* for 50 *kurus*[5]…"

"Alright, thank you," Gülay managed to state, eyeing the boy's lean yet sturdy, tanned arms scoop some to wrap for her. Something from his upper arm- peeking underneath his gray top caught Gülay's eye as she placed the coins on the counter. A drawing of some sort?

"What's that?" she asked, intrigued beyond herself.

"What's what?" the boy asked, handing her the packet of sweets. His eyes followed where Gülay's had been focused. "Oh, my *dajvatsk.*"

"Your what?" Gülay raised her brow.

"My tattoo," the boy smiled, rolling his sleeve further up to reveal the outline of a full rose. "You like it?"

---

[4] Outdoor bazaar

[5] Measuring units- for weight and currency, respectively

"I do," Gülay smiled. "I like flowers. My own name means a flower. Well, partly. Gül-as a matter of fact. What a coincidence- right? It means a rose…" *I am an idiot.* She just wanted to run home and throw herself on her bed in embarrassment.

"Gül? Is that your name? My name's Tigran," the boy reached out his hand.

His smile simultaneously managed to excite her and yet calm her nerves at the same time. "Gülay," she shook his hand. "Nice to meet you."

"Gülay…Gülay…" Tigran scratched his chin. "Not necessarily your name- but your face. Why do you look so familiar to me for some reason?"

"Well, we are seemingly neighbors," Gülay shrugged. "And my mother has been supporting my studies. I go to *Istanbul Kız Lisesi.* It doesn't allow boys, of course, but perhaps you've seen me around there?"

"You mean- glimpsing you, perhaps- while I was sneaking around there to check out girls or something?" Tigran let out a hearty laugh. "Armenian boy must be doing so to corrupt nice Muslim girls, is that it?"

"Wait- what!?" Gülay placed her arms on her hips. "I said no such thing! I just meant… I don't- you know- go around anywhere else much except school. And you appear around fifteen years old like me…"

"Or is it that I must not be getting an education in secondary school myself, being an outcast with my tattoo and all. Is that it?" To Gülay's joy, Tigran's face appeared to be teasing her only.

"No, I didn't think that at all," Gülay raised her chin in defiance. "You actually sound quite well-spoken- with the intelligence of a fox, in fact, with these things you're throwing at me here, Tigran."

Tigran. Why had simply saying his name aloud rushed a flow of blood to her nether region all of a sudden?

"Well, I am fifteen, but, in any case- no, I don't believe I could have seen you anywhere else except today…" Tigran shrugged, his smile still on his face. "We just moved here from Kars…My mother and I, I mean. My father has had this market established for three years now, as you must know. You come here often?"

"Oh, yeah," Gülay fibbed. "All the time. Best vegetables in town!"

"Hmm, yet you weren't too sure about our chocolates, huh?" Tigran smirked.

"Well, I just never had the occasion to require chocolates," Gülay began, hands flying in the air in a multitude of directions. "I mean, my mother and I go often to visit *Sevil teyze* where Ceyhun and I often try to play chess. But you know. We don't really get her chocolates or anything. Usually, my mother cooks something to take over there, but she's been tired lately, and…"

"I get it. You and this Ceyhun kid must have some special friendship," Tigran moved his eyebrows up and down.

"No, no! He's like a brother! Trust me!"

"I trust you…" Tigran winked.

"So, thank you for the chocolates," Gülay managed to get out after a deep breath. "Welcome to Istanbul. I hope to see you and *Hrant amca* around here again soon. You said he's your father, right?"

"Yes. And Where's your father, Gülay?"

"He, umm, is in the military. He doesn't live with us…"

"Oh, yeah?" Tigran's voice turned serious. "My aunt back in Kars recently wrote that several local Turkish fathers have gone to Tblisi to join the Tatars."

"What? That's absurd!" Gülay yelled. "How could you believe such lies without any knowledge? Through just gossip?"

"You said he's a military man, didn't you?" Tigran continued in a steady, calm voice. "It'd figure he'd fight to support other Muslims instead of our side…how else do you explain his absence? And just why are you getting so defensive?"

"He left us for another woman!" Gülay blurted, sprouting tears. "Okay? Happy? Satisfied? Not for some stupid war! Not in anything against any of your people. Nothing but a man leaving his wife- and daughter, too- to go live with someone else in more comfort! Alright?"

"Gülay, I'm so sorry…" Tigran inched closer to her, shaking his lengthy black hair strands off of his face. "I really didn't mean to bring up such a sad topic."

"My mother was right…" Gülay muttered under her breath, unable to meet Tigran's eyes.

"About what!?" Tigran raised his voice.

"I shouldn't have come to this market!"

"Oh, because we're Armenian?"

"No, because you don't like *us*! How did I just meet you and you managed to make me cry, already?"

"Maybe we simply affected each other…" Tigran's voice said, even softer now.

"I have to go…" Gülay inched closer to the wooden door.

"Gülay, don't go, wait up…come back into the store. My dad makes good tea. It's fresh."

"No…"

"You don't drink tea?" Tigran raised his brow.

"Not much."

"How am I more Turkish than you?" Tigran snickered. "All you Turks are supposed to love your little tea in the little glass cups, aren't you?"

"For your information, I prefer fruit juice," Gülay crossed her arms, wiping her tears. "Freshly squeezed. Besides, tea and coffee are more for adults," she tossed back her long hair. "But then again, I'm talking to a young boy with a tattoo! Like an adult! An actual tattoo! How did your father allow for this?"

"Psst...he didn't," Tigran winked. "It's not exactly sinful or anything, like I know it is for you Muslims. But he still doesn't approve. So, I had to get it secretly. This woman friend I had…French…very professional. Always helped me with novel…experiences."

The look on his face had Gülay discern his implication at once. "Yuck! Gross. You had sex with a prostitute, didn't you?"

"It is a custom...all young men do it. And I *am* a young man, Gülay. Not some virgin boy. Like your Ceyhun, I imagine." He added with a smirk.

"Leave Ceyhun out of this," Gülay placed her hands on her hips. "We're all in the same grade! I'm leaving… I guess I'll see you around soon."

"You're welcome to stop by our store any time," Tigran placed his hand in his pockets. "For chocolates….or just for someone to have fun with to fight. But, hey- *all is fair in love and war.*"

Gülay crossed her arms. "Hmph! What did you do- read Shakespeare, or something?"

"That is a sixteenth century poet named John Lyly, Turkish girl," Tigran snickered. "As I was saying- *do* stop by again. It really looks like I can teach you a thing or two, now. We can even read together…"

"You…tattoo boy… *read*?"

"I can read you." With his hazel eyes locking themselves on her own amber ones- a minute longer than Gülay would otherwise have been uncomfortable with from anyone else. She found herself unable to leave.

"Oh yeah? And what do you read?" she asked.

"Our life story…I don't need to see your palm like the gypsies on the street," Tigran leaned closer to her face, placing one hand on the door behind her. "We are going to become very good friends. Very close, in fact. Friends with love. You will see."

"I'm …going home. It was nice to meet you, Tigran."

"Enjoy the chocolates, Turkish rose," he winked.

Who does he think he is? Gülay's mind was racing as she ran toward her home. What did Tigran know about love? A voice inside her said he'd probably know much more than Ceyhun.

Gülay snickered but stopped in her tracks soon afterward. The part that had begun to scare Gülay was the subsequent thought in her mind, as she inched closer to her house to accompany her mother for dinner at Ceyhun's house.

The thought that her whole being- her titillated mind, palpating heart as well as the throbbing wetness that had surprised her in his presence- was telling her; she *wanted* him to teach her love. The joy, the pain- all its forms.

Gülay could not wait to purchase chocolates from Hrant's market again.

§

1915

"Are you ready boy?"

"Yes, let's go uncle," Tigran replied. He looked around the trenches.

"The uprising will not be in vain…" his uncle continued, fixing his gun firmer on his belt. "The Russians are right. We deserve our own land here in this portion of the empire too. *Ararat* mountain belongs to our people! The Turks love claiming everything as their own."

"Yeah," Tigran smirked. *Like Ceyhun.* The man who'd married the only girl he ever loved. His Turkish rose- his Gülay.

How giddy they'd been for those precious two years, sneaking out of their homes to meet…making love at any opportunity they could. Until that fated day, behind the train tracks- when her mother caught her, and forbid them from seeing each other. And that Ceyhun had married her for her 'honor'.

Himarut'yun![6] Tigran had known the real reason. It was for her to get over him and marry a Muslim man instead. Over a decade

---

[6] An expletive in Armenian

had passed, and he could still smell her hair- sweeter than the flower after which she was named.

§

1952

"*Anneanne,* you're back from Bursa," Elmas smiled at her grandmother.

"I know why you're really kissing me, *minik kuş,*" Gülay chirped. "Mehtap, you really have to cut this girl's hair. It's growing so thin- you have to let it grow thicker…"

"Mother! Please leave me be! I am a grown woman, and can decide for my own daughter, thank you very much!"

"Alright…" Gülay shook her head with a smile at her daughter. She tied the ends of her headscarf tighter underneath her chin. "Speaking of a woman making her own decisions…there's something I'd like to announce to you, my girls. After Ceyhun's death, you are the only two people I have left in this whole world… And I do hope you can visit. But… I have decided to move out East. I will live out the rest of my remaining days in Kars!"

"Kars?" As little Elmas asked her mother where her grandmother would be going, Gülay closed her eyes and smiled at the memory. That day on the trenches in Kars, where she'd insisted to Ceyhun she'd wanted to teach English.

"Our life story…" She could still hear the sound of his teenaged voice when she'd first met him at his father's market, nearly 50 years ago. Tigran had told her he could 'read' their story. He'd referred to them being as one- coupled up- though they had just met. Had he had powers to foresee the future?

Her mother, Ayşe, would smirk at such things, chastising her for saying such things were not *caiz*[7].

---

[7] Permissible according to Quranic law

If he had indeed seen their future- would he have done it all over again? Or would he have left the Turkish girl who'd entered his family market that summer alone, instead?

A single tear dropped on her cheek, and her granddaughter, Elmas, looked at her with sympathy. She yanked her mother's arm for attention, as they both looked back at Gülay. Mehtap did indeed catch her mother's eye and asked if she was alright.

Gülay smiled and nodded, but in her heart- she knew Mehtap had sensed what she'd been thinking. She was long told the identity of her father. Gülay had had many regrets- but loving Tigran and carrying his child as a fruit of their love had never been one of them. The child that would have certainly had her on the streets had her friend Ceyhun not sacrificed his own conservative ideals in a woman for his love- and married her immediately after finding out about her condition. He'd been gracious to pass Mehtap off to their families and circle as their own, following a swift marriage ceremony.

1915. That year of her Kars visit. Ceyhun had called her 'crazy' to do so, but she'd insisted it was even more noble to educate the children in such a volatile region. She'd witnessed his body dying. It'd been years since they had seen each other- yet there they were. It'd been fated for them to be together at least in death, Gülay knew.

A crescent moon had now been tattooed next to the rose- she stroked it as he'd recognized her and rolled up his sleeve. She'd given the tattoo a kiss, right before doing so on his dying lips as well. He had reached his hand across her face and whispered her name whilst she'd stroked his tattoo- now of her full name.

"We're yours, Tigran..." she'd whispered. "Mehtap and I...Always yours."

Tigran had nodded, closing his eyes with a satisfied smile as he took his last breath, his head falling back on her hand while Gülay laid it gently onto the blood-streaked ground.

Ω

THE DRIVER

MARCO RAMIREZ SQUINTED TO SEE through the foggy window, the rain pounding the glass stronger than his heartbeat did so through his chest. "Oh man, I've gotta get these slow-ass wipers fixed before they remove my Lyft eligibility."

He eyed the alert on his phone from the corner of his eye, signaling to switch to the right lane. 'Delilah'. Two miles down.

"Damn…" he muttered aloud. The customer had chosen the more expensive ride option rather than waiting a bit longer. "This lady must be in a hurry."

Whatever. Marco needed the money. The summer camp his wife had had her eye on for their son came at a hefty price- just for three lousy weeks of painting and dancing. Something about steeper prices due to less kids being allowed. *Damn coronavirus restrictions.*

He halted the car upon spotting a rather plump woman with an attractive face framed by rain-soaked black hair pulled up in a bun. She was holding the hands of a little boy around his Peter's age. She had on a yellow coat that was easy to spot.

"Good evening, ma'am. How are…"

"Please, just drive," her voice interrupted him in a panic-loud, even from behind her pale blue mask. "Scooch over, come on!"

Marco noticed the boy's slumped shoulders and sullen, brown face. He didn't protest as he wriggled his body toward the corner of the seat. "Okay ma'am, just tell the boy to keep his mask on, please. It's the company rules…"

"We left very fast...no mask..." the woman's voice was stern. "Can't you see he's been crying? Because of my husband...just please, let's go already!"

"Oh, okay," Marco saw through the window reflection just then that this 'Delilah' lady had something red on her cheeks. Lipstick she had put on haphazardly, perhaps? *No. Blood!*

Oh, shit! Marco thought. Had her husband beaten her or something? "Ma'am, are you alright?"

"I'm trying to be, thank you," she replied with a sigh, adding quickly in exasperation. "Please, just drive...We need to get away, now..."

Mami! Ay Dios mio! No, papi, por favor, détente! The image of his drunken father slapping his mother before his six-year-old self flashed through Marco's mind just then.

A loud car speeded by, allowing him to reconnect to the present. "Idiot! Speeding through the rain like that! Sorry, Ma'am. Please excuse my language."

"That's alright. Some people don't care about endangering others..."

Marco noted the woman was staring out the window. "Would you like me to take you somewhere...special? You know, where workers can help victims in your position...?"

"What do you know of my position?" she barked.

"Sorry," Marco held out a hand to the mirror so that the passenger behind him could see, the other still on the steering wheel. "You're right, you're right. I just want you to know you have options, and that, you know- you and the boy can be safe."

"The address we're heading to is the one place he'll never dare go to find us," Delilah's voice stated, calmer now despite the smirk on her face. "Believe me."

"Alright, ma'am, we're almost there." Marco glimpsed his phone- mere minutes were indeed left of the ride. A distinct text message tone alerted his attention back to his phone from the road. He caught snippets of the notification as he drove.

EARTH UP YOUR ROOTS

Child abduction. East Hills Police.
Victim: Pedro Ramirez, 12 years old, 5 ft, short black hair, last seen wearing a Knicks jacket
Suspect: Delilah Gomez, 34, 5 feet 5 inches, 160 lbs., long black hair, last seen wearing a yellow jacket and matching rain boots

Marco's hands began to tremble as he cleared his throat, whistling a tune as the notification disappeared. *Mierde.*

"Are they expecting flooding?" the woman asked him. He met her intense gaze from the mirror. "Sounded like a weather emergency alert."

Marco took in a deep breath, glancing at the boy's shiny navy-blue jacket, with orange block-letter writing that read 'New York'. He wasn't much of a basketball man, but he had a pretty good feeling that had been the logo and coloring for the Knicks. "Nah, I doubt it, ma'am," he responded as calmly as he could. "They always exaggerate in 'em weather alerts, you know what I'm saying?"

"You saw the message, didn't you- *Marco*?" Something about the way she pronounced his name shook Marco to his very core. And just how could she have known his name? *Oh, right- Lyft displays our names and car information.*

"What do you mean?" he managed.

"I'm not stupid, Driver. Shit! I can't believe the bastard survived to fucking issue an alert…"

"He's alive!" the boy spoke excitedly and for the first time. He wiped the silent tears that had drenched his face.

"You shut your mouth!" the woman warned him in a quiet but stern voice, placing a finger on her lips.

Survived? Had this woman been the one to try to hurt that man? His mind raced to his Uncle Juan and his crazy wife, Maria; Marco knew violence didn't only pertain to male perpetrators.

"Are you driving to Exit 37 or not?" Delilah stormed, interrupting his ponderings. "I paid for your services, you're obliged to take me to Roslyn…" Delilah flashed what looked to be the corner of a large kitchen knife from the corner of her handbag, holding it high toward her chest in a way that was visible to Marco.

Crazy bitch!

"Oh, of course, of course, ma'am," Marco knew he had to play smart if he wanted to survive another day to hug his son and wife again. "I…I was just worried about the crying boy you've got there with you. Other than that- yeah, I received the message, but it's none of my business. We never know what goes in a private domestic situation. It's just my job to drive. Please, relax…relax…It's okay…"

"I suppose you're going to tell me to trust you or something now, aren't you?" Delilah quipped, adding a little laugh. "I can never trust a man. I did once- and look where it's gotten me. On the run from the cops, accused of kidnapping my own son- by a man whom I had to fight off in self-defense…Of course, he has to go and twist it against me. Trust a man…Bah!"

"Self-defense," Marco nodded rapidly. He looked at his phone again- one minute was left. *Thank God.* "Yes, of course, I understand."

He took another glance at the boy. His face was now looking to him like a physical mixture between his son Peter's as well as Marco's own younger self.

Papi, no!

Could Delilah have been telling the truth? Could she really have been a victim of domestic violence who simply had to fight back in order to protect the life of both herself and her boy?

Gomez. The woman did have a different last name than Pedro. Then again, he knew women had not always taken their husband's last names- if they were even married at all, that is, which this woman had earlier implied she was.

Marco saw that Pedro was eyeing him curiously- not shying away when he caught it in the mirror. This woman wasn't particularly very warm with him either. Criminal or not, he was hoping Delilah would be a satisfied-enough customer to leave him alone once he drove away from their destination. That knife in her bag certainly wasn't the last image he wanted to see before closing his eyes to this world.

Nothing was making sense to Marco anymore as he pulled up to a one-story, white-brick private house very close to the exit. A small, rather run-down front lawn displayed a couple of gnomes, and little else. Something about the place looked familiar to him, but Marco couldn't quite put his fingers on it.

"Goodnight, ma'am," Marco feigned a smile, turning genuine when he looked at Pedro getting out of the car. "Stay safe, Pedro." The boy smiled.

Was it foolish of him to use the child's name that he'd read from the alert? *Oh, what the hell.* Delilah had already known about Marco's newly acquired knowledge.

As an elderly woman treaded toward them from the front door of the house, Delilah didn't utter a word. She shut the door behind her.

Marco clicked the locks and was just about to speed away when he heard *her* voice. That all-too-familiar, warm, high-pitched voice, coming from the elderly lady whose face was becoming clearer now as day as she came out of the shadows of the evening, and closer to the streetlight to welcome Delilah and Pedro.

Marco opened his door at once, and got his body outside.

"Mami?" Tears rolled down his cheeks as a million thoughts sped through his mind at once. The knife! Was his mother in danger?

Hugging? What was his mother- whom he'd known to be in her Florida home- doing in Long Island? Embracing these people- one of whom was just listed as a kidnapping suspect on an Amber alert, for Christ's sake?

"Ma!" He turned off the ignition and got out of the car fully this time. Finally, the woman's ears heard him.

"Mi hijo!" his mother put a hand around her mouth, the other still around Pedro. Delilah turned to shoot Marco a confused glare. *"Mi guapo hijo!* You guys have met?"

"Met?" Marco walked toward them slowly. "How do you

know these two, *mami*? And what are you doing up here in New York? You didn't tell us anything!"

"Your aunt Rosa is inside, mi Marco," his mother said, ushering him closer into a hug. "Come here. Come inside. All of you. Before anyone sees."

"Aunt Rosa?" Marco took another look at the house again, his thoughts now traveling to a different time. The faded, decorative marble gnomes caught his attention again- a male and a female one in an embrace. *Si, no estoy loco!* He hadn't imagined it at all- he really *had* been at this house before. A long time ago, as a little boy, holding his mama's hand.

"*Si, mi hijo*," Isabella answered her son, caressing his cheek while glancing between him and Pedro.

She turned to meet eyes with Delilah, who returned her smile. "I see it too, yeah. There is a little resemblance, isn't there? Wow! Oh, man! I had no idea our driver Marco could be…*the* Marco…"

"I knew it!" Pedro exclaimed, releasing laughter as they all had entered inside. The laughter sounded to Marco like it'd long been held back. "I knew he looked familiar when I saw him in the car, mom! I recognized him from his picture!"

"Si, *mi amor*," Isabella chuckled. "You and your mom had a blessing today from the hand of God- meeting my Marco. Take a seat. Aunt Rosa will be out of the shower any minute now- you poor things can wash up after she's out. In the meantime, you can wash your faces in the small bathroom we've got here downstairs…Oh, what has that *monstruo* done again…"

"*Mami*, I don't remember an Aunt Rosa?" Marco whispered, watching Delilah and Pedro be ushered toward the guest bathroom around the corner. He crossed his arms across his chest, watching as his mother returned to join him on the living room couch. Marco managed to take a look around; modern art and furniture decorated a theme of black/white/red around the space. This 'Aunt Rosa' had pretty good taste.

"Could you please finally tell me why you're here? Why any of us are here? How do you know Delilah and Pedro? And you called her husband 'monster'- do you know him or something? What in Heaven's name is going on?"

Isabella caressed his arm, her expression turning serious for the first time that evening since Marco had spotted her.

"Rosa is my cousin, *mi hijo*," she started with a sigh. "Not really your aunt, as you already know my sisters back in Colombia. We haven't kept in touch much, but you did meet her once as a young boy. She's done good for herself here, and I knew Delilah and Pedro could count on her assistance with your monster of a father. Just as you and I had done once, when we arrived here. Desperate. With no one else to really turn to in New York…"

"My…father?" Marco inquired.

"Well, yes, Marco," Isabella patted his arm playfully. "Don't you remember what he'd do to me? Surely you were old enough…"

"I meant, mom- what does my father have to do with Delilah and Pedro? Didn't he get deported back home?"

"That's what I told you, to keep your fears at bay, *mi hijo*," Isabella explained. "But, no, unfortunately not. Though that bastard should have long been arrested and deported- at the very least- if not downright have dropped dead…he's been around. Securing little jobs here and there. Marrying Delilah- his tax accountant- after me. Rosa said I was crazy, at first, to help her. But she was no mistress. Esteban and I were long *finito* when she entered the picture."

"Delilah…married my father? And Pedro? He's…?" Marco could not brave the words to come out of his mouth. Not quite yet.

"…Is your half-brother," Isabella nodded, right as the twosome started walking back toward the living room.

"Hola!" Pedro waved with a sheepish smile. Marco smiled at him, giving him a fist pump. He turned to face Delilah. "Ma'am…um…my bad. Delilah- how long has my father been hurting you? What did you do?"

"Too long!" Isabella cut in before Delilah could say

anything. "That *monstruo* has been allowed to inflict his venom for too long! I'm so glad Delilah found my information and contacted me. She's going to get revenge for all of us, Marco-all of us!"

"By…murder?" Marco began to shake his head.

"Marco, I understand you," Pedro said. "I didn't want Papi to die, either. I'd rather he rot in jail!"

"Pedro, maybe you should head upstairs, and let the adults talk about this…" Delilah said.

"Mom, I want *him* to rot in jail, *not* you!" Pedro stood up and stormed toward the kitchen.

"Baby…" Delilah began, but Isabella got up to head toward the kitchen behind Pedro.

"I'll calm him down," she said calmly. "You two- talk."

To Marco's surprise, the woman who'd appeared to be tough as a rock until that point began to weep like a baby before him.

"My Pedro is right," Delilah began to shiver. "He's issued an alert against me- but the knife really got to his artery! Or at least, I thought so! I don't understand how he could have survived! They're going to come after me now. I don't want to go to jail! Esteban had already made my life worse- so I don't care about serving time- but I can't stand to do that to Pedro! Your mother and I had had the perfect plan… it was going to look like a kitchen accident. We were all going to restart our lives here. Rosa lives alone, and she was so nice to offer to help us. Just like she once helped you and your *mami*. Esteban hates her. I…"

"No one will be going to jail, Delilah," Marco gently placed his hands on her shoulders. "You hear me? No one except maybe my father, at least. If he survives. I'll give my testimony, too. I'm familiar with criminal law. I was going to be a cop; you know? But my wife said it'd be too dangerous, so I took up other jobs. But I know enough to know that self-defense is real. You've got nothing to worry about, Delilah. I got you."

"Thank you," Delilah mouthed.

EARTH UP YOUR ROOTS

there once were two villagers
who, upon herding their sheep
and harvesting the crops
would look up at the sky every night
and dream of traveling the world
accomplishing 'worldly feats'
viewing their simple lots as defeats

one night
when the stars were huddled together
seemingly in close proximity
to both one another
as well as to the earth,
the villagers asked:
'What must we do?
to make it out of this scene, accomplish something beyond the routine?'

they reaped from the earth only what was meant to be reaped and no further
didn't harm it beyond necessity
in an attempt to accumulate, or explore their services, taken for granted
provided nutrients for so many
urbanites going about their business, never making time
to look at their lives among nature in all their busyness

yet they've catalyzed the seeds
they- the villagers- as the enabling roots of
urbanites' deeds

EARTH UP YOUR ROOTS

as poets,
we love beauty
not the physical one of a person or a flower
as anyone would naturally love those things
but the lesser appreciated-
beauty of the miracle called life
beauty of sorrow
beauty of frustration
beauty of pushing our art
like a miraculous baby after strenuous labor

there's obvious beauty in success
but a lesser obvious one in failure
in the humility when you lose
in acceptance when you come up short

your empathy increases with your fellow sisters and brothers of the
earth

beauty of aging
beauty of having experienced life
beauty of gratitude
for even having a hand to record your contributions with
beauty of being given a body to inhabit
to experience all the miracles on this planet before our transcendence
into the next realm
beauty of ignorance before life's meaning and plan
the beauty of surrender
we're beautiful
when we're in this together

IV. MAINTAIN

to be called ungrateful
for being given everything
but the simple things you actually need...
is the worst kind of mental torture

EARTH UP YOUR ROOTS

we tend to reflect back on our teenage fights
with ridicule

backstabbed lives…
lover stolen
words like knives…
hearts left broken

yet at least they'd made sense
now you can become devalued
for no apparent reason

grown teens trading gold for mere cents
unanswered texts feeling like treason

yearning for the grievances
of the teenage years:

more logic behind the shed tears
less of the silent, intimidated fears

EARTH UP YOUR ROOTS

beauty can blossom
as fast as seasonably wither
a tree can sprout and scatter greens
just as rapidly as it can become jaundiced
and diminish into smithereens

empty twigs like arms can embrace with florals
suddenly blocking your cross-street view…
"Had those fences been there, and of that hue?"

duality exists…not only in quality
dark…light….'I won't'… 'I might'
but rather a process: set, until you intervene
creating your destiny

the rose in bloom only *whispers* for attention
as does the wind, splendid in its zephyr,
into your ear
things, in May, you may or may not want to hear

the grass awaits for you to lay
for a terrestrially-cooled nap
making a king-sized bed feel like hay

oh, to be in the moment…
have we ever seen such a magnificent film,
playing before our eyes daily…?
if we can drop self-imposed duties
and heed to nature embracing us gently…

EARTH UP YOUR ROOTS

ORDINARY

IT WAS AN ORDINARY DAY LIKE ANY OTHER during a New York October: unseasonably cold with the winds, and unseasonably warm under the sun. The heavy rains of autumn had not yet begun, and Janice for one was feeling glad that Monday morning.

"I hope he notices my blown-out hair before any winds ruin it," she thought, observing her straightened, chocolate-brown long hair in her locker mirror. It had merely been a week since she had turned 14 years old, yet Janice had been feeling like she was much older for about a decade now.

Ever since her father had left her and her mother to fend for themselves in a run-down, one-bedroom apartment in Queens when she had just been a preschooler, she'd had to overhear more adult conversations than she could fully understand. For the past year or so, however- things had taken a turn for the worse, ever since her mother found out that he'd remarried a woman with a son from another man.

Suzan, her panicky mother, would constantly be on the phone with either her sister- Aunt Louise- or her lawyer friend, Jack. "Find out how much he is spending on that woman and her boy, now," Suzan would suggest, often mistaking Jack for a private detective. "He'd better not be neglecting both his child support *and* spousal support in order to accommodate for someone else's bastard child! And find out if his company really *is* in trouble this quarter as he claims…"

Janice never understood why Jack would allow himself to be subjected to such extra labor, and for such a small legal fee at that. As everyone knew- lawyers were supposed to be money-hungry folks, weren't they? *He must have had a crush on my poor mother ever since they used to work together*, she'd secretly suspected. *Why else?*

Men were interested in only one thing, her mother would continuously warn her- especially as she had just entered high school that previous month. *Whatever,* Janice thought, her heart beating faster the minute she heard Scott's infectious laughter as he rounded the corner. He was joking about something with one of his football teammates. She shut her locker door and cleared her throat as Scott approached. "Hey Janice, how's it going?"

"Hey Scott, can't complain actually…" Janice stammered, flipping her hair over her left shoulder. "And you? This weather has been so weird, hasn't it?"

"Hey, yeah, I've got to go…Sorry…I'll see you tomorrow in Chem," Scott said as he hurried down the corridor to catch up with his friend.

His friend, Janice thought to herself, with an exasperated sigh. *That's all I'll probably ever be as well. His Chemistry partner in class…while he remains the quarterback of my dreams.*

§

"Mom, this is absolutely delicious," Janice exclaimed over dinner later that evening. "This is a different sauce you've used on these chicken cutlets. Do I taste oregano? Basil?"

"It's just a bunch of spices thrown together over some extra olive oil drizzle, honey," Suzan stated with an expressionless face. She'd already cleaned off her plate and was just accompanying her daughter at the table as she ate. "I just wanted to liven it up. I'm glad you like it."

"…Okay. Mom? Mom!" Janice didn't like the subtle sadness she heard in her mother's voice. "Are you okay?"

"Oh, I'm fine," Suzan started, grabbing a slice of toasted bread from the basket in the middle of the table. "It's nothing…just that Jack was supposed to stop by for dinner tonight, too, and, well, I haven't heard from him yet…"

"Oh, I see" Janice started to feel her blood begin to boil. "So, this atypical, non-bland chicken was for Jack, apparently, and not me. Cool."

"Don't start, Janice," Suzan warned, nibbling nervously on her slice. "You know he's got his report on your father ready and was just supposed to come over to discuss it, but…"

"Speaking of the devil…" Janice mocked, peering at her mother's cell phone after a text message made a sound.

"Yes- your father definitely *is that* for putting us through this…" Suzan started, picking up her phone with excitement.

"I meant Jack, mom" Janice said, rolling her eyes. "Mr. Lawyer-of-the-year has some excuse for being late, apparently."

"Stuck in traffic…I'm on my way. My apologies…" Suzan read with a smile.

"Joy," Janice said. "I'll be in my room while you two discuss how *devilish* my father apparently is."

"Don't you take that tone with me, young lady," Suzan started. "Do you really want to see your mother continue to struggle while your father is frolicking with some woman, and…?"

"They're *married*, mom!" Janice exclaimed. "And, yes, of course I'm not exactly thrilled he left us…and I appreciate your two part-time jobs, trying to make ends meet. I mean, hey, I'm going to start babysitting soon. But dad does *still* care. I mean he got me my laptop for my birthday…"

"Clever, honey," Suzan started, standing up to pace back and forth around the kitchen. "That's what that man is. For *buying* your acceptance and affections!"

"Looks like our savior is here," Janice mocked as she heard the 'ding dong' of the doorbell.

"Shh, not another negative word from you," Suzan warned with a whisper. "Please. We need him to extract extra financial support from your father, you know this…"

Janice pretended to zip her lips, rolling her eyes once again toward the ceiling.

§

"Mr. Stevens…you really didn't have to…" Janice started to say later over coffee in the living room.

"*Jack*. I insist, Janice, please call me by my first name," the lawyer said with a smile, as he fixed his designer-brand glasses on his angular face.

"Ok…Jack," Janice continued. "I mean, I've forgotten about my birthday already….And, this smart phone…It's the latest model! It's really too much, I can't accept this…"

"You've raised a really humble teenager, right here, Suzan," Jack smiled, turning next to him to face Suzan- who was grinning from ear to ear.

"She's one of a kind, my Janice. But, she's right. This is awfully too sweet of you…You've already been so kind, and…"

"Nonsense," Jack insisted. "Ladies, ladies…believe me…you both deserve nothing but the best. After everything you've had to go through as mother and daughter…"

"Would you like another cup?" Suzan asked, pointing at the coffee machine.

"No, thank you," Jack interrupted this time. "Please, just, sit down…"

Suzan did as she'd been told, exchanging an equally nervous and silent look with her daughter.

"To start off with the good news," Jack began, taking out a printed photograph from the backpack which he had placed next to his feet, "Here, you can see Bob and Laura leaving an IKEA, holding hands…"

"Just wonderful," Suzan mocked.

"*IKEA*, Suzan," Jack retorted, pulling out another computer-scan of a different, close-up photo now. "Not buying some fancy, expensive furniture like you had been imagining. And- if you look closely at Laura's ring finger here in this photo- you can tell that she's wearing a simple wedding band, nothing too..."

"Ok, ok, I get it, Jack, thank you...." Suzan was shaking her head and covering her eyes with her left palm now. "I know you must mean well- but honestly seeing them isn't helping..."

"Suzan, look," Jack started with a sigh. "You asked me to ensure he wasn't spending more money on them while refusing to increase his child and spousal support for you and Janice. Not, may I remind you, to appease your apparent jealousy over their relationship!"

"You... You've misunderstood," Suzan exclaimed, clearing her throat. "Of course, I'm grateful for the truth. And I could care less about
what Bob feels anymore...It's just..."

"...What I believe my mom is trying to say, Jack, is *thank you*," Janice cut in, sarcasm audible in her monotone voice. "I've been telling her- it's all in her head..."

"Janice, that's enough..." Suzan started with an angry tone.

"Let her speak, Suzan," Jack stated. "She's not a child anymore- listen to your daughter...Go ahead, Janice."

"Um, thank you," Janice continued. "I mean, I actually met up with my dad for my birthday recently, and we had a long and honest discussion. He is working extra hard to provide for everyone. He seemed happier than I'd ever seen him..."

"Thank *you*, Janice," Suzan said in a softer, exasperated voice. "You've embarrassed me in front of Jack. And thanks for sympathizing with your father's *holy* search for happiness, while I'm..."

"Mom, please stop needlessly victimizing yourself," Janice stood up to sit next to her mother on the opposite end of the couch, placing her hand on her shoulder. "I love you...and I want nothing but for you to move on with your life and find happiness, as well..."

"I'm...embarrassed...," Suzan said with a smile now.

"Ok, Jack, please tell us the bad news, I suppose, before we take any more of your time tonight."

"No worries," Jack said with a smile. "Well, the only bad news, I suppose, is- yes, like Janice has learned…I found out further details about his extra hours, actually. Bob has been doing some extra research apparently on the computer- the details of which I couldn't get yet. But- here's the catch- he's definitely working on it with Laura. I've seen them going over details at various coffee shops. They may have been able to land some well-paying side project, for all we know…"

"This is it?" Janice mocked, after observing her mom's silent, acceptant nodding. "Mom- this is pure speculation and guessing…"

"I really don't know what to say…" Suzan started, putting both of her hands in the air.

"…Mom," Janice cut in, taking a peek at a text message that had just arrived on her old cell phone. "Clara is asking for help with our Social Studies homework. Can I stop by her place for half an hour?" Clara was her best friend who lived just two buildings down her block.

"Well, you know the rules," Suzan started. "As long as you make it back before 11…"

"I've got to get going too, actually," Jack said as he got up. "I'll walk the young lady out. If you guys need, I can even catch up on some e-mails in my car and wait for her return, to walk her back. You can never know what kind of shady people could be looming out there during these late hours…"

"Oh, thank you, Jack," Janice started, grabbing her backpack from her room, where she'd gone to fetch her textbook. "But I go there all the time, I mean…"

"We'd love that, Jack," Suzan cut in. "Very kind of you to offer, actually- thank you. I would feel a lot more at ease…"

"Alright…I guess. After you…." Janice said, putting on her

jacket as she shot her mother an annoyed look over her shoulder. "I'll see you soon, mom."

"Good night, Suzan," Jack called out from the elevator doors as they opened. "Everything will be alright."

§

As Janice started to hurry back home forty minutes later, she cursed her luck when she noticed just then that soft rain had started. "Oh, shoot!" she exclaimed, trying to make sure the hood of her coat was enough to cover most of her hair as she walked to her apartment building. *So much for the sleeker style I was hoping Scott would perhaps notice better tomorrow in class*, she thought.

"Janice.... how was your study date?" Jack's voice called just then, rolling down the window of the passenger side of his new-looking Toyota sports car, sparkling with the rain drops.

Oh, darn! I'd forgotten all about him, Janice thought as she rolled her eyes. *Why couldn't he have just gone home already?* "It was good, thanks for waiting," she muttered. "I've got to go inside. This rain..."

"Of course," Jack called out. "Could you come inside for a second, though? I wanted to discuss something I couldn't do so in front of your mother, actually..."

Oh brother, thought Janice. "Well.... Can it wait? It's almost 11...and you know my mom..."

"It's important...," Jack insisted.

Maybe he's learned something important about my father, Janice thought as she nodded and opened the door to take a seat on the passenger seat- which had been warmed up, to her surprise.

"How does that feel...do you like that?" Jack asked her with a smile, looking at the seat.

"Um...yeah, I guess," Janice stammered. "So, what is it that you wanted to tell me?"

"Janice…Janice…Janice," Jack started, picking on a strand of her hair from her face, as he slowly lowered the hood of her jacket back over her shoulders. "You have so much pressure on your shoulders, with all the additional stress your mother's causing with her excessive worrying. You know, I've known you for years now…I practically watched you grow up. I really admire this strong, amazing, *beautiful* young woman you've become…"

"Mr. Stevens…thank you," Janice started, a sudden chill of nerves running throughout her body, as she tried with her right hand to locate the handle of the car to run out. "But if you're not going to tell me something about the research case, then I really have to go…"

"You have no reason to feel nervous, Janice," Jack said with a smile as he started to massage her shoulders. "I just wanted to make sure a young lady like you feels relaxed and strong in times of stress like this. I can help you. I'm your friend, you know. You can call me anytime. Why haven't you started to use your new phone already? You deserve nothing but the best…"

"I don't need a massage, Mr. Stevens," Janice insisted, raising her voice now. "…Or a new telephone. I can return it to you, if you'd like. Now, excuse me, I'm going back home."

"…Alright," Jack said with a serious face now, retreating back to his seat. "You think about it, alright? I don't need the phone back. I really want you to have it…I could just use friendly conversation. Your mom can be a little too much sometimes, as you know…"

"Please don't talk about my mother like that. She actually values you and your friendship. Goodnight…" Janice stated angrily as she shut the door behind her and ran inside her apartment, not daring to look back. Her hair was getting really wet now, but she no longer cared. She didn't want to touch the hood of her jacket to cover her hair- not since it was something he had touched.

§

"Janice…Janice!" Suzan shouted the next morning, placing the porcelain plate of cheese toast and blueberries loudly in front of her daughter. "Can you please tell me what *exactly* has been bothering you ever since you returned home last night?"

"Mom, I told you," Janice said with a soft, defenseless voice. "Clara just said something that had me a little upset, but I'll get over it. It's no big deal. Chill. Would you let it go already?"

"I will not let it go!" Suzan exclaimed, taking a seat across from Janice at the table now, sipping from her warm tea mug. "You always share with me everything that bothers you about your friends. Why can't you share with me today? Is it something about a boy?"

"Oh, it's about a…guy…alright," Janice said with a mocking chuckle, still staring at her toast.

"Could you please start eating, honey?" Suzan asked in a softer, satisfied tone now. "And let me know who this mysterious guy is that you apparently had a fight about with Clara?"

"Mom, I didn't have a fight with Clara over some boy, alright?" Janice exclaimed, taking a bite of her toast and chewing on it for longer than necessary. "Just please don't push it today…"

"But you *did* just say it was about a boy…," Suzan insisted. "What else could it be? I hope you didn't give a similar attitude to Jack after you left your friend's house all angry like this…"

"Jack?" Janice retorted, standing up from her chair. "*F**** Jack! I'm going to school, mom!"

"You watch your mouth, young lady," Suzan stood up after her. "I told you there will be no cursing in this house! What is *with* your hostility towards Jack? He's been nothing but good…"

"Oh, he's trying to be *good* alright, mom" Janice started to say right in front of the door with her backpack over her shoulders now. "He's trying to be *really good*- especially to me- to *me*- mom. I'm freaking 14 years old! Don't you see? The guy is a creep! Okay? Are you satisfied?"

"Whoa, there…" Suzan said, as she blocked the door so that her daughter couldn't leave just yet. "What exactly are you trying to imply here, Janice? That because he bought you a birthday gift…and, wanted to wait for you to make sure you got back home safe…?"

"Mom, no!" Janice started, throwing her backpack on the floor. "The phone is still in its box in my drawer- you can go ahead and use it if you'd like. I don't want it! I don't want anything that man touched- not after he touched my hair
and my face in his car, and my shoulders..."

"Janice?" Suzan yelled. "Did he downright do something inappropriate…?"

"Mom!" Janice exclaimed in shock. "I'm telling you the man touched my face…and he massaged my shoulders. How much more *inappropriate* does he have to get…?"

"Jack has always been just a friendly guy," Suzan said, holding her daughter's shoulders now. "Now, listen to me: you will not breathe a word about your silly suspicions to anyone, alright?"

"Mom, he admitted he watched me grow up," Janice said as she started to tear up. "He was never particularly friendly with me when I was younger! Why won't you believe me?"

"I'm not saying that," Suzan said. "I'm just afraid you may be exaggerating…That's all."

"I'm going to school now," Janice said with a loud sigh, wiping her tears on the sleeve of her coat. "All I know is, I don't ever want to be alone with that man, ever again. Alright? Please…"

§

"Are you OK?" Scott asked, sorting out three different test tubes at the laboratory table. "You've been pretty distracted today…I mean, you're also *pretty*, as always, but distracted." He added a smile.

"That's sweet, Scott" Janice said, returning his smile. She couldn't believe her luck. Scott was finally paying closer attention to her- it seemed- and despite her frizzed-up hair, at that. Yet, she couldn't help but continue to be traumatized over not only having been hit on by her mother's long-term friend in his car, but also by her mother's apparent denial. "I just had a minor spat with my mom, that's all."

"Ouch!" Scott said. "I have those all the time too, believe me. My mom and I have been increasingly more and more awkward with each other, especially since we just moved in with her new husband in Brooklyn. Which reminds me, I may have to switch to a new school closer to the new place, soon."

"Brooklyn? Are you serious?" Janice's day was looking like it'd be becoming increasingly sadder.

"Kids! Back to work! No chatting!" Mr. Brown called out from the front of the class.

"Sorry!" Janice and Scott called out to their Chemistry teacher, giggling.

"But, Janice, you've got to check out my new room, though," Scott said in a lowered voice, showing pictures from his cell phone to Janice now from under the lab table. "It's so cool- the way Bob and my mom decorated it- and much bigger than my room here in Queens."

Bob! Janice felt a chill run up her spine the minute her father's name had been uttered by Scott.

"Scott?" she asked. "Do you happen to have a picture of your new stepfather as well?"

"My stepfather?" Scott asked with a confused face, reaching for his cell. "Oh, you mean Bob? He's cool, I guess. Hold on, let me see. Here you go! They're like teenagers. It's so awkward…"

As Scott showed her a photograph of himself as the witness for his mother and her father at their court wedding ceremony, Janice got a sinking feeling in the pit of her stomach.

"I'm afraid it's about to get more awkward, Scott," she stated softly. "Let's wrap this up before Mr. Brown sends us to Detention, and talk after class…"

§

"Wow!" Scott exclaimed later that afternoon, sipping on his

Java-Chip cold drink at the Starbucks two blocks from their school. "We...are officially...stepsiblings: my good old Chem partner and I, huh? Oh, man!"

"...Yup...," Janice replied with a nervous chuckle. She couldn't even bring herself to order anything to drink. She was feeling shocked at both the surprising news, as well as the speed at which her little crush had begun to feel more platonic the moment she realized the truth.

"I mean, he told us he had a daughter," Scott continued. "But he never gave any details. It doesn't really surprise me, though. He and mom are always busy working on secretive stuff together...If I didn't know any better, I'd fantasize they were CIA agents or something," Scott chuckled.

"Secretive...stuff?" Janice asked, recalling the curious project Jack had told them he'd seen Laura and her father working on, thinking it could potentially have been some side hustle.

"Well...it's actually not so secretive, I guess," Scott explained, putting his drink down and letting out a big sigh. "It's actually kind of gross, but necessary...Are you ready to hear this?"

"Gross...but necessary?" Janice asked with a raised eyebrow. "Curiosity killed the cat. Tell me!"

"Well, my mom is an attorney, you see..." Scott began. "She is particularly passionate about putting pedophiles behind bars- that sort of thing. And Bob- your dad- is good with computers, as you know. So, I know they most recently received some tips about some pervert that's been showing his face in Queens. Apparently, the guy served a little time for child pornography distributions and gross things like that, and had practically been shunned from Elmhurst, Woodside, Corona, and the entire area here basically! But one of the victims' mother swore she started seeing him drive around the neighborhood in some fancy car- in disguise apparently, wearing glasses..."

Just as Janice started getting goosebumps at the memory of Jack touching her in her car the previous night, she also couldn't ignore the need she felt for her next question. "Scott...does this guy have a name?"

"Well, I'm supposed to keep quiet until they've collected more evidence ..." Scott continued sheepishly. "I mean- you know, with the whole *innocent until proven guilty* thing..."

"Scott, please," Janice pleaded. "There's this creepy friend my mother brings over to the house sometimes, but he sort of hit on me and he wears glasses and drives a fancy car, like you said...."

"Whoa," Scott exclaimed. "Janice, that's some serious stuff...Did you tell your mom?"

"I did..." Janice began, tears welling up in her eyes. "But she's sort of in denial...Scott, please! Tell me the name!"

"Jack. The creep's name is Jack Stevens. Does it ring a bell?"

§

The subway ride to Brooklyn (after Janice had to plead with her mother to allow her to go see her father for 'bonding time' after her 'car trauma') was mostly quiet in awkward silence.

"Would you like some lemonade while we wait for Bob, honey?" Laura asked once they'd reached the humble two-bedroom place where she lived with Scott and Janice's father.

"No, thanks," Janice said with a smile. "And thank you again for agreeing to see me and listen to everything, on such short notice..."

"Oh Janice, of course," Laura started, smiling at her son who'd been eating his sandwich next to Janice at the kitchen table. "Scott's always talked about you as one of his favorite friends at school. And I recognized your name from the teenage daughter Bob always talks so fondly of-but I never thought it would actually be *you*...you know? Life works in mysterious ways..."

"I agree," Janice said, looking the plump woman up and down. She seemed like a humble lady- the complete opposite of her mother's thin frame always adorned with extra accessories. Each time Laura mentioned her father's name, Janice could hear the sound of affection in her voice.

Janice sighed as she recalled her mother's warning on the phone as she very reluctantly agreed to allow her to go to her father's house. *Don't you dare complain about Jack when he hasn't done anything bad to you. We still need him. Please Janice...Be smart.*

"...This is him, yes...?" Laura asked after she'd opened some files on her laptop. "This is the bastard. Jack Stevens."

As Janice took a deep breath and braced herself with what she was about to see, she was pleasantly surprised when Scott gave her arm a reassuring pat. She smiled, as she felt just then that it had truly felt brotherly. As an only child, she'd often wondered about what it would have been like to have a sibling. *Who knew?* She thought. *I guess something was bound to connect me to him after all.*

Looking at the familiar face on the screen- a current photo of Jack with glasses, as well as an older photograph of him posing without glasses with some former students- Janice sat down on a nearby couch in their living room and covered her eyes with her hands.

"Hey, hey, it's alright," Laura said as she came to sit down next to her. "If it's him- you'd be helping us catch a predator we'd been looking for, for so long. Mrs. Nunez for one would be very happy to meet you- a catalyst in the capturing of the pervert that traumatized her daughter. That little girl still has nightmares, apparently..."

This is it, Janice thought. *This is where I can lie and say I don't recognize him, or tell the truth, and make a difference in people's lives: perhaps even in my own and that of my mother's.*

"Stop needlessly victimizing, yourself Janice," Suzan had told her on the phone before she'd gotten on the train. "That's what you told me too last night- remember?"

Her mother's voice had sounded more vengeful- for somehow embarrassing her in front of Jack- rather than concerned.

I'm not victimizing myself, mom, Janice thought just then. *Just the opposite, in fact.*

"That's him," Janice said confidently.

As the doorbell rang and Scott allowed Bob to enter, Janice looked at her father with a smile. "Dad…" she called out.

"Oh, honey…honey…Laura filled me in a bit. Never doubt your instincts, sweety," Bob said as he walked over to hug his daughter. "I wish I could have warned you guys sooner…I wish you'd told me right away."

§

The events of that following week after the revelation were still fresh in Janice's mind, even now that almost exactly an entire year had gone by. Janice, a sophomore in high school, with her stepbrother Scott now attending school in Brooklyn- where they'd continued to hang out from time to time whenever she'd spend time with her father- was eating spiced-chicken with her mom for dinner again. "I hope this delicious chicken isn't for another man again, mom," Janice said with a playful wink that particularly cold October evening.

"Oh, hush," Suzan replied with a smile. "It was never about a man…Especially not that a-hole, whose name will never be uttered in this house again- may he rot behind bars. You know, I just wanted to believe I could somehow marry again and provide a family for you again…Like your father did so easily, you know…"

"Mom," Janice said, taking her mother's hand in hers. "We *are* a family."

"When did you grow up?" Suzan asked with a tear forming in her right eye as she squeezed back her daughter's hand. "I'm so proud of you. *Nana* would have been proud, too."

"Sometimes adults are the children, and the children have to be the adults…" Janice retorted with a laugh.

"Yeah, yeah" Suzan laughed. "You and your sayings. My daughter's going to be a writer…a famous writer. She's no ordinary girl, I know it. You know: my friend Tim is actually a published author…I'm telling you; you have to send him some of your work sometime…"

Janice didn't reply. She just smiled and allowed her mom to continue talking, and later changed the subject.

Ω

EARTH UP YOUR ROOTS

the glistening raindrop
clings to the grass
capturing attention
which the mind can
but the spirit will *not* deny

this drop will soon perish
in the heat of the sun
when the clouds part
while its fleeting memory
will remain in the flooded heart

the rooted grass, of course, will stay
going about its day-to-day
even when the snow will come, cover,
and eventually melt away

moments gone by
will always be the most admired
nostalgically desired
until we die

EARTH UP YOUR ROOTS

the familiar sounds of the morning
the hammers doing fixing
the birds doing chirping
the employees commuting

the familiar view
or the familiar smell, a nasal hue
the stench of brewed tea or coffee,
the moist soil lingering from rain, lovely dew

mentally organizing your daily tasks
not realizing it may be your last
death could come indeed
at any moment
pray, take heed

death of the body…death of employment
death of love…death of enjoyment

you're prepared for anything on this earth
as long as your mind is prepared for its rebirth

V. BLOOM

*those who overestimate themselves
will underestimate you,
likely never having been told
the story of the tortoise and the hare as a
child*

EARTH UP YOUR ROOTS

the rain nourishes the hopping, content sparrow
fulfilling its most natural need
through this occurrence, unpredictable
but nonetheless reliable

the rain
which brings harmony into the soul
accumulating subtly at first…drop by drop
until the sudden outpour…floods now with joy
unpredictable…undeniable

it washes away settled dust on cars
and creaky fences
the rain creates chances
to glow
where you can tolerate the chill
or give into the thrill
of a subsequent *rainbow*

EARTH UP YOUR ROOTS

I got a bruise yesterday
not sure how
but it spread, dark and throbbing-
sure as I know where my head I lay

some bruises have a mysterious root
better those
than wounds remnant from youth

I wear the scars, invisible, though tattooed
I smile away the chagrin;
when there's a will, there's a way

I apologize
for all the times

I didn't listen
to the little girl
begging for my attention

both to my daughter
and to my reflection
in the mirror

life repeats
until your lesson
becomes clearer

ZELLE

A Play

Prologue

1889. Leeuwarden, Netherlands. Dutch music is playing. A teenage girl with long wavy brown hair is dancing alone in front of a sunny window overlooking a meadow.

Adam Zelle: M'greet! M'greet! Come down for dinner, please! Your brothers are already at the table. Your ill mother has managed to still prepare a lovely dinner for us all- do not anger her!

Margaretha: I'm coming, father. *(Smiles proudly at her silhouette's reflection on the window. Turns to her mirror in movement. Whispers under her breath)*

As if you haven't angered her enough.

(Humming a melody, holds up her skirt and twirls)

I cannot be to blame…. I am merely dreaming….

EARTH UP YOUR ROOTS

ACT I

Living Room. 1897. Java, Dutch East Indies (Indonesia). RUDOLF and MARGARETHA are in conversation.

Rudolf: *(clears his throat)* Margaretha?

Margaretha continues folding some napkins distractedly. Her focus is outside the window.

Rudolf: *(adds louder)* Margaretha Zelle!

Margaretha: Hmm? Oh, sorry. I was lost in thought about something Lady Bella said over dinner. What is it?

Rudolf: You were distracted when our guests were here, too. Yes. Don't think your husband hasn't noticed. I can tell when you're daydreaming again, even by a flutter of those eyelashes.

Margaretha: *(puts the napkins, in a pile, back in a cupboard)* No, not at all, Rudolf. You've got it wrong, this time. I was merely still thinking about what she'd mentioned about those dances for the gods. I wonder what they look like. Otherwise- no dreams of working again. Do not worry. I've promised you.

Rudolf: *(satisfied, picks up his newspaper again and plays with his mustache)* Good girl. If you remain honest like this with me, then I should count my blessings once again that you've answered my ad for a spouse, and not some other gal.

Margaretha: *(rolls her eyes and forces a smile)* You can rest assured, Rudolf. I'm well aware of my duties to you and this household, in return for this fortunate life here with you. I have, after all, been reminded countless times. You can concentrate on the news once again.

Rudolf: Oomph, the news isn't very pleasant, I'm afraid. Drums of violence and aggression are sounding from the West. As a man of the military- I must be confident that I have a loving wife at home, focused on growing our family and performing her tasks. So that I may have my load lightened and be able to focus on my mission.

Margaretha: *(under her breath)* Yes, that's also the job description of a servant, isn't it?

Rudolf: *What* did you say?

Margaretha: Nothing. Simply that I understand.

Rudolph: *(grabs her arm)* I heard you, Margaretha Zelle. You mentioned that word again. 'Servant.'

Margaretha: It was merely a joke. Let go of my arm, please. You're hurting it again.

Rudolf: *(relentless):* You are never to equate being a dutiful wife with servitude again, Margaretha Zelle. Do you understand me? Servitude is being loyal to one's nation. I hope to be clearer this time.

Margaretha: *(whispers, her eyes looking at the head of the house maids in the other room)* Maria will hear. You are clear. Now, let go. I apologize.

Rudolf: *(softens his grip, transforming it into a graze on her cheek)* Good girl. That's the one I married. This side of you. The side of you who is aware that some sacrifices are made in a marriage by both sides. I always return to you my side of the marriage contract too, do I not?

Margaretha: *(changes her voice tone into a playful one)* Oh, do you? But you've been too distracted lately, Rudolf MacLeod. For 2 months to be exact. Yes, I've been counting. You haven't even really touched me since you began that new…

Rudolf: *(pulls her torso closer to his and whispers into her ear)* I will make it up to you, my Zelle. I told you. I'm an older man- I need my rest. The long hours have been taking a toll.

(kisses her softly on the lips). Let us sleep tonight, and you'll be a happy girl over this coming weekend. In the meantime, did you try on the new bracelet?

Margaretha: The golden one? Oh, yes, it was very exotic. Thank you. I adored it.

Rudolf: It's a specialty of the Indies.

Margaretha: (*sighs and locks eyes with MARIA, who's closer to them now, fluffing some pillows*) Yes. You've got quite a taste for this island's specialties, indeed.

Maria: I'm done for the evening, sir. Madam. May I be excused?

Rudolf: (*smiles*): You may go, Maria. Thank you.

Maria: (*smiles back with a bow, meeting his gaze for a long moment with blushing cheeks*) Goodnight.

ACT II

Scene 1

Paris, France. 1905. Fancy restaurant. Music playing. LOUISE and MARGARETHA are dining.

Louise: You have got to show me those moves again, *chérie*. I could use one or two of them on good old Mr. Hubbert. Our anniversary is coming up. Lord knows we need a little spice (*she laughs and sips her wine*)

Margaretha: (*laughs confidently, throwing her hair back*) I could. But I'd have to charge you, *ma chérie amie*. After all, I'm a professional entertainer now, educated in this art of dance. Have you not noticed?

Louise *(laughs with her):* Oh, I've noticed. I think this entire restaurant has noticed. Simply even that hat of yours is enough!

Margaretha: Oh, Louise. Soon enough, it will not just be my clothes or my hats. Or just this restaurant. Soon enough this entire city and the entirety of France- and perhaps even Europe- will know my name. They'll know my face. My story. My dance.

Louise: *(looks around and lowers her voice to a whisper)* Of course, *chérie*. You know I'm your best supporter. But surely you know, you've got to be careful. They're talking about you, too. You know. How you've left your surviving child with your ex-husband and come here for your- and I quote- 'selfish, promiscuous striptease.'

Margaretha: *(bursts into tears)* I'm working on it, Louise. And of course, I am aware of the pitiable slander.

Louise: *(gets up to sit next to her and caresses her arms)* I am sorry. I just wanted to ensure your preparation before any potential conflict these jealous folks may concoct.

Margaretha: *(wipes away a tear and waves her fingers dismissively)* It's not just their hurtful words, my dear friend. Even your name- Louise. I'm constantly reminded...*Ma fille...* My Louise Jeanne. I miss her so terribly. I couldn't afford to keep her; despite being given custody. But it is even more than that. After losing our dear, little Norman to that sickness... I couldn't bear not giving Louise a better life! And I knew...she'd be better off without me. Prouder, perhaps- hopefully- of a happier mommy, making a name for herself across Europe. Rather than a sad one back in Java- or even in the Netherlands now - living with that monster.

Louise: You're sure Rudolf can be trusted as a father, right?

Margaretha: Oh, yes. Of that, I'm certain. I'll admit he was a formidable father- if not a great husband. As for me- I'm afraid I couldn't be either- neither an ideal wife nor a mother. Perhaps that's why I'm trying so hard to be a good dancer, Louise. To be good at *something*. Once I'm ready- I know she will come live with her mommy. I just know it. I will earn her heart. I will deserve it.

Louise: *(rubs her back)* Of course, *bien sur*.

Margaretha: *(clears her throat, adds a sudden smile and a wink)* Now, where were we? Oh, yes! My performances. And yours in your marital bed next week. I'll show you everything I've studied. The moves of the Orient, India and the Sumay combined! I tell you: they're not only an aphrodisiac on the eyes, but also on the soul. That's one of my plans, dear Louise. You see?

She inches closer to her friend, clutching her wine glass tighter in her hand.

They cannot continue to spread *femme fatale* rumors about me, if they know the pure and spiritual stories behind the dances! I am not merely some stripper- Lord knows there are thousands of French models here with more enticing curves than mine. It's the *story*, Louise, that these viewers also love. Beyond just the striptease. The purity...the innocence they enjoy seeing on the woman's face at the end of her seduction. It's poetry.

Louise: *(nods)* The poetry…The purity…Got it, M'greet.

Mata Hari: *(waves a finger seductively)* Non, non. *Mata Hari.* N'oubliez pas! No more *Marghereta* or *Zelle* or *M'greet*. I am ready to embody my stage name wholly now. It shall bring me luck. I will speak it- and dance it- into existence!

Louise: *(chuckles)* No resistance! Cheers to Mata Hari. What was it? Oh yes! L'oeil du soleil. Eye of the sun! Mata Hari!

Mata Hari: Cheers!

She locks eyes with all the men in the restaurant sneaking looks in the direction of the loudness from their table. Instrumental Eastern music plays in the background.

Scene 2

Streets of Paris. GABRIEL and MATA HARI are having a casual stroll.

Gabriel: May I have a word, Mata?

Mata Hari: Of course! What is it, dear Gabriel?

Gabriel: Mata, you have not only been a great client of mine to book over the past year, but also a great friend. There for me with the anti-Semitic battles I've had to battle…

Mata Hari: Oh, of course. Argh! It has surely been the most absurd thing to me- to not be accepted as a human being simply for being who you are. Go on…

Gabriel: It gives me immense pleasure to announce to you the good news…

Mata Hari: Oh, prey do tell already!

Gabriel: You, my dear, are now a regular at the Paris Olympia!

Mata Hari (jumps for joy and the two hug)

ACT III

Scene 1

EMILE ETIENNE GUIMET and MATA HARI are in a Parisian hotel room.

Emile: *(looks at the B&W photograph in his hand)* A Hindu priestess, huh?

Mata Hari: *(hugs him from behind)* Oh, hush, Emile. The crowd at your precious museum gobbled it right up! The public of Europe simply adores such exotic background stories, you know that!

Emile: *Oui, ma belle*. They adore it- but do they *buy it*? That is my concern. If you begin to lose credibility, that could become the end of our business arrangement.

Mata Hari: *(plays with his hair)* Oh, no, we wouldn't want such an ending. And especially not an ending of our *personal* arrangement as well, I hope?

Emile: *(gives her a passionate kiss)* Never. I'm just concerned and you need to work extra hard to…

Mata Hari: How's your family doing, Emile? How's your old lady?

Emile: Why remind me of that now? Are you trying to make me feel bad again, after we've just made love?

Mata Hari: Well, are you trying to make *me* feel bad for my stories…?

Emile: I'm simply expressing concern….

Mata Hari: So am I, Emile! Just a *petit* reminder that it is not only I who has to be careful of the revelation of the truth, is it…?

EARTH UP YOUR ROOTS

The two turn their backs toward each other for a moment.

Look, Emile. Do not worry. Even if they are suspicious- this is my art. People can temporarily suspend disbelief for the beauty of the art in a given moment. How else do you explain the utter insistence of the story of Santa Claus around Noel?

Emile: That's a tad bit different, my silly darling…

Mata Hari: Stories are stories, Emile. And art is art.

Emile: This is work. This is life.

Mata Hari: And just what is life, if not a temporary work of art?

Emile: (*kisses the tip of her nose*) Ok, you win.

Mata Hari: I always make sure I do.

Emile: Stubborn girl. My woman-child. I want to obtain my divorce, and marry you already.

Mata Hari: *(lets out a sigh)* Doesn't always work out so easily, Emile. Look, I'm sorry for being sensitive. But…that photograph…Please throw it out…

Emile: I need something to dream about you with when we have to be away, my darling.

Mata Hari: It's just that- I know Rudolf is always up for using anything he can against me with regards to our Louise Jeanne.

Emile: I understand. Very well.

Mata Hari: Thank you. And give me another favor, will you, Emile? Don't ever talk about leaving your family for me. I never asked for it- you know that. And I never would. Your children need their father. They don't have to pay for our sins.

Emile: Darling, there's always a price for everything worth having in life.

Mata Hari: Don't I know it…

Scene 2

Performance space surrounded by crowds. MATA HARI is dancing with five other women in black around her. Wears a metal breastplate, flowing fabric tied around her hips and little else to cover up her nearly nude body. She rattles her entire torso in a spiritual trance. At the end of the dance, she drops herself on the floor. The crowd is mesmerized, silent. She suddenly puts an arm up with flair, throwing her head back in an 'innocent' smile. The crowd goes wild with applause.

ACT IV

Scene 1

1916. MATA HARI is 40 years old and chubbier now. She hasn't danced since 1915. Meets her friend LOUISE again in a home setting.

Mata Hari: I'm afraid it may be over, *mon amie*. Ten years. I've peaked. Now, it's as if I can only hang on to the sides of a steep mountain while I continue my decline…

Louise: You are still a great dancer, Mata Hari. Youth is but an illusion. You have inspired me so much! I've left Monsieur Hubert. I've got the kids. My bakery is doing well. I am standing on my own feet. All because of you- Margaretha! You're my inspiration. My hero. You cannot give up now…Not you…

Mata Hari: That's wonderful. You've got your baking talent to hang on to. What do I have? Rudolf was right- I couldn't cook for *mierde*. But did I deserve to be mistreated?

Louise: No, of course not…

Mata Hari: Men can get away with everything. It is simply not fair, Louise. Women like you with a talent or trade can certainly get more ahead now than they could before. But, regardless, at the end of the day- we are still looked upon differently…As the lesser sex, somehow.

Louise: You *do* have your trade! Maybe…you can open a dance school for girls? Teach all you've taught yourself for years?

Mata Hari: But what is a woman without her dignity, Louise? I've been hanging on to my anger for so long…Getting revenge on all the men I've seen do me wrong. My father. Rudolf. Countless lovers involved in their ridiculous politics. By doing the same…I've been using the men back, just as they've used me! But I am not happy, Louise. I cannot go to sleep with a clear conscience like you can.

Louise: It's never too late. You were not the only free-spirit of Europe. You've had countless imitators…You're a living legend!

Mata Hari: What is the worth of having a 'legend' if one couldn't actually *live* while alive?

Louise: To inspire? Through your story?

Mata Hari (*smiles*): I've always liked that…

Louise: How's the young captain?

Mata Hari (*rolls her eyes*): Vadim? Oh, you know, just being… young. A Russian pilot providing service for the French. And me as his lover- can you imagine? Old enough to be his mother… He wouldn't be with me if he hadn't had such a reckless character to begin with…

Louise: You are not that much older than him, come on. Men take on young lovers all the time, and no one cares.

Mata Hari: I'm telling you… It's a man's world! But I *am* worried about him…It's dangerous out there.

Louise: You love him…

Mata Hari: I love the way he makes me feel…

Louise: M'greet…

Mata Hari: *(sighs, lowering her head)* Alright. I love him…I have always needed an object of affection as motivation, haven't I? I've replaced dance- which I'm no longer appreciated for- with him, I suppose.

(The two women chuckle)

Scene 2

It is summertime in France. At the military intelligence agency. MATA HARI and the director of the agency- COLONEL LOUIS- are talking.

Mata Hari: Vadim Maslov! I have to see him! His eye…I've heard what happened, and…

Colonel Louis: With your Dutch citizenship, you cannot, Madame!

Mata Hari: But it is neutral in the war- I've been able to travel freely everywhere…

Colonel Louis.: It doesn't help you on the front lines, Madame. (*Adds in a whisper*) We may be able to help you, however, if you agree to spy for France. We could use someone with your neutrality. We've heard of your closeness with the German Crown Prince Wilhelm- we are in need of intelligence on the German plans. Particularly from a certain Captain Georges Ladoux…

Mata Hari: I care not for such arrangements, nor about sides during this terrible war! Please! I simply have to see Vadim! It pains me…

Colonel Louis: You shall be able to see your Russian pilot…and be provided with one million francs. Do we have a deal, madame?

Mata Hari: (*sighs*) We have a deal.

ACT V.

Scene 1. Madrid 1916. MAJOR ARNOLD KALLE and MATA HARI are conversing in an office setting.

Major Arnold Kalle: I have read the transcript of your interrogation by Sir Basil Thomson in London. You admitted your work for France.

Mata Hari: I was…under tremendous pressure. I do not care very much for France. I am haunted by the memory of the lies and gossip- allowing me to fall down from such a high place of exaltation. I've been backstabbed, I tell you. I now only wish to help Germany.

Major Arnold Kalle: What would you want to tell the Crown Prince if we allow you to see him? You swear it is your real intention to *provide* him with information, and not *obtain* on behalf of France?

Mata Hari: I know so much about their leaders. I've been personally hurt, as well. Of course, I can provide his highness with whatever information he needs- in exchange for a fair sum, of course…and discretion.

Major Arnold Kalle: Very well, Agent H-21.

Mata Hari: Who?

Major Arnold Kalle: (*smiles*) I'm looking at her.

EARTH UP YOUR ROOTS

Scene 2:

St. Lazarre Women's Prison, 1917. Paris, France. MATA HARI is writing a letter to her daughter from her cell. She read the words out loud to herself as she writes.

Ma Cherie fille,

How I long for some miracle of clemency or justice by the forces that have placed me before my oncoming death, and for me to be able to tell you how much I love you in person in place of this letter. But, alas, life has turned your idealist mother into a realist- and I'm afraid these words will likely be the last words I shall be allotted to provide you with.

I've tried, my darling, to be a warrior…. To make you proud…But they are punishing me for something that a man in my same position and shoes would have been able to scrape through without having to pay with his life….

My Louise. I hope you go on to live a life of more honor and accomplishments as not only a woman but a human being in your life than your mother was able to….

I have only done whatever I did out of love. Love for you- knowing you'd be better under your father's traditional-minded care. Love for dance…for obtaining bliss from this life given to us by the Almighty. Love for inspiration…. Love for a man- a love that led me down dangerous roads I had no intention of ever going on…May you never love as foolishly and deeply as I have…especially someone who cannot return it…Choose a safer life…

They're accusing me of giving names…. of betraying France. They say information I provided- to whom I thought were business partners and friends- caused the death of tens of thousands of soldiers! The absurdity! How could I have done that as one woman? It was all due to their own greed and violence! I was simply trying to make a living…To utilize my neutral citizenship. I was trying to help everyone- and in turn I ended up hurting myself.

I long so much for you to be proud of me…Remember this; ultimately, it was only I who had been betrayed…Betrayed by them all…Not even my friend Vadim agreed to testify in my defense.

Never sacrifice yourself for a man, my dearest! Never! You hear? Never sacrifice your dreams, either- as long as your feel in your heart they represent your true being and are not purposely harming anyone.

'Tis better to have lived an entire book of life in short years, than a couple of chapters into prolonged years of a dull existence.

Stay well. Stay in school. And please don't believe whatever terrible things you may hear about me. They only ever wished to see me as an extension of their own evils, and as a scapegoat- remember that. I was merely creating art, my Louise. And I merely wanted to earn enough to get in your good graces once again in my older age. Stay well…stay true to your being.

Your loving mother,

M'greet

Scene 3

MATA HARI is standing before a firing squad- *sans* a blindfold. They've begun to fire away at her. After a round or two, she blows smiling, acceptant kisses at her executors and collapses on her stomach in a similar pose as one of her most famous dances. In her last thought, she imagines she's at the end of a performance on the ground instead and raises her arm- for 'applause' in her imagination. She collapses following the death of her physical body.

Ω

EARTH UP YOUR ROOTS

PHOTOGRAPHY: Engin Tufan Sevimli

write in the way
you want to read...
cook in the way
you want to eat...
love in the way
you want to be loved-

stand before your fears
as they stand before you

EARTH UP YOUR ROOTS

confidence blossoms
from knowing who you are
not based on what others claim
but by heeding to your own inner star

as a child the seeds had been sprinkled
but never planted firmly
always a question remained,
you'd never been satisfied entirely

you never felt thin or curvy…
                                      never cool or wholesome enough
neither just the right kind of emotional…
                                      nor just the right kind of tough

you grew limbs like stems
from seeds barely nurtured
dependence on another's judgments
had taken place of being watered

who you were and who you've become
can now unite with
who you realize you've always been…
                         age and experience bringing comfort
                               into your unique skin
your indivi***duality***-
your inner compass pulling you to the truth
                       like a magnet, toward your destiny

EARTH UP YOUR ROOTS

like a miniscule traveler into the vessels,
brain and membranes;
dive deep

all the way to the root
of the issues and pain
running through your veins

face your flaws, caress them
plant affection into those unfavored seeds-
the ones you'd hidden around the stem

acceptance breeds evolution
watch your imperfection… **_blossom_**

you are more than your past
you were purposely created…. **_awesome_**

AFTERWORD

Grow your rose....in the form of prose

Dear reader,

What hasn't been said about a rose- mostly as a symbol for youth and fleeting beauty...of love and fleeting emotions?

Like Mata Hari- a *rose,* too, is legendary. Wasn't it Shakespeare who'd asked, "What's in a name? A rose by any other name would smell as sweet…"

Well, talking about 'roots,' we *could* discuss such concepts as people changing their ethnic names to assimilate into different cultures, for instance, to argue whether that's true or not in today's world…

But what about a less-famed flower? Namely, the picture on the cover of this book- a *tulip.*

> *the wilting*
> *the pricking*
> *oh, I would rather be the tulip, than the rose:*
> *cyclical,*
> *cultural,*
> *perfunctory in the kitchen, in place of an onion*
> *growing despite being cut*
> *bending toward the light*

Beloved reader,

If you're familiar with anything regarding Turkish culture and history, the tulip on the cover represents my roots in Türkiye; the tulip, originating in Anatolia and Central Asia rather than the Netherlands as many people think, is the country's official flower.

It is a flower that has culturally come to represent perfect love, rebirth, royalty and forgiveness. Tulips are also known for their rather fleeting periods of bloom in the spring. Aren't we all ultimately fleeting in existence on this terrestrial realm? I often write about aging in my poems, and more from a reflective perspective rather than a mournful one; I find myself rather more confident in my skin and identity at my current age, in fact, than I did in my 20's. I agree, for instance, with those who often say they wish to be able to have had their older mindset and wisdom in their younger selves and bodies.

In my previous collections, I'd written two personal poems regarding turning 35 and 36.

Well, in this one, dear reader- these 'ROOTS' are being earthed up at 37, blooming as I turn 38.

this is 37
many have delivered hell, while promising heaven…

…and this is 38
extinguishing flames
while circling heaven's gate

of mistakes, I'm aware
naivete gone- both the 'truth' and the 'dare'

enemies of emotions, beware

I carry still the childhood-stemmed burden
I've taught while still learning- of this, I'm certain

loving words becoming shamed
with claims of keeping sensitivities protected

EARTH UP YOUR ROOTS

endangerment of the body
and peace of mind ignored-
actions of desire instead getting respected

in this generation where benefits get exalted:
wear at least your conscience on the sleeve
even if the heart must be kept vaulted

just as words, we too are rooted

consider a *Hippocratic* oath- rooted as 'horse power'
versus a *hypocrite*- rooted as an 'actor'

distinctly reputed

inform: set free your own form
don't conform to the norm

make peace with ease

earth up your roots
if you cut yourself off from them, you may become ornamental
like roses in a vase

but with a cause and an end,
ultimately detrimental

EARTH UP YOUR ROOTS

Dear bud,

In this collection, we saw different characters affected by their 'roots' in diverse ways…

May you always earth up your roots and your essence, accept your unique self and your lineage with the good and the bad…

Focus on and manifest *only the good* from here out…

> FOCUS ON WHERE YOUR SOUL IS ROOTED
> NOT WHERE YOUR BODY IS
> LOCATED

Thank you, dear reader, for continuing this 'sowing' journey with me.

May you always **write out your drops**, **set free your flow**, and **earth up your roots**.

right now, what's visible
may be the rotting
they can look and not see
the fruits you are slowly bearing
and the beauty you are creating
let them assume…

while you're about to bloom

FIRE UP YOUR FLIGHT

Y OU MAKE THE DARK MAGICAL:
reluctant, curious firefly.
Just a flap of your wings can
catalyze change: hesitant,
unaware butterfly

Embrace the fuel burning within
no way out but right through and in.
Yearning….learning.
Illuminating…*transforming.*
The Source within *glowing, providing*

Undim that light: *make bright your surrounding.*
Soar off the lift and thrust *take off follows unloading.*

Your torch- your might…*feel the joy in the fight*

For neither glory nor fame…rather live to ignite

Fly off your Flame. Fire Up Your Flight.

FIRE UP YOUR FLIGHT

"A great fire burns within me, but no one stops to warm themselves at it, and passers-by only see a wisp of smoke…"

-VINCENT VAN GOGH

PHOTOGRAPHY: Dayanch Kakabayev

FIRE UP YOUR FLIGHT

Dear resilient rocketeer,

Here we are. I have arrived at the final, 'fire' element of what has ended up gushing out of my soul as a four-part, 'elemental' poetic series. If you're familiar with my works, you may know by now that I had never foreseen writing my debut novel, *'The Catalyst'*, as part of a trilogy…let alone adding three more poetic collections after first publishing *'Write Out Your Drops'* in 2021- compiled of the poems I'd shared on my Instagram handle of the same name. I especially never thought I'd go on to publish poems fused with other creative writing styles (short stories, autobiographical essays and even a play script). And yet, as I've always believed: life truly is what happens when we're busy making other plans…and God really must 'laugh', as the Yiddish proverb goes, when mankind 'plans'.

Kısmet. The only real Turkish-origin word in the Miriam-Webster dictionary (aside from the word 'bosh' eluding to nonsensical talk, derived from *boş*- the Turkish word for 'empty'). *Kısmet*. One's 'pre-destined lot'. Many believe in it, while others believe humans create their own fates through individual choices. The truth- as I've often surmised *('Set Free Your Flow: A Centered View'* readers, I'm looking at you)- must lie somewhere in *the middle*.

That's right. Human lives, in my opinion, are determined through this sort of a 'happy medium' between paths destiny lays out specifically for us as unique individuals- based mostly on our genetics and environments- and our subsequent choices that lead us down different paths at various points in our lives. As if following different branches of a tree leading us into different directions; we decide, indeed, yet the options we choose from are precisely ones designed and predestined for us (by a power higher than us, whatever you may call such divination).

Here is another Turkish word: *'hayırlısı'*… translating roughly to '…may only whatever will ultimately be for the best happen'. A 'religious' word I was 'secularly' raised with, never delving too much into it until becoming an adult and becoming further interested in the faith conditioned from birth. (*Hayırlısı* is sort of like a mystical version of the famous Western song lyrics: *You can't always get what you want....but if you try sometime, you'll find...you get what you need*).

The Quran tells Muslims to be 'grateful' to Allah not only in times of joy and victory, but also adversity and disappointment. We're told, if we are believers, that we must also believe that what may appear to be something 'bad' happening to us can also have another 'good' purpose which may not at first be evident. Social or professional rejection could be divine protection, for example- saving us from what would actually have become a terrible reality in comparison to the dream we'd had of the thing that we initially desired.

So, dear reader- where does *choice,* then, come in? And how can we choose? Especially in our modern age when, due mainly to rapid developments in urbanization, globalization and technology, each passing year appears to bring on more choices available to us (and in even more categories than ever) than thousands of years of humanity ever had. Call me old-fashioned, but I'm actually of the belief that this can become truly frustrating and even be detrimental to mental health- leading to continuous cycles of dissatisfaction and regrets over our possibility of having chosen 'something else', etc.

Journeying through life can symbolically begin to feel (post-communist regimes, of course) as if one's shopping in a supermarket or clothing store with a myriad of options competing for our attention through various 'attractive qualities.' *(Pick me, I'm on sale this week....Pick me, I'll make things easier for you...Pick me, I may not be healthy, but I'll make you smile in the short-run, and you've had a hard week and deserve it).*

The proverbial placement of 'multiple eggs' in one basket can also tire: *We can light up multiple fuses and yet 'burn' ourselves out- literally!* Yet if one is lucky enough to have discovered their calling early on- they can not only ignite that fuse, but actually work toward adding fuel to it until it gradually takes off and takes flight. Just as with picking an educational or career path for optimal self-actualization: the same can hold true for various relationships and connections in our lives. *Discover your fuse, and let it become your muse* for a colorful and meaningful life, focusing on a beautiful journey rather than some unguaranteeable destination. Believe that there's been a path laid out for you to arrive at (your *kısmet*) - regardless of which roads you may 'select' (leading you to the variety in experiences you live through) on your way there. Believe that, if you 'ignite' what sparks your joy and intrinsic interest, and use that fire within to illuminate and enlighten your path rather than burn you up inside: you will live the optimal life divinely intended for your particular personality and set of talents and ideal contributions meant for the world. Thus, whatever outcome you experience will feel that much more like it was all for the best and ultimate good (*hayırlısı*).

Dear reader…If you've read any of my works enough to know my opinion on our place on earth as human beings- the answer to flying through fire just may lie in our observation of nature (other living things around us, visible or not to the naked eye). I've 'poured' out my heart and struggles through 'Drops', 'aired' out the polarizing forces that have pulled me throughout my bi-cultural upbringing in 'Flow', and 'earthed up' all parts of my identity- the uprooted dirt *and* the nutrients- in 'Roots', along with all of you. It's time to conclude with *fire*. The element common to *The Catalyst Trilogy* as well, interestingly enough- binding all my published works thus far together.

The flames raging inside of us can take over, if we allow them to engulf and incinerate us into ashes. But the flames may also become alchemized to ameliorate our lives, through balanced management. So, how can we fly through burning? Through consistent self-questioning leading to various self-actualizations, followed by consistent recognition of signs by the universe. And, of course, as always, through challenging work- labor which will never feel burdensome if we discover the ideal occupation for our personalities. The fire can thus transform into useful fuel, 'burning' to allow us to soar.

Like a wildfire in nature- as tragic as it can become (if unchecked) for trees and wildlife- it can ultimately, if managed, also provide nutrients for the soil and revival opportunities for other living things in its environment. (Oh, the things this mother has become inspired by through reading along with her young daughter's *National*

Geographic non-fiction series). We're *miniscule* in comparison to some creations, yet *grand* in relation to others. We're neither special nor irrelevant in the grander scheme of things. We are not angels of light, nor jinns of fire (any readers of *The Catalyst Trilogy* with me here on my poetic musings as well?). We are humans of clay, of earth; molded by our Creator to be formed perfectly in our multitude of imperfect ways. We can smolder- smokeless- like the jinn…emit light and brightness, like the angels. Yet, ultimately, humans are somewhere in the *middle.*

Too often, we ignore the only real, guaranteed beauty of *the moment* and *the present.* Our human ancestors have often quipped that happiness and joy truly lie in 'the journey'. And yet, from birth on, we tend to get caught up in growing up through accumulations- checkmarks of certain socially-conditioned 'milestones'…only to mourn when we don't 'meet them' by certain time periods, after which we 'keep busy' by staying afloat…often staying alive without actually living and reveling in the moment.

If you're reading these words, it's 'too late' for a different you with a different past. We exist as we are in the present, and therefore must not allow what we have no control over to have power over us. Instead, we must allow our kinks and flaws- through acquiring lessons from the pains of the past- to empower us as we fly on our journeys.

And how to recognize your journey? Look for signs in the universe. Repetitions and patterns. Messages from Nature are all around us if we stop and breathe daily to fully utilize all our senses, as well as consider all the elements. What brings you joy? What brings you discomfort? What do you find yourself drawn toward, and what do you find you rebel against? Are you hurting anyone with your choices, including yourself? If yes, it's never too late to change unhealthy habits. And, if you're not, then it's never too late to follow your own compass. What you experience, thus, on your 'path' will precisely be your 'journey'…your 'mission'…your 'purpose.' Listen to your dreams and your intuition; you'll know.

Many associate 'fire' and 'flames', through religion, to the concept of 'Hell'- as I highlight in a dream I had as a child that

FIRE UP YOUR FLIGHT

'coincidentally' coincided with a trip described in a story I'd only first read as a university student (see my first poem in the first chapter entitled 'signs'). Had I been, subconsciously,

influenced by the 'burning fire' I'd heard of throughout my Muslim upbringing, based on 'punishment for sin' ? As deeply as I believe in Allah (God) and the continuation of the spirit after the body passes on (there's even scientific proof of corpses losing similar weight- thought to be the weight of 'the spirit'-immediately upon death), I'm not sure if 'Heaven' and 'Hell' described are more allusions to the 'punitive pain' of the conscience (along with various levels of social shunning depending on the severity of our wrongs), in comparison to the 'bliss' ('Heaven') we'd experience upon making 'kind' and 'authentic' choices....rather than actual places our souls would potentially travel to upon death.

Well, no one's died and returned to tell us for sure: in the meantime, we have spirituality...and creative writing :) I'd like for my collection to allow you, dear reader, to put aside whatever your faith (or lack thereof) may be, and think of 'flames' instead as energizers for change and 'fuel' to reach your utmost potential. Flames allowing you to soar high and create a self-satisfied 'paradise' on this earth through virtuous deeds (which, I believe, include being good to yourself, as I feel God would want for us as His creations). May you enjoy this collection consisting mainly of poems (some new and some old, never before published ones), bringing it back full circle to how it all started with 'Write Out Your Drops'.

burn the old and revitalize....take charge as you're charged
it'll provide propulsion...your redemption can follow conflagration
divine intuition ... will lead to the solution
we can burn- both ourselves & others- yet also learn as we teach
we can become the traumatized, or catalyzers for change
*we each have a **role**...over which we have partial control*

how will you discover, and then play out yours?
how can one part be in hiding, while the other one explores?
how can one wing be held down, while the other one soars?

FIRE UP YOUR FLIGHT

perspective

Hell
doesn't require the much-discussed
dogmatic place of flames and the anguished

Heaven
doesn't require the much-preached
cinematic place of waterfalls and the vanquished

God
is said to be as near as our artery vein:
remembrance and gratitude will replenish

bliss…as near as joyful bursts after fights
penance…as near as tears of sleepless nights

Ignite

*admit it:
wouldn't life,
without conflict,
be like literature
without one?
… lifeless*

Musings & Ponderings

FIRE UP YOUR FLIGHT

life can end in a minute

even before the very last heartbeat
life can lose its joy and hope for tomorrows
oblivious to meaning and purpose
drowning in one's sorrows

life can end in a minute

in a tsunami, hurricane
a catastrophic heartbreak
accident, health failure
shattering earthquake

life can end in a minute
appreciate everyone in it

leave behind golden memories;
precious stones that shall remain
even among the dirt and casualties

dedicated to the victims of the deadly double earthquakes in Türkiye and Syria in February of 2023

FIRE UP YOUR FLIGHT

signs

I'll never forget a childhood dream I had- sometime around the age of ten or eleven, if my memory serves me... Though of that dream itself I'm as certain as day;

I was walking, slowly... led by the hand of someone not discernable to me, you see, through a locale of cobalt-blue walls: a place with bars like prisons-behind which people were reaching their hands to us, as if asking to be rescued.

I was told, by my mysterious leader, that this had been 'Hell'- after which I casually inquired about Heaven... I was then at once taken toward a bright golden light, as my companion and I began to gradually walk up some steps on a staircase heading toward the sky.

I awoke at that moment.

Later, in university, I took a random Italian literature class to fulfill a requirement. And one of the readings was the classic by Dante Alighieri- whom I'd never heard of until that course.

I felt chills reading through the *Inferno...Purgatorio...Paradiso*; the cantos were introducing new characters to me from history...and yet, the gist of the story was familiar.

...that childhood dream...

Could it be? And wouldn't that really be-a most Divine Comedy...?

Are heaven and hell- merely, on earth,
previewed? Or actually lived...encountered?

One of my few dreams:
         that shall forever remain... vivid, unfettered

FIRE UP YOUR FLIGHT

metamorphosis

from a dull caterpillar
to the winged beauty

leaving all in awe
despite a short lifespan,
it does all it can
to transcend
representing the soul
before the prison of a body

with its attraction toward the light
the butterfly spreads its wings into flight

script

the pen
is said to be mightier
than the sword

with a process-
through the recorded word-
its own reward

this one aims only to slash misperceptions,
 judges only judgements…
it edits unhelpful rerouting,
needless corrections,
misdirection and interceptions

aiming, through healing, *to heal*
yearning, through revealing, *to deal*
to unleash what the soul's tended to conceal
what it can't always explain, yet most certainly feel

FIRE UP YOUR FLIGHT

torrents

sometimes
it oozes,
   the poetry…
like blood
    subtle and quick
    akin to a finger upon a prick

at other times
it overflows,
the poetry,
like a high tide
overbearing and encompassing
before the waves subside

the unspoken, but written
the unlived, but imagined

it's all apparent
for all who can see, to see

these verses shall be free
to be recorded for humanity

                                from me to you, dear reader
                                    and from you to me
                                what's shared…
                                                    is *infinity*

FIRE UP YOUR FLIGHT

roles

the loving loner
the studying teacher
the entertained amuser
the bored borer

the done and the doer
the secretive sharer
the conducting straphanger
the dreamed-of dreamer

the self in its entirety
can be your own epitome-
harboring contrary forces in harmony

you are duality and duality is thee

discover your propellant
uncover your destiny

FIRE UP YOUR FLIGHT

righteous

when you've run out of the excuses,
mouthing 'I was young'
whilst knowing inside
it was the possibility and the fun

the responsibility to uphold
a choice between the moral and the selfishly bold

clear now as day…
choose the lighter-on-the-conscience way

more satisfying to be doing what you say
it becomes no longer even fun to stray

occasions

"why flowers?"
he asked
"those gifts die…"

"better them than showy flatteries"
she answered
"those lie…

…I can smell and reminisce,
'tis better to miss
fleeting bliss

than being lifted high in the sky
and later thrown, though you don't fly
…only to cry…"

FIRE UP YOUR FLIGHT

foretold

it's seldom that people disappoint us
without our allowance

wanting to see the fruits of its labor,
the soul disregards their lack of compliance

we turn a blind eye, let them get close
be they wolves or fools in emperor's clothes

yet
they've shown their true selves
from the onset
they dreamt of their benefits
while we dreamt of watching the sunset

reflect back on the beginning
my friend
for how it started is often
how it'll end

FIRE UP YOUR FLIGHT

sleepless

                                                                                                         bumpy wall
                                                                                                          off-white,
                                                                                                           piques me
                                                                                                              despite
                                                                                                      lack of light

I sit up in my bed
and stare

Nature's canvas
versus
man-made artifice

                                        I peek at both through the window
                                                                  to one, I smile
                                                        while to the other, I glare

images of mere days
as well as of years
gone by
both play out before my eyes right then and there

                                                            dissipated but remnant
                                                            through their casualties
                              seeking genuineness over mere pleasantries

FIRE UP YOUR FLIGHT

opaque

before us:
the snow…pure
which sometimes provides the cure
for what we endure

before us:
a blank page
a new chapter
the certainty of the present-
with conscious will and gratitude-
as the only 'happily ever after'

fame? fortune? nay
I pledge
a page
sentiments fused with rage

raw emotions…expressed
what's felt…confessed

disregarding barriers
except those of our own,
self-imposed shields
are the most painful
and the least shown

FIRE UP YOUR FLIGHT

memorialized

when you're uncategorizable,
'fitting in' can make you
unrecognizable
from one member
or other

remember
your unique glow,
surrender
and accept that inner flow

don't follow others on social media
without following yourselves
…'like' and 'save'
your own lives
…be the written,
not the shelves

be authenticatable…
the superficial, in retrospect,
the most regrettable

FIRE UP YOUR FLIGHT

fortuitous

seeing your reflection in your child's eyes
is a great teacher

you face your own traits-
both positive and not

crediting- finally- the prior
accepting- finally- the latter

unique

is it the prohibited that attracts the rebels?
or have they merely been unable
to believe in the potential
of finally belonging and discovering a home
rather than make-do shelters made of pebbles?

rebellion anchors identity,
unmasked authenticity
provides stability

individuality over conformity
except when
necessity breeds adaptability

linguistics

even the word 'compromise'
includes 'promise'

a pledge to meet halfway
doesn't say
'stray'

FIRE UP YOUR FLIGHT

jigsaw

'the one', overrated
'the present', underrated

you can fit well
on paper
and in principle, only
with someone whose expectations
are things you've always hated

coexisting in a zone
where technically you won't be alone,
but most certainly lonely

authenticity
won't make you feel depleted

the less perfect piece,
despite edges that may be jagged,
can make the puzzle of life feel completed

FIRE UP YOUR FLIGHT

phoenix

lower your standard
and you can be slandered

                        someone who won't even bother to rise
                              in order to meet you halfway
                                isn't worthy for your focus to stay

you can die each night when hit by reality…
intrusive thoughts
and narcissism
murdering your vitality

but you can be born again soon after…
with renewed fidelity
to morality

ah!
to feel as light as a feather
with regards to your conscience's clarity

rising from the embers…
                                        …what sweet serenity

FIRE UP YOUR FLIGHT

masochistic

it's a sad testament
of our society

when we get used
yet tolerate abuse
of any kind

get wronged
yet look the other way
as if blind

…just to keep away the loneliness
…despite knowing something's amiss

                                                           another new year

                                                             lonelier still
                                    …advanced by technology
                                    while held back in body:
                                            we are confined

                                           are we progressing,
                                           or falling behind?

FIRE UP YOUR FLIGHT

first-person

I despise labels
labels restrict
labels contradict

I despite loneliness
'lonely', too, is a label
with labeling too strict

I admire being alone
self-reflection breeds creativity
self-care is enlightening

I admire unlabeled authenticity
breeding freedom and felicity

truth is mighty
it is power

truth is lightning
it can devour

…and uncover innately in a minute
a lie concocted in an hour

revolution

I've been rebelling
for so long
that it's become
a go-to state by default

                        maybe I should rebel instead
                            against my own mindset

                                purging the norms
                              fixed from upbringing

                      maybe I should be re-labeling
                         things I've been witnessing
                                and repressing

abiding by nature
with pure intentions
can rarely be at fault

FIRE UP YOUR FLIGHT

infuse

with strong leaves allowed to seep in heat,
nature's awakening fusion-
a most flavorful diffusion-
takes over
bliss with the first sip
fully damp after the dip
the tastebuds drown in flavor

the subtle hint of citrus or thyme
black breakfast, colored with undertones of
English rose, raspberry, or lime

let it all sink in … must be shrewd

can't let life hit you-like coffee-suddenly
like good tea, life is to be brewed

FIRE UP YOUR FLIGHT

machinery

I listen to the passing speeder
and crackling heater …
usually unheeded background noise
now growing louder as the lights get dimmer …

…until eventually out, 'tis no longer bright
…say your prayers, say your "good night"

I appreciate allowing for this rare quiet moment

laudable

taking notice of sensory enticers otherwise

inaudible

-not the din of mechanical commotions
 but a revelatory aria of hidden emotions

Spark

…why doubt yourself due to the mere opinions of fellow humans who, also, by nature, doubt themselves?

Musings & Ponderings

FIRE UP YOUR FLIGHT

seism

…and aren't some connections ever-changing, unreliable roller coasters?
repeating merry-go-rounds
or tornadoes…twisters?

one party spinning loosely on the top,
while the other hovers closer to the ground,
begging… "stop!"

you can close the park
when you're motion sick,
take refuge as the storm wears itself out:
picking a peace of mind,
over waiting to become their pick

purposely or unintentionally:
masters of double standards and hypocrisy-
with rudeness and selfishness galore-
their nonchalance disguises manipulative tendency

you can evade the earthquake zone
where you found temporary joy in times calmer
…for how long can you walk on eggshells,
anticipating an aftershock or another tremor?

FIRE UP YOUR FLIGHT

unsavory

beware the flatterers: their technique always begins the same
making you feel special is their game
they get you when you're down
flipping around your frown
their acting deserving a crown
they swear you're their God-sent
you agree to their arrangement
their promises expire
their smiles retire
the flatterers let go of your hand
when you need support the most
as you're no longer complacent to mediocre performance,
they become a ghost
and turn into a cold host:
implying indirectly for you to 'get lost'

they flatter the next in the same ways: you find one day you've been
replaced
only when distanced from illusionist haze
'you recognize you've always been special
you're prime-time, not a commercial

you find you never needed their flattery
as your confidence soars,
so does your ability

you've actually been set free

FIRE UP YOUR FLIGHT

company

among these lavenders
that bloom but once a year

the stench of the remnant beauty
of a less dared and less common rarity
infringes upon the olfactory organs here

linking to the smile-inducing memory

that of a primal urge for a connected adventure,
a secret between two…purer than often thought:
an unexpected gift from nature

I've missed the latest bloom, it seems
it's evaded the nonetheless still beautiful scene

one no longer comes undone at the seams
when sharing the days creates lilac from black-
colorizing routine

FIRE UP YOUR FLIGHT

engulfed

behind the smiles
lie the miles
of riverbeds that would be formed
could these teardrops be gathered…

behind the masked eyes
in disguise
lies the soul's flow…
the roots that continue to grow
the fuel and the flames …
despite passing games

                                                                                   linger

the inner light that burns?

                                        … don't ever let that get dimmer

FIRE UP YOUR FLIGHT

365

allow us
experiences to become fragments of bittersweet
 yet beautiful, future nostalgia

allow us
memories created to inevitably become
moments frozen in time
with hands intertwined
I, yours…and you, mine
singing to the innate tune of love
without meticulous rhythm or rhyme

knowing well that one day most lovers must part
moments still freeze in a cozy corner of the heart

recycling in our minds…
less 'fast-forwards', more 'rewinds'

                                      images of us
                              in every holiday and season

                            disregarding the thieves of joy
                              like common sense or reason

FIRE UP YOUR FLIGHT

loyalty

nature's trusty cycles and beauty:
undeniable

humans' self-serving attentions:
unreliable

before your hurt-
believing themselves not liable,
but when they're in need of rescuing
holding *you* accountable …?

unless you're suiting their needs-
less value is placed on your worth or deeds?

turn that precious, twinkling attention
inward
let the flimsy and fickle go
backward

advance your unique dance
let them remain
wayward

                remain the sun…
                      stars will eventually fade
                      despite having more fun

FIRE UP YOUR FLIGHT

self

greetings

to the awkward young bud your soul has remained despite the grown petals,
the added thorns through the years
and dew from the tears

greetings to the tulip-
hey, listen, please do
know that somehow you always pull through

you weren't of you-
but this me now …
this future *you*…
can matter-of-factly assure:

she's proud of you

buzz

some people should be noted
and kept around …   like a bee
best observed behind nets…   for safety
welcomed only occasionally… rare honey

FIRE UP YOUR FLIGHT

athenaeum

I'm a library
with a variety of books to borrow,
stories of verbal beauty to visualize
alongside only secrets to keep

my collection can enthrall
or make the reader weep

people proving to be shallow
whilst I'd thought they'd be deep

but I'll let flakes be lakes
I'm literary emotion…devotion
                an entire ocean

barred

a myriad of flowers can conceal behind gates, rusty
                        steel bars and bricks built on foundations, shaky
  …what's inviting to the outside can include those   locked
                          inside, screaming for release quietly
                …what's inviting to the outside can exclude
the dwellers' inability to escape…prohibited from remedy…a silenced,
                          haunting melody

identity

I am a poet
wouldn't you know it?

I am an observer
an active liver… breather … feeler …doer

I'm a recorder
the sinner and the savior … the smiler & the crier

an appreciative prayer

both prey and predator- a played player

an attention-giver
to the most minuscule details of nature

I'm a poet
and
I love it
reaping nothing but pure joy of it

life is worth it
so, unearth it

knowing me
wouldn't you know it? I am simply…*a poet*

FIRE UP YOUR FLIGHT

tattoo

just as the brave lover
can carve a beloved's name
into their heart's interior
it should be realized that, upon betrayal-
once held dearer, suddenly made to feel inferior- that same warrior
can just as easily carve a Brutus name back out- exterior

achingly…yet permanently
pride is survival…a necessity
when faced with selfish, narcissistic tendency

if you don't know how to love,
                                        leave such warriors be

FIRE UP YOUR FLIGHT

redemption

you light the fuse…
they can't refuse
their muse

don't let them misuse
have they even gotten the news?

those who've survived the abuse

                                        create…overcome…produce

propulsion
           after
                  conflagration

                                          duped

                some seduce us with empty promises
                    we smile upon as entertainment
                          and not out of belief,
           though they must surely believe us to be fools

FIRE UP YOUR FLIGHT

journey

I long for the minimalist joys

further and further away
from prying eyes
I'd once thought were positive attention
which have since proven themselves
to be merely for gossip and comparison

jealousy…
sometimes of nothing except
your self-sufficiency

selfishly
calculative for their own deeds…
while you're calculating
melodic songs from once-wooden reeds…

less views
more art

don't overthink
or overshare

just start

FIRE UP YOUR FLIGHT

gossipers

fear stagnation:
the enemy
of life's purpose,
and of gradual-elevation

        allow conflagration

                        if you must

better to break free
from their self-projections
and comfort-zone expectations

        before you yourself

                        turn to dust

un-settled

some unions are akin
to a job with benefits
and a lifetime guarantee

mere comfort…passionless

FIRE UP YOUR FLIGHT

suburbanite

reveling in subdued beauty-
an industrial, traffic war zone
redeemed through the subtle nature
of this island-
fauna and flora less tropic, more suburban

encompassing various lakes
and wooden paths of unkept planks…
throwing in a few memorials,
and sprinkling family-friendly
playground addends…

benches with graffiti
pollute the eye
from the corner of which
you notice a disheveled passerby

you preemptively reach for protection:
pocketed mase only,
hating guns
and
hate crimes

as a myriad of birds chirp loudly
distracting from concerns
with their colors and uniqueness
                the island…always attempting amends

purple flowers peek through cemented cracks
yellow florals bloom into dandelions

we walked in circles
as had become familiar
trying this way and that …gradually circling back

the path wasn't perfect

but somehow always worth it

FIRE UP YOUR FLIGHT

the ecology…always improving psychology.

to belong- the desire
cyclically rekindling- the fire

a now occasional trip back into the city
feeling exciting-
once on its own merit,
but now only so
because it's a temporary change of scenery,
from which you'll return to suburbia-
        some calling it a trap, while others-   *home*

FIRE UP YOUR FLIGHT

visitors

my grandmother talked to birds
not in a way which contemporarily would likely be likened to insanity
but they'd visit her Istanbul balcony
and she'd replicate their sounds
reverberating their hymns with her own melodic voice:
it would both lessen her loneliness,
this nature-human interaction that'd gone beyond merely feeding, as is
more popular…but also, symbolically, ease her sense of entrapment,
as the birds would then fly off…
she'd had no sense of belonging there, I now reckon- in her balcony
she'd worked so hard for after being born in a foreign land,
from which her family was one of many expelled for their ethnicity
and faith…
the birds would take her with them in her imagination
perhaps even to her childhood in Plovdiv
I sit in the yard
observing the variety in the birds' tones
and I understand-
solitary tranquility, and assuredness, through nature
can hold your hand
…far beyond those whom you'd once called 'friend'

ever can

FIRE UP YOUR FLIGHT

sensory

some words can evoke multiple senses at once
lavender…cinnamon…champagne…you

secret

what's less often realized is:
the breaker can hurt just as much as the broken

thieves

you can steal innocence, but lose humanity
you can tear through pages
shatter down walls
…but never integrity

FIRE UP YOUR FLIGHT

messenger

the trees, in the night breeze, talk
without saying a word
quivering evergreens
and the seasonably meager-leafed
united now in howling song and movement

too-rapidly these images flash before me
blurred
images- from media usage-meant to evoke *fear*
yet how can I do so,
when it is pure nature I hear ?

what is it?
speak, Nature's majesties,
what are we humans not getting?
why are we still immersed in our suffering?

to the spirit,
your message is clear as day,
not blurred;

must savor the unseen,
tune into the unheard

FIRE UP YOUR FLIGHT

chai

the liquor of unexpected sweetness
through encircling the entirety of a being
from all directions
intoxicates
endlessly
and will do so,
ceaselessly

open minds
open limbs

deepening souls
as longing caves
become waterfalls

more bittersweet
than satisfied

but with the most intimate endings
and with the softest, truest landings

FIRE UP YOUR FLIGHT

imperfect

thorns
protect the flower

don't complain
when pricked
if you wanted a taste
of its power

a herbivore's inner fire
to experience
that which only the rose
could extinguish

thorns highlight
thorns distinguish

FIRE UP YOUR FLIGHT

protagonist

one must look at naysayers
whose negativity can hit out of the blue:
disclosing their falsehoods,
when one would have thought they'd be true

and, if in possession of a clear conscience,
one can come to realize
that the unimportant opinions of the naysayers
are based merely on their illusions-

                                            their own struggle,
                                               their own issue

one must actively think:
"...*you* don't have to like me
I do
and I don't have to make you feel bad
to claim some false triumph
over a passing fad..."

                                          rest assured- and be glad
                             you'll be the among the best memories
                                    they will have ever had

FIRE UP YOUR FLIGHT

trinket

'hanging in there'
your answer to their daily 'mode' inquisition

you're hanging on
like the fragile,
ornate ornament
on the tree

in a most delicate condition

valued and shining
only to be taken down at the season's end-
thought to be reliably recyclable,
when it's needed again

until one day
it shatters
breaks

oh, how the transparent,
glass heart
aches

Emblaze

…one of the healthiest things you can do in life is to respect the inevitability of change, and let go of stagnant situations that have had and are done with their time in the sun…where all that's left is the shade…under which a branch which once bloomed with scented flowers is now but a brittle twig that's neither glowing nor growing- merely awaiting its turn to drop to the ground, like an ash at the end of an incense stick…for letting go of what no longer serves or brings joy isn't selfish: holding on is

Musings & Ponderings

FIRE UP YOUR FLIGHT

assumption

one can search the world for 'the one'
yet, in one, they could experience the world
love, ever the two-way street,
requires the question:
"before asking even further sacrifice from another,
what am I myself really offering the lover?"

denying the realness of a connection,
calling it merely a toxic attraction
youth- and false leadings from envious friends-creating the illusion
that there'll be more chances,
blushful glances, or mirror dances

as if a locomotive train…station after station
"…if one stop is passed, there'll be another…"
but what if that station had been home-
your heart and soul's cozy shelter …?

one can search the world for convenience,
in actuality…
and label that 'love' for the world to see

but in only one can they find themselves with
skin glowing, spirit smiling, hands trembling…
no lies…whilst staring into the lover's eyes

FIRE UP YOUR FLIGHT

mastery

I learned what love is
a subjectivity at once warm and familiar….
realizing for others it might not be the same or similarly linear

I'd thought it to be settlement, unison in aging…
socially embraced, divinely protected,
routine-dependent and unrejected…
more of the rearing and breeding
less of the panicking and bleeding

I learned what love is
I learned it through the pain endured
pride ignored
ego bruised
sleep and sanity sacrificed-
yet quietly so…
for its persistent expression-
I also learned-
was obsession…
and obsession, misusing admiration- faulty adulation- contrary to many ballads,
could also not be love

I learned it to be more of an acceptance
of their truths, and their reactions to your own
vulnerability on blast…

until faith was restored
upon their return,
like a boomerang or a magnet

for I learned love always beckons back
without loud calls needed-
an innate comfort in their company
is instead heeded

FIRE UP YOUR FLIGHT

I learned what love is
when I'd taken risks
cyclically
just for another chance-

even if at their whim-
to throw another glance

up close
into their soul…relinquishing control

I learned what love is
through accountability…
and the throwing to them of the proverbial ball
…as I learned to let go…
                        and love- if true- would always, then, linger near
                                            like a shadow

FIRE UP YOUR FLIGHT

queue

one by one
they line up
the birds
in late autumn
awaiting
the holidays

I stand back
avoiding
my usual swing chair,
and respectfully observe them
to preserve them
in my future memory

I presume they're here
for the feed I'd laid out-
particularly to reattract
the Cardinal, with his blessed feathers red

yet they're more interested now
in the crackling leaves and diluted pond water
I worry for the koi (goldfish?) swimming about
after subduing the urge to feed them, too,
(their hibernating digestion momentarily escapes me)
I then laugh myself silly,
for how could the tiny birds eat living fish?

disturbing nature is bold
watching nature is gold
one by one
we recycle routines
avoiding being misled
awaiting, instead,
to be fed
…satiated
…elated…emancipated

FIRE UP YOUR FLIGHT

cyclical

nature is humble

it is content, overall,
with repetition;
tears of rain
sun rays of joy
changing leaves
and the first snow fall

nature is resilient

it adapts
to maladies and punctures
in its atmospheres
despite wounds and lacerations

nature is inspiration

we, too, consist of routine duplication:
perspiration, inhalation and exhalation

giving up is annihilation

surrender to the flow
adaptability over resignation

FIRE UP YOUR FLIGHT

fork

the sun peeked
if only for a brief moment
a brevity nonetheless so intense
that the rays of the majestic star lingered
despite their dissolution back behind the clouds before the frosty chill
remnant since the morning
lingered on

we walked among frost
which did not even create puffs of visible air before our faces
typical of winter's unofficial beginning
for not even the heat of our breaths could compete with that cold

yet our glances were warm
memories of which fill our eyes now
with tears of gratitude
despite any storm

FIRE UP YOUR FLIGHT

aurora

What's the point of living in a three-story villa, thought the Beverly Hills star, *…when you've just had to tiptoe to your kid's bedroom to borrow cash from her piggy bank?*

Aurora Adams was no longer in demand as an actress as she once was, but she'd been getting by thanks to 'the mother' roles on cable holiday movies, with quite a bit of a loyal social media following boosting her morale, albeit not her pocketbook.

Named after the northern lights, she was presently on a late-November flight to try to catch them in Reykjavik, and her bank account was just short of the remaining $100 or so from the ticket she needed to get there.

Her agent, Liam, had landed her some European commercial gig, where she'd be filmed in a bathing suit with the lights dancing around her-something cheesy, as far as she was concerned, about the skimpy clothing brand being 'durant' in all temperatures. But Liam had been unable to also land her a free flight, as would often be the case. *Bastard*, Aurora cursed him mentally, plastering on yet another fake smile at the stewardess handing her a second plastic cup of wine.

As if on cue, Liam reached across the blank seat between them, holding out to her his Jell-O pudding. "Chocolate is more your thing, Aurora. Here, have mine…"

Aurora smiled with a sigh as she grabbed the plastic cup. She supposed it wouldn't be fair to blame anyone else for her poor management skills of various kinds. She knew that deep inside.

"Can I come with you, mommy?"

Tears welled in the corners of Aurora's eyes as the image of her daughter, Melody, came to her mind. *"I want to see the no-thing lights…"*

"Nor-thern, my sweet," Aurora had enunciated, giving her angel of brown curls a kiss on the cheek. *"You be good with grandma, okay? I'll be back in a few days. I'll take pictures of them for you with my phone, if I can. They're pretty hard to catch, you know, depending on cloud coverage…"*

FIRE UP YOUR FLIGHT

"I'm hard to catch, too, mommy. Catch me if you can!"

"Aurora?" Liam's waving hand before her face awoke her from the nostalgic reverie of that morning before she'd headed out to the airport.

"Sorry…I just miss Melody already." Chocolate Jell-O was also her daughter's favorite. "Can I have a spoon?"

Aurora fumbled through the handbag she'd laid on the floor. Her hand brushed something metal, and her droplets transformed into full-blown tears.

"I'll ask the stewardess for one," Liam interrupted her thoughts.

"Never mind, Liam, thanks," Aurora wiped her face. "See? I left her spoon in my bag. I always carry it with me so she can have a fruit yogurt snack in case she gets hungry on-the-go…"

"No need to use her spoon," Liam said softly, as he proceeded to request one for Aurora from the flight attendant. "She knows you love her… She's proud of her mommy. Don't you worry."

The pilot announced some turbulence somewhere over the approaching Icelandic airspace, and Aurora put on her seatbelt. Her nerves had already long given up on any sleep. She gripped the armrests harder, lifting her window shutter ever so-slightly… when her eyes became bedazzled by something sparkling green.

Aliens? Her first thought, as she quickly then laughed at her silliness. Her palm slowly raised itself over her mouth. *Oh my God!* The dancing images caught her breath as another announcement came over the speaker.

"Ladies and Gentlemen. This is your Captain speaking again. I apologize if you've been asleep… But you may want to lift up your window shutters, as we're currently flying among a most fortunate and rarely encountered display of Aurora Borealis, at an altitude of…."

Everything will be alright. Aurora Adams started recording. For Melody. For herself. For them. She smiled.

Somehow, someway… It just will.

FIRE UP YOUR FLIGHT

ophidian

serpent…
come hither
be bold…
don't slither
world history may repeat
but this bond won't
when forced in another

                                                          illusioned

                                                                         please
                                                                           halt!
                                                             don't come near
                                                            …the idea of you
                                                                 I imagine
                                                             in my head
                                                         while sleepless
                                                              in my bed
                                              is so full of beauty
                                                                  I fear
                             losing that company
                               with a harsh reality

riviera

what is it about the scent
of being near a natural body of water
that energizes
and mesmerizes?

a most curious mixture of saline sweetness
 and sugared bitterness
shocks the nostrils,
with the nasal passages
being foreign to the everyday-sniffed
fragrances

FIRE UP YOUR FLIGHT

lunar

for millennia people have looked
both *to* and *at* the moon

                              for reliable cycles to calculate months,
                                    for beauty….for proximity
                                for companionship…for loyalty

I gazed tonight at the moon,
and I could swear I saw the outline of continents

a reflection
of earth

a reflection
of us

FIRE UP YOUR FLIGHT

suffix

admiration
stimulation
absolute elation
while in duration
…fixation

                                                          trepidation
                                                          hesitation

cessation
tribulation…

                                                          sedation
                                                 procrastination
                                                     stagnation

redirection or reconnection
anticipation…reciprocation…reverberation

                                      preservation…if there's gratification

self-amelioration…divine protection
empathic humanization…divine salvation

FIRE UP YOUR FLIGHT

de-voted

the radio announces the exit of the last Castro,
and my thoughts drift to democracy…vis-à-vis …
capitalism…human rights…
and sometimes, sadly, hypocrisy

healthy competition
needed for improvement and motivation…
nonetheless should exclude imitation
and mendacious, misleading justification

not a healthy rivalry
if you're competing in an un-level playing field
contending at times with unfair trends
and at others- with utter injustice, lacking a shield

sometimes revolutionizing is required,
but in the minds of the people:
                     a good coup can only be a mental one, bloodless

for democratic change
                   can still house undercover autocracy, regardless

the people must persistently demand
a just leader for all in their homeland

FIRE UP YOUR FLIGHT

jazz

a unique set of sounds through wood and metal
combining to create beauty through chaos
a mélange of emotions conveyed
only seldomly through accompanying vocals…
more so through facial expressions,
surprising hand placements and string plucks, muting the ends of a brass
wind

unity despite the lack of repetitive melody
neither a beat you'd expect to sing along to
nor choral verses or bridges to be anticipated
…the end of the piece remains mysterious…
forcing you to be in the moment and pay attention

not trending on the radio waves…
despite the golden history and valuable contributions to society
wider known as a sophisticated category
creating a myriad of storylines like a movie
playing in viewers' heads without words spoken,
only music

a soundtrack of lives, as differences intertwine
at least jazz enlivens…and those who are jazz, live

abide

a high expectation
lowers satisfaction,
an elevated fixation
lessens actualization

remain in the flow
for beauty to grow,
trust you'll know
when…where…how to stay
when…where…how to go

trade-off

I haven't seen the moon tonight;
can't enter slumber content
I haven't heard the voice
which has mesmerized, like a curse;
I can't rest easy…depleted,
like coins accrued but unspent

I don't want to seek any further
you're untradeable-no barter
be still my heart
at least I've got my art
I will not bother

FIRE UP YOUR FLIGHT

dynamite

a limit was reached
certain boundaries, breached

> you've wronged…all you could
> you've longed…all you could
> tried to see 'the good' in alone time…
> all you could

faults, different from your own
yet affection, was still shown
despite secrets being known

> here it remains still
> this friendship on fire
>
> the rare reliability in a quickly-passing world
> with increasingly less left to admire
>
> where we're left to ponder
> if social acceptance is worth
> sacrificing the soul's desire

FIRE UP YOUR FLIGHT

luminary

be an angel only to those in need of one

a child or an injustice sufferer
a genuine friend or grateful lover

not a speaker
with inaction out of cowardice…
nor one immune to sensitivity
until they're in need of it themselves
after they too fall victim to artifice…

for your wings,
unappreciated and unrecognized
among all those devils in disguise,
will be clipped

remain bathed
in the heavenly pool
while they drown in the cheap wine
that they've sipped

meaning

…and in this world
 without safety nets,
          we shield up
                and feign toughness

taking chances
placing bets

the soul,
through the body as a vessel,
never forgets

and after a loss, the mind…may
…but a heart that's loved?
never regrets

success,
regardless of circumstance,
is what a heart that's loved
begets

Ascend

and why do some run from developing connections
faster than they would from diseases?
…evading beating hearts, uncontrollable smiles or even platonic vulnerability,
more urgently than far more menacing fevers and dangers, with the power to ultimately hurt more…?

Musings & Ponderings

FIRE UP YOUR FLIGHT

seatbelt

I've boarded
roller coasters
all my life, often without the overhead vests

I shook and rambled
more than I made audible, though surely it'd been visible…they never believed me…
they'd gotten used to seeing me smiling 'pretty' & 'happy-go-lucky'; that mask was a necessity,
not my reality

I boarded roller coasters knowing the likely consequences
for the beauty of an experience that would nostalgically make me smile

ignoring the excruciating pain
all the while
of one from a world different from my own,
plans in their mind different from what was shown

rides aren't dependable
they aren't as reliable
as the sunrises & sunsets
where no one regrets
overexposing their truest self without games or trickery
…your vulnerability
pushing away their feigned chivalry

life is already a bumpy ride…are risks worth losing your stride?

FIRE UP YOUR FLIGHT

life

it takes a mere, but real and long look
at the grand sky above

to grasp our purpose on earth;

unlimited space to fly and appreciate
      limited by morality, time and the elements

                                     marine

                                     sometimes
                                 you're glorious-
                                     swimming

                                       at others-
                                   merely floating

                                   refuse to sink

                           intuit, before you feel
                                   or even think

FIRE UP YOUR FLIGHT

recipe

I fear less what I feel
and more the ramifications of expression

I express less than what's real,
hide more than reveal

Pandora's box could cause either destruction
upon its outer shield's disruption
or
to my malady-
a most beautiful remedy
…a prescription
for reconstruction

there's no zest nor zeal
one'd be able to conceal

when the soul finally knows
the path to its depth…
and how it glows

enthusiasm will flow
one's essence will show

FIRE UP YOUR FLIGHT

innate

I feel this thing
looking at the moon
reflecting
prisms, shades of light yellow ahead
a halo shape encompasses my bed
while the birds after midnight sing

I feel this thing
strangely not wondering
what you're then doing
…and whether it's something alright
or off-putting
more accepting than suspecting
I smile…while recognizing
my naïve but strangely comforting
sense of fulfillment… merely feeling

this ability to naturally emote was,
I suppose,
the something missing
for which I'd been yearning

FIRE UP YOUR FLIGHT

creatures

sometimes
the animals are to be envied

survival…their only drama
survival…their only trauma

                                            so much we can learn
                                    even from an entire universe
                                                under the ocean

                                      co-existence and survival
                                    its inhabitants' only devotion

patronage

Mona Lisa's smile curved higher
after she'd left this earth
                                    her absence added to her worth

                    couldn't anyone tell her, then, in a timelier fashion
                            …that maybe she was never broken?
                      …that she never had to suppress full joy,
with words left unspoken

FIRE UP YOUR FLIGHT

beach

…caught it!

within the glance
sideways
(squinting) imitating my own
as the setting sun was also caught

appearing to disappear into the horizon
though the orange star had remained still-
the earth's capricious moving
thought it would simply fade into oblivion

the catcher's dream for a unique path,
too, had set
and felt done
…until moments were caught
witnessed by insects and egrets
and-sparkle!
a revival had begun

FIRE UP YOUR FLIGHT

joy

what could simultaneously be so insignificant
as to not hold any relevance in the grander scheme of things…
yet also possess the power to change an entire theme
or a life in need
through a matter of minutes?

what could never pay the bills, but fulfill a soul…
summarize so much with so little,
create meaning from seemingly nothing at all?

what could formulate a rainbow
out of a torrential storm?
…a refreshing chill when things surpass
a comfortable warm?

poetry = colorimetry

caged

the canary has had enough of distance-
nothing historically romanticized about it, about the
heart growing fonder, can hold true in the modern-age
of forced shields making them colder

the canary, since being a chick,
has already lost so many…
attachment issues linger,
 of the 'anxious' variety

loneliness…
rapid, distracting technology…
leaving hearts a mess…no nest…
…emptiness…
keys of devices
touching the fingers
more than another's embrace
the glare of a visual screen
more than a physical kiss
lighting up the face

they hear the canary's cries from afar
and flatter, as 'strength', its wounded tune
…never offering medicine
or positioning themselves
to join the golden cage to spend incalculable, limited days on earth
as much as possible
in unison

migrations

birds of a feather
flocked together,
until the cursed one
dropped down with its wing wounded
whilst it had been on a sky high-

gazing up
at the continuing flight
of the other

their
'forever'
apparently had meant
in
'fair weather'

FIRE UP YOUR FLIGHT

breathe

reflect on how often we give up
on what brings us genuine joy
purely because it is inconvenient and not easy

and then fool ourselves with the label of
'not meant to be'

like planting a flower,
you can hold most power
to reap beauty
as you patiently water

classic

like the flower
crinkled
between the pages
of your favorite chapter

…beautiful…even after its death

we wouldn't have wilted
had you not plucked it

solar

burn sage in your soul
your sacrifice has taken its toll,
they've used you to feel whole
whilst pulling you down a hole

turn your head toward the sun

let them continue to chase their fun
stars are many, and can fade into none

the sun is everlasting…and one

FIRE UP YOUR FLIGHT

organ

the beautiful buzz
flowing through the veins:

post-exercise
endorphins kick in,
your beating pumper within
enlightening you to
the simple daily reminder
of what's underneath your skin

you've survived
you're alive

pat on the back,
a high-five

FIRE UP YOUR FLIGHT

chapters

there was a wooden door
she remembers from childhood

she's hid behind it
all the burning secrets
and embers
that she could

there lay a garden behind picket fences
displaying roses of all shades-
dove-white to heated reds
each stem…
the thorn
the scorned

the forlorn
the mourned

she's still got a lot to learn
she's still got bridges left to burn:

*the ones who only chastise or yearn
yet never quite really earn*

FIRE UP YOUR FLIGHT

present

the past is the past

the mistakes of yesterday or yesteryear,
perhaps clearer
as such
only in retrospect,

have been made

they can't be undone
like your bed, or make-up at the end of the day

make the most of the errors
only matters that you utilize and color the gray

to contribute to your growth,
allow what's been actualized
to strengthen your wings
more than you'd realized

applying lessons learned,
self-realization points earned

self-actualized… *catalyzed*

FIRE UP YOUR FLIGHT

teacup

the pastel porcelain
has beheld such warmth
over the years
….and sweet

weary through time
…it's taken the heat

chipped around the handle
yet there's nothing it can't handle

…other cups can't hold a candle

FIRE UP YOUR FLIGHT

festival

when the body dies, the soul remains awaiting

the day when all committed will return full-circle
in accordingly designated places
the day when those meant for us
and whose souls we've missed
will once again be before our faces

the essence of the spirit lingers each time
we remnants on earth commemorate,
they sense what's said and prayed
in another realm
though their souls aren't literally with us:
it isn't some 'ghost haunting'
if in our scripture we trust

value the iron- of an otherworldly meteorite before it turns to rust

the irony of love:
giving in fully only
after its ashes have turned to dust

FIRE UP YOUR FLIGHT

larva

the butterfly,
with an average lifespan of merely a month or two
spreads its beauty, a good luck charm
as different as their wings are from one another-
from clear to black
and gray to multi-color…
they affect us all

you can crow with the crows
flocking all day in flocks

or soar like an eagle-
more dignified, solitary….
               alone, but not lonely

nitrate

you'd thought it 'revival'
whilst they'd mused 'rival'

feed your truth
starve your confusion
you're your only challenger
don't fall for illusion

FIRE UP YOUR FLIGHT

purgatory

as we spend our lives searching for meaning
let's not lose sight, that life is precisely meant for learning
& the test of faith consists precisely of those questions still lingering

stay in the living
no one's all-knowing

ensure it is kindness you're spreading
and there can be peace in the
ending

Catalyze

…and sometimes you don't need any externality to blame for wanting to leave a situation…sometimes, merely not liking who you've become in a circumstance is enough reason…when you've stopped being able to catalyze growth, and stopped becoming catalyzed yourself: you must shift…and revitalize

Musings & Ponderings

FIRE UP YOUR FLIGHT

fueled

you're burning
 and
  yearning

working
earning

enduring
learning

engulfed
without ashes
or embers

a soul ignited
forgets more than
it remembers

letting go and
soaring

no simple floating- boring

allowing
the fire
to burn as fuel

allowing the sweetest most natural high
and the life inside to fly

by this given miracle- mesmerized
by adapting and catalyzing- *catalyzed*

FIRE UP YOUR FLIGHT

grip

if you can get through that hour
of your lowest vibration

you possess the power
to rebound stronger

when depression is temptation
daily steps for self-worth is redemption

                                                unexpected,
the quiet that ensues
bittersweet,
the soul crying silently
to be sought and found
while you feign retreat

what you conceal,
since you can't reveal,
feeling more real

FIRE UP YOUR FLIGHT

holder

I was gifted
a cracked vase
with its split spiraling downward before I provided the glue…opening
it to the possibility of seeing life more maturely, to feel
and visualize anew…
ignoring how it'd gotten that way in the first place:
its unhealthy habits and old ways

    figured it'd want to prolong feeling whole for as long as it could…
   valued it like ceramic, ignoring its insistence it'd been made of wood
                      tested my loyalty to my role as the gluer
                disregarding the misuse of the wrongdoer

and once it'd found reassurance, the
supply of glue was met with annoyance
a mirror to the truths wasn't needed
…a darker, numbing, hedonistic call was heeded
                      Through the unspoken, instincts were awoken

    Trust- no longer even cracked- but, rather like the vase's essence-
                                                  broken

FIRE UP YOUR FLIGHT

mousetrap

I've often empathized to tears- even upon hearing of, let alone seeing,
something hurting a member of the animal world

even a 'pesky' pet
a cockroach…a rodent
a cockroach…a rodent

and now…witnessing my daughter's reaction
to such natural truths she observes
in the neighborhood,
I find myself pondering human beings
in reflection

driving home I see the 'sneaky' raccoon
dart across the street
was that a cat, instead?
…no… the face
appeared to be darker in a mask
…can't bet

I slow down on the busy street
by instinct, without glancing in the rear mirror…
worried more about my potential to slam into the animal…than a car
slamming into me

living things are parts of our lesson and worldly test
unless survival instincts are ignited- mustn't trap what wouldn't trap
you- *must be at your best*

FIRE UP YOUR FLIGHT

redeem

focus on the lesson
after your errors

no use being stuck
on what's caused the tremors

nightmares still causing shivers…

you've been shamed- more by the self
than fellow brethren, fellow sinners…

salvation through service
can aid your repentance

forgive for forgiveness
it can heal your penance

FIRE UP YOUR FLIGHT

floral

thorns
protect the flower…
don't complain
when pricked
if you've wanted a taste
of its power

a herbivore's inner fire
to experience…
that which only the rose
could extinguish

thorns highlight
thorns distinguish

home

I didn't leave you…
just the torn part of myself

transformation gets me through,
you're still a beloved book on my shelf

geometry

I learned to love myself as a *whole*
through allowing myself to dislike *some*
of the *segments* that come undone
despite the gluing of *fragments*

as the *sum* of all our parts,
we contribute more than our minds…
our bodies and our hearts
the dark and the light, combined…

…make the ordinary, divine…

born perfect, yet in tears
live to die smiling, imperfect,
but content
rather than merely accumulating years

FIRE UP YOUR FLIGHT

anti-social

share less,
live more

reduce stress…

let them assume you're a bore
posting shouldn't be a chore

> **intuition**
>
> it hurts
> because they called it 'love'
>
> and made you believe it, too
>
> all the meanwhile
> to your instincts
> you should have been true

seen

we fight ourselves for external validation…
only to grow
and discover its occurrence
contingent upon the termination
of that inner quarrel

self-negligence…   *shows*
inner-confidence…   *glows*

FIRE UP YOUR FLIGHT

rest

title-worship and hustle culture are nearing 'over'
dust off that pressure to 'triumph'-
according to someone else's standards-
from your own wary shoulder

'tis a more satisfying thrill to smell the flora
on a brisk-wind nature stroll
than to party hard and then show it off,
with substance-filled, sleepless nights
taking their toll

who ultimately cares?
which brands label your tables and chairs?

if they do, they're competing
                                                not completing,
                                                merely depleting

maintain your energy:
a work-life balance makes your mental health more sustainable

the fewer yet truer…the less but the best
are always more pleasurable

FIRE UP YOUR FLIGHT

egret

that tender embrace
this can't be some chase

hearing that it may just be a phase
but the subtly crimsoning moon
would fully blush
with one gaze upon your face

down by the bay
where affections grow
and connections flow

some mourn a lack of a significant other
others mourn the inability to reveal…undercover

we reap the seeds which we sow
trying our best is all we know

FIRE UP YOUR FLIGHT

shelled

had prayed for felicity…serenity, proximity
a random praying mantis, one night
a freak chance of nature, instead
took it all away from reality

the insect signaled the end of a season-
a rare and twinkling one,
warm only in the sun,
with which has terminated the illusion

…a dream that perhaps this could be real:
through the definition of which
would mean in the rougher days
as well as in the days of zeal

the one still skeptical
of what was clearly unique and magical;
pragmatic, too, though unconventional
simultaneously logical and emotional
their words cutting deep, surgical
and they found *you* unethical?

said they craved your face
scorching embrace
yet they threw you into the pit
once you gave in to their chase
will misusing, losing love
ultimately be worth choosing
the easy way out?
pushing the manifested out of sight?
saying 'this isn't right'…
was it, then, when night after night
they'd begged for the darkness to feel like light?

harming a harmless little girl inside

FIRE UP YOUR FLIGHT

simply begging for attention
pulling a cozy rug from underneath
putting her in unwarranted detention…
an otherwise beautiful 'stillness' rattled,
fears and the need for control
put severance into motion

sacrificial plans and meaningful glances
now shattered
oh, the actual little one
you'll realize one day
that this had all mattered

an otherwise beautiful trust
they've lost and will now have to earn
when for the much-craved
unrivaled passion from the wronged
the wrongdoers always yearn

FIRE UP YOUR FLIGHT

pride

indecision…
do I cut out my heart
and wallow in submission?

a world I cannot condone,
beyond my upbringing or preparation,
yet drawing me in without contemplation

thoughts, overthought-thoughts…
whom you thought were your people
sneakily becoming ghosts…

sobs, silently-wailed
and sobbed

daylight can disguise
what the late night
has robbed

FIRE UP YOUR FLIGHT

prompt

I've always adored the seaside at dusk:
that point in the day
at which it is no longer light
yet darkness still has not devoured the heavens

the birds audibly prepare to sleep-
at an hour when you know you should too…but don't…
too distracted, of course…
modern-day 'tasks' and streaming shows await

the magenta remnants of the day linger
stubbornly, in the ether
silently ensuring you remember
before, by nature, they too must disappear
and take their place in the past

the tranquility of the near-quiet thrills
enthralls more than could liquor or pills

the encroaching nightfall –from another perspective-
gives hope of another approaching sunrise
 rather than symbolizing some abysmal dimness

waves crash onto the shore slower than the higher ones
of the afternoon-when the rays, like flames,
had been burning red-orange…
radiating from our majestic star

those tides now
give in to their states of rest

FIRE UP YOUR FLIGHT

alongside the birds and other creatures of the wet sand

I watch in awe
of nothing but the beauty of the moment

nothing grandiose about that routine
but it is momentous indeed
for my lungs can draw in that chilly, brisk air by the water

the sun winks its last wink before the goodbye-
more a 'goodnight' rather than anything that will be an end

night has finally fallen
and the day's etched forever into memory

                                            infinity…long after the reality
                                                fades into the oblivion

FIRE UP YOUR FLIGHT

elemental

you've got your body
as your vessel on earth
to tread through floods of water

and push through shifting currents of sudden change

and to grow from your seeds
with a spirit to rise from the ashes

a phoenix of inspiration
following lessons learned from life's lashes

AFTERWORD

Dear reader,

In this final 'elemental' component of the namesake compilation, I've experimented a bit with free-verse poetry (*Dante, Aurora*) and non-rhyme poetry (*Prompt*-an actual #nanowritingmonth prompt)- of which I'm not too habited- being self-contained by the art of rhyming I've always been fond of.

It's been a different experience, and I enjoyed it. It's also inspired me to write- InsAllah (God-willing)- my next novel after The Catalyst Trilogy from the first-person perspective (something else I haven't yet tried).

Will I keep 'lighting' that fuse, and change my writing style altogether? I doubt it. Experimentation from time to time is nice, but I don't dwell there. I continuously experience enough changes in my life that I think I want to stick with at least one constant in writing- my love of rhyming verses.

Fire causes negative change- no doubt about it- as does 'too much' of anything. ***Water*** nourishes but can cause floods….***Air*** allows for flow yet can cause storms and floating adrift off course…***Earth*** can grow life yet also take it by sliding and shattering…Fire? It can illuminate and spark, yet also, of course, engulf.

when life engulfs you into flames…of desire…you perspire
…avoid trouble: there's only one you and one life
…allow fire, instead, to illuminate you and take you higher

you're the one dealing…experiencing
what they are judging, opining- not knowing…naïve to suffering
when you prioritize yourself, it is never a waste
we're born and die alone and bare…make haste…in good taste

FIRE UP YOUR FLIGHT

write out your heart- bleed out your art through the DROPS,
painting over their dark existence:
set free your FLOW, your inner glow
authentic blooms versus synthetic flowers:
your essence will have them yearning
for your presence
as you earth up your ROOTS
be ever as in awe with life as a sprout
never too late to bloom...or too late to shout
fire up your FLIGHT
and you'll be led to your calling, you will know

EPILOGUE

Dear reader,

I've always found comfort in symmetrical things- including the concept of closure, where the end and beginning both feel 'right.' As noted in several portions of my writing as well, I grew up with OCD- undiagnosed and suffered by myself alone (Googling symptoms wasn't prevalent as it is now). It could be due to that, but also my need to share and seek a grander meaning beyond what affects only me and those around me.... And, so, I end with poetry what I began with poetry as well.

Are we protected on this planet? Are we limitless, beyond the elements- once our soul has escaped the body?

blue skies
for miles

are nice
but can
scare me

no clouds to disguise
fake smiles
over dreams that either haunt me
or betray me

May you always find the opportunities and time required- however brief- to 'take advantage of your youthful (even if not necessarily young) bloom', as quoted by the French writer Pierre de Ronsard in his famous *Ode A Cassandre* (a poem I learned in my junior high school French class I can still recall by heart).

THE ELEMENTAL COLLECTION

May you root your body (yes, even try walking on grass/soil barefoot in colder months), allow your attention to hear nature's sounds floating in the breeze, emblaze your thoughts warm by the fire or other sources of heat and coziness, and allow all five of your senses to interact with pure waters.

May you look up at the stars with gratitude as you inhale the nightly air, and, despite the potential for clouds, have faith that they're there.

I'm grateful always to Allah above for sending signs when I pray for them- answering my calls in what I ultimately later recognize as having been most 'favorable,' or '*hayırlısı*' for me.

Things are certainly not perfect- as my dear daughter, Dalya, and I still wait for justice for her innocently-imprisoned father in Turkiye: where he remains along with countless other such innocents under the authoritarian regime. Yet we've been doing our best to make the most of it, with the help of a small but special circle of supportive family, good friends, and sometimes even kinder strangers with their messages of appreciation and support.

May justice and empathy prevail in the world. I leave with a haiku, inspire by a short social media contest winning poem I'd written using a prompt. I would also now like to dedicate it to victims of needless violence in Ukraine and Gaza.

> some steal innocence
> claim ends justify the means
> …lose humanity

May you always act live wholly, authentically, and with humanity, dear reader, and be on the right side of history. Never forget all the elements that make you…*you.*

Blessings,

Selin

THE ELEMENTAL COLLECTION

like honey- you flatter, my dear
sticky…though not as sweet

you praise parts of the flower that serve your pleasure
but not the parts that serve the world, and make it unique

words that can create
a momentarily warm smile
but not warm a heart
with humility and vulnerability

is fleeting positivity…worth a sour eternity?

Ω

ever a rebel
the edge-walker

pulled only to the exotic:
to what's foreign
but with a sufficient speck of the familiar

with red flags
that would divert another
(signaling danger)
attracting her,
their flames signaling warmth
rather than conflagration
the 'strange' and unordinary: her shelter

THE ELEMENTAL COLLECTION

nature always beckons
louder than whimsical calls
of benefiting folk
encircling

like the hawk
that focus on its prey
tricks and reckons

nature's call is defiant
not compliant
yet nonetheless reliant

nature embraces the weary
when fellow kind feel more scary

Ω

the snow is honest
it never promises warmth
it can't deliver
like sunshine
in winter

Ω

dear bird-
unique one
piquing my interest this celebrated morning
with your slender tail and proud beak, shapely head
I wonder-
are you reflective, too, as this, yet another year nears its conclusion?
have you, too, tried to flock and provide for others of your kind,
seeking inclusion?
worked endlessly, relying on the feed provided daily
until one day it stopped, inexplicably?
have you, as well, welcomed…
to seek solace in the affection of a friend
whilst they saw you as means to a different sort of end?
dear nestling-
at least, I've tried….have you?
at last, I seek now only peace
I'm tired…and you?

THE ELEMENTAL COLLECTION

Photography: Marissa G.

THE END

ABOUT THE AUTHOR

SELIN SENOL-AKIN is a social activist and adjunct language instructor, aside from her creative writing and featured spoken/published poetry.

The Catalyst, which reached the online new release chart at #1 during the pandemic, has since become a part of a reader-requested trilogy: with *The Penance*, and *The Nestlings*, respectively.

Her acclaimed, #1 released poetry-fused books, *Write Out Your Drops, Set Free Your Flow, Earth Up Your Roots* and *Fire Up Your Flight* make up the multi-genre *'Elemental'* collection.

She lives in Long Island, New York with her young daughter and family.

Visit selinsenolakin.com for updates

Collaborations including the author:

- 'Versos Estivales' (2019), *Books & Smith Publishing*
- 'Flash' (2020), a poetry/short-story anthology
- 'The Media High School Journal of Academics & Fiction' (2021), New York
- 'Write Out Your Drops'- audiobook version (2021), with narrators Selin Senol-Akin and Esra Gultakin
- 'The Catalyst'- audiobook version (2021), with narrator Katherine Schooler

THE ELEMENTAL COLLECTION

THE ELEMENTAL COLLECTION